Scottish Law of Leases

Scottish Law of Leases

An Introduction

Angus McAllister MA(Hons), LLB, Solicitor
Senior Lecturer in Law in the Department of
Land Economics, Paisley College of Technology

Edinburgh
Butterworths
1989

United Kingdom	Butterworth & Co (Publishers) Ltd, 88 Kingsway, LONDON WC2B 6AB and 4 Hill Street, EDINBURGH EH2 3JZ
Australia	Butterworths Pty Ltd, SYDNEY, MELBOURNE, BRISBANE, ADELAIDE, PERTH, CANBERRA and HOBART
Canada	Butterworths Canada Ltd, TORONTO and VANCOUVER
Ireland	Butterworth (Ireland) Ltd, DUBLIN
Malaysia	Malayan Law Journal Sbn Bhd, KUALA LUMPUR
New Zealand	Butterworths of New Zealand Ltd, WELLINGTON and AUCKLAND
Puerto Rico	Equity de Puerto Rico, Inc, HATO REY
Singapore	Malayan Law Journal Pte Ltd, SINGAPORE
USA	Butterworths Legal Publishers, AUSTIN, Texas; BOSTON, Massachusetts; CLEARWATER, Florida (D & S Publishers); ORFORD, New Hampshire (Equity Publishing); ST PAUL, Minnesota; and SEATTLE, Washington

A CIP Catalogue record for this book is available from the British Library.

ISBN 0406 105 898

Typeset by Pindar (Scotland) Ltd, Edinburgh
Printed and bound by Thomson Litho Ltd, East Kilbride

Preface

This book is intended primarily as an introductory students' textbook on the Scots law of landlord and tenant. For this reason, I have aimed mainly for conciseness and clarity of exposition, rather than a study of the subject in depth. However, I have also kept in mind the needs of practitioners – not only lawyers, but also chartered surveyors, whose trainees I have been teaching for the last eleven years.

Landlord and tenant is a field where there are still substantial differences between the laws of Scotland and England. Moreover, the amount of legislation in recent years has left some of the standard texts out of date on certain aspects of the topic, and it is hoped that this book will at least partly remedy the deficiency. In particular, I have been able to include the radical changes made to the Rent Acts and the residential sector generally by the Housing (Scotland) Act 1988.

I would like to thank Professor Will Fraser for advice and encouragement during the period of writing the book, and also Mr John Irvine for his meticulous help with checking the proofs.

The law is stated as at 31 March 1989.

Angus McAllister
May 1989

Contents

Bibliography

(a) **General texts on landlord and tenant**

1 Gloag and Henderson *Introduction to the Law of Scotland* (9th edn, 1987), ch 33
2 Paton and Cameron *The Law of Landlord and Tenant in Scotland* (1967)
3 Rankine *A Treatise on the Law of Leases in Scotland* (3rd edn, 1916)
4 Walker *Principles of Scottish Private Law* (4th edn, 1988), ch 5.15

(b) **Other books on landlord and tenant**

5 Connell *The Agricultural Holdings (Scotland) Acts* (6th edn, 1970)
6 Duncan and Hope *The Rent (Scotland) Act 1984* (1986)
7 Gill *The Law of Agricultural Holdings in Scotland* (1982)
8 Halliday *Conveyancing Law and Practice*, Vol III, *Leases and Heritable Securities* (1987)
9 Law Society of Scotland (Various Authors) *Aspects of Agricultural Law* (1981)
10 McKerrell *The Rent Acts: A Practitioner's Guide* (1985)
11 Megarry *The Rent Acts* (11th edn, 1988)
12 Ross and McKichan *Drafting and Negotiating Commercial Leases in Scotland* (1985)

(c) **Other Relevant Textbooks**

13 Gloag *The Law of Contract* (2nd edn, 1929)
14 Himsworth *Public Sector Housing Law in Scotland* (2nd edn, 1986)
15 McBryde *The Law of Contract in Scotland* (1987)
16 Walker *The Law of Contracts and Related Obligations in Scotland* (2nd edn, 1985)
17 Woolman *An Introduction to the Scots Law of Contract* (1987)

List of Abbreviations

AC	Appeal Cases (Law Reports)
All ER	All England Law Reports
CA	Court of Appeal
Ch	Chancery (Law Reports)
Cr App R	Criminal Appeal Reports
CLY	Current Law Year Book
D	Dunlop (Court of Session Reports, 2nd Series, 1838-62)
EG	Estates Gazette
EGLR	Estates Gazette Law Reports
F	Fraser (Court of Session Reports, 5th series, 1898-1906)
FSR	Fleet Street Reports
GWD	Green's Weekly Digest
HL	House of Lords
HLR	Housing Law Reports
Hume	Baron Hume's Reports of Decisions, 1781–1822
JLS	Journal of the Law Society of Scotland
KB	King's Bench (Law Reports)
M	Macpherson (Court of Session Reports, 3rd Series, 1862-73)
Mor	Morison's Dictionary of Decisions, publ 1811
P & CR	Property and Compensation Reports
QB	Queen's Bench (Law Reports)
R	Rettie (Court of Session Reports, 4th Series, 1873-1898)
RVR	Rating and Valuation Reporter
S	Shaw (Court of Session Reports, 1st Series, 1821-1838)
SC	Session Cases
Sc Jur	Scottish Jurist
SCLR	Scottish Civil Law Reports
SLCR	Scottish Land Court Reports
Sh Ct Rep	Sheriff Court Reports

Table of Statutes

List of Cases

1 Introduction

There must be few people in Scotland, whatever their position in life, who have not encountered a lease at some point. Many are tenants of dwellinghouses, having leased them either from private landlords or a public authority, probably the local council. Many others are tenants of business premises, whether they be shops, offices or factories. It is also common for a farmer to be the tenant of the holding he cultivates. Landlords too come in many guises, from large financial institutions, such as banks, insurance companies or pension funds, which have bought property as an investment, to the private individual who leases out his house for a few years while he is absent abroad.

Not only is a lease one of the commonest types of agreement now, but it is also one of the oldest: we will see shortly that statutes going back as far as the fifteenth century are still good law.

Indeed, so familiar is the concept of a lease, that to spend too much time on a definition might be to run the risk of making the basic idea seem less straightforward than it actually is. However, it is necessary to take a brief look at its main features, so as to properly mark out our field of study.

1. MAIN CHARACTERISTICS OF LEASES[1]

A lease is a contract by which a person, known as a tenant, is allowed to occupy someone else's property for a finite period. In return for this he pays to the person granting this right (ie his landlord) a periodical payment known as rent. Rent usually takes the form of money, but may also (though not commonly) be paid in goods.

Several points arise from this that require to be developed:

(1) The subject matter of a lease is **heritable property**. This

---

1 Rankine *Leases* (3rd edn, 1916), Introduction; Paton & Cameron *Landlord and Tenant* (1967), pp 3-5.

means, broadly speaking, land and buildings and rights pertaining to them. In a strict sense it means land and its pertinents, including buildings and any other fixtures attached to the land; however, although it is subsidiary in legal theory, it is often a building rather than its site which is the most valuable element in a lease, and therefore the main subject of the contract. Heritable property is the equivalent (though not the exact equivalent) of the English concept of real property. Where moveable property is rented, the contract in strict law is not one of lease but of **hire**, although the term lease is sometimes loosely used in connection with the hire of some moveables.

(2) A lease is a contract. This means that, as well as the special legal rules relating to landlord and tenant, the general law of contract also applies to leases. It is not within the scope of this book to look in any detail at the law of contract, for which there are several excellent textbooks at various levels[2]. However, reference to contract law will be made from time to time where thought necessary or appropriate.

(3) The tenant (or tenants, where there is a joint tenancy) normally must be given an exclusive right to occupy the subjects of let. Where the landlord has reserved the right to share occupation in some way, the contract may not be a lease at all but a mere licence. This is an important distinction which we will return to later. However, there are certain exceptional types of contract which do not involve exclusive occupation by the tenant, but nevertheless have been traditionally considered as leases. These include leases of shooting rights, salmon fishings and the right to extract minerals.

(4) A lease usually confers only a temporary right of occupation upon the tenant. The right of ownership remains with the landlord and possession reverts to him at the expiry of the lease. In strict theory this need not be so, as in the old case of *Carruthers v Irvine*[3] where a lease was stated to endure 'perpetually and continually as long as the grass groweth up and the water runneth down'. Such a perpetual lease, however, is really an anachronism and extremely rare. A lease will generally have a definite date of expiry, although its duration may be extremely long, eg 99 or even 999 years. Moreover, a lease without a definite termination date (known in Scotland as an

---

2 Gloag *The Law of Contract* (2nd edn, 1929); Walker *The Law of Contracts and Related Obligations in Scotland* (2nd edn, 1985); McBryde *The Law of Contract in Scotland* (1987); Woolman *An Introduction to the Scots Law of Contract* (1987).
3 (1717) Mor 15195.

'ish') would not qualify for the considerable benefits conferred by the Leases Act 1449[4].

There is, however, a much more important qualification to this concept that a lease confers only a temporary right of possession. In certain cases, mainly agricultural leases and house lets, the tenant may have a statutory right to security of tenure, ie the right to remain in occupation of the property for an indefinite period beyond the stated termination date. These cases will be discussed in much more detail in chapters 12, 13 and 14.

2. ENGLISH LEASE LAW

Although Scotland still has a separate legal system, there has been a tendency since the Union of the Parliaments in 1707 for the law of the two countries to be assimilated. Nowadays many areas of law are governed by statutes that apply to both Scotland and England, eg employment legislation or company law. In other areas there are separate Scottish and English Acts, but with substantially identical provisions, eg the statutes relating to town and country planning or compulsory purchase and compensation. However, in the realm of landlord and tenant there are still many important differences between the laws of the two countries. It is true that many common principles of contract law underpin lease law on either side of the border; however, Scotland and England traditionally have quite distinct systems of land tenure and this has tended to create a fundamental divergence that is still very much with us.

One manifestation of this is found in the English distinction between freehold and leasehold tenure. In England when one 'buys' a property by paying a capital sum, it is sometimes acquired outright and the purchaser becomes the owner of the freehold. In many instances, however, what is being bought is only the tenant's interest in the unexpired portion of a very long lease, perhaps for 99 years or 120 years or even longer. A nominal amount of rent may be payable, but the main consideration is the capital sum, and the transaction will externally resemble an outright sale. A form of 'leasehold' tenure was traditionally possible in Scotland, but was much less common, particularly in the case of residential property. This was because the Scottish system of feudal tenure allowed landowners to obtain a similar type of monetary return without granting leases: thus an owner could grant a right of perpetual

4 See ch 2, pt 4 below.

ownership to another person while retaining the right of superior, enabling him to charge the new owner (now his vassal) an annual feuduty. The amount of the feuduty would have been comparable to the rent payable under a long English lease and in both cases a capital sum might or might not have changed hands when the property was first disposed of; this would probably depend upon whether the site already had buildings or whether these were to be provided by the new owner or tenant.

Nowadays, long leases are common in Scotland in the case of commercial and industrial properties, where there has been much English influence. However, long leases of dwellinghouses (always comparatively rare) have now been expressly forbidden in Scotland for periods of more than twenty years[5]. In England, on the other hand, long leases of residential property remain widespread.

Despite the English influence on Scottish commercial and industrial leases, it is here that we find another fundamental difference between the countries. In landlord and tenant law generally, much of Scots common law has been supplemented and in some areas virtually replaced by statute. This is particularly true in the case of residential and agricultural leases, where Scottish and English tenants are both protected by separate but substantially similar legislation. Many of these statutory provisions cannot be contracted out of, ie if a tenant is induced to sign a lease with a clause denying him his statutory rights, such a provision will have no effect. In England, tenants of business premises are similarly protected by a substantial statutory code; for example, under the Landlord and Tenant Act 1954 a tenant often has the right to renew his lease, even where his landlord wants him to move out. In Scotland, with one minor exception[6], there is no such statutory regulation and the parties enjoy virtual freedom of contract.

There are many other differences, the more important of which will be referred to when they arise. Nevertheless, there are enough common areas for it to be expedient to quote English cases where there is no equivalent Scottish authority. This is particularly so in the chapter on rent reviews, where the sparse Scottish authority is almost swamped by the deluge of English decisions. Such English authority, however, should always be treated with some caution; English cases may often be highly persuasive, but are never totally binding in Scotland.

---

5 Land Tenure Reform (Scotland) Act 1974, ss 8-10; see ch 6, pt 4 below.
6 See ch 8 below.

3. TYPES OF LEASE

Not all of the following categories are mutually exclusive and there is some overlap between them:

Urban and rural leases

The distinction between urban and rural leases in Scots Law is traditional, operating independently of the other classifications described below. It does not mean, as the words might suggest, that one kind is found in the town and the other in the country, though that is a possibility. Where the main subject of let is a building, and there is either no land attached or the land is subsidiary (eg garden ground), we have an **urban** lease. However, where the main subject is land it is a **rural** lease. A lease of an agricultural holding is therefore a rural lease: there may be farm buildings, but they are subsidiary to the land as part of the subjects of let. The distinction between urban and rural leases is still important in some cases where we have to apply the common law of landlord and tenant. For example, whether or not a lease is an urban or rural one may determine whether or not it can be assigned without the landlord's consent[7]. Other incidences will be noted as they arise.

Commercial and industrial leases

Commercial and industrial leases are urban leases, as they relate to the let of buildings. 'Commercial lease' is the term generally applied to leases of shops or offices. An 'industrial lease', as the name suggests, is the lease of a factory. In England, they all may be encountered under the term 'business leases'. As noted above, commercial and industrial leases in Scotland (though not in England) are almost free of statutory regulation. Commercial and industrial subjects are generally the most valuable types of heritable property, and are commonly acquired by large financial institutions for the purpose of investment. It is in this area, because of the amount of money that is often at stake, that the fast developing law relating to rent reviews is most alive[8].

7 See ch 5, pt 1 below.
8 See ch 10 below.

Agricultural leases

Agricultural leases are, naturally, rural leases. Leases of farmland are closely regulated by the Agricultural Holdings Acts, which confer many important rights upon tenants; these include the right to claim security of tenure (ie to stay on after the expiry date stated in the lease) or, where that is denied, the right to be compensated for improvements which the tenant has made to the holding. In the case of smaller holdings, the lease may instead be governed by the legislation relating to crofts and small landholdings, but the type of protection enjoyed by the tenant is similar[9].

Residential leases

Residential leases are leases of dwellinghouses, including flats, and they are of course urban leases. Like agricultural leases, they are extensively regulated by statute. Until early in this century, the most common types of residential let were those from private landlords. Such leases (apart from a comparatively small number of lets of houses with a high rateable value) have for many years been governed by a series of statutes usually known as the **Rent Acts**. The Rent Acts protect tenants by giving them security of tenure and the right to have a fair rent registered for the property; these rights are now in the process of being modified, since the passing of the Housing (Scotland) Act 1988[10]. Over the course of the present century, the incidence of private house lets has gradually decreased in proportion to the rise in public sector tenancies, mainly in the form of local authority housing. However, there are still many private residential leases, notably in the realm of bedsits and other short furnished lets. Statutory regulation has more recently been extended to the public sector itself, in a separate series of Acts giving a tenant, among other things, security of tenure and the right to buy the house he occupies from his landlord[11].

Leases of certain uses of land

Scots law has traditionally given the status of lease to certain types of agreement under which the tenant does not have an exclusive

---

9 See ch 12 below.
10 See ch 13 below.
11 See ch 14 below.

right to occupy the property, but the right to use it for certain purposes only. Many of these have fallen into disuse in modern times, but others still occur, mainly in rural areas. They include **mineral leases**, which are less common since the nationalisation of coal, but can still be found in respect of other types of mineral. Logically, a mineral lease should really be regarded as a type of sale, as the subjects are gradually removed by the tenant. For this reason, instead of rent, the mineral tenant generally pays a lordship or royalty, based on the amount of minerals taken. Other special uses of land that may be leased include **salmon fishings** and other **sporting rights**. Readers who wish to explore the above in greater depth, or to investigate some of the more rare and exotic varieties, will have to consult other references[12]. Finally, it should be noted that in deciding whether or not these, or any other borderline cases, should be called leases is no empty exercise. It will determine whether, in addition to the general law of contract, the special legal rules relating to leases will apply; in particular, it will decide whether the tenant will enjoy the benefits conferred by the Leases Act 1449[13].

Long leases

There is no prescribed length that determines whether a lease should be regarded as a long lease or not. Twenty years is perhaps as good a figure as any, as it is the maximum length for leases of residential property and the limit above which leases may be recorded in the Register of Sasines or Land Register. Long leases of commercial and industrial property are common, as institutional landlords want the financial security of having a tenant committed over a long period, and business tenants have to rely on the lease contract to give them the security of tenure enjoyed by their English counterparts under statute. A common type of long lease is the **ground lease**, whereby the landlord leases the ground only, for a relatively modest rent, and the tenant either buys the buildings outright or provides them at his own expense; obviously, a tenant will agree to this only if he is given a reasonable length of tenure (eg ninety-nine years) which will at least match the useful life of his buildings. The various implications of long leases are sufficiently important to merit a chapter on their own[14].

12 See *Paton & Cameron*, pp 73-84.
13 See ch 2, pt 4 below.
14 See ch 6 below.

Other types of lease tenure

The rich and variegated Scottish legal tradition has bequeathed to us certain special types of lease tenure which, although rare, are still to be found in certain areas.

The Crown's kindly tenants of the four towns of Lochmaben. This is a strictly local phenomenon found in Dumfriesshire near the Border, originating historically from grants by King Robert the Bruce to vassals on the lands of his castle there. It is a strange hybrid of tenancy and ownership, under which the 'tenants' have a potentially perpetual right along with an absolute right to sell, but can be removed if they don't pay their rent[15]. Eventually transfers of kindly tenancies will be registered in the Land Register of Scotland, which will have the effect of making the tenants proper owners, and absorbing them into the general system[16]. However, this will happen only when the area becomes operational for registration of title, which has not yet occurred[17].

Tenancy at will. This tenure is a little more common. It is an informal type of ground lease to be found particularly in fishing and rural villages on the north-east coast, in highland villages, and in a mining village in Lanarkshire[18]. The tenant rents the land from the landowner in order to build his own house, but is given no formal title and can be removed for non-payment of rent. This rather insecure position has been somewhat alleviated by statute and the tenant at will now has the right, if he wishes, to purchase his landlord's interest[19].

Licences

Licences are not in fact leases at all, but often resemble them and occupy a grey area that may be exploited by unscrupulous landlords. The concept of a licence to occupy is much more developed in England, where it has been extensively used as a device for denying tenants of dwellinghouses the protection of the Rent

---

15 *Rankine* ch VII; *Paton & Cameron* pp 69-70.
16 Land Registration (Scotland) Act 1979, s 2(1)(a)(v), s 3(3)(c).
17 See ch 2, pt 4 below.
18 *Paton & Cameron*, pp 68-69.
19 Land Registration (Scotland) Act 1979, ss 20-22; see also *McCann v Anderson, More v Anderson* 1981 SLT (Lands Tr) 13, *Ferguson v Gibbs* 1987 SLT (Lands Tr) 32.

Acts, which strictly apply only to leases as such. For this reason we will consider licences in more detail in the context of Rent Act evasions[20].

4. LEASES AND THE COMMON LAW

We have already seen that for certain types of lease, mainly those relating to farmland and dwellinghouses, the common law of landlord and tenant has been largely superseded by statute. In the field of commercial and industrial leases, there is not the same statutory presence, but the common law, unlike many statutory provisions, can generally be contracted out of, and often is; this means that the legal relationship between the parties is mainly governed by the terms of the lease document itself.

However, the common law of landlord and tenant remains important for a number of reasons. Some common law requirements are so fundamental that no lease can feasibly be without them, and these are considered in the next chapter. The common law will also be required to fill in any gaps that occur when statute law or the terms of the lease document are silent. Thirdly, the party most likely to try and contract out of the common law is the landlord, who is generally in the stronger negotiating position when the lease contract is being drawn up; however, it is unlikely that he will readily give up the powerful traditional rights he enjoys against his tenants, such as irritancy or hypothec[1]. Finally, it is salutary for parties drawing up lease documents to have in mind what might be the consequences of failing to create a clear and unambiguous contractual agreement, covering all important areas. The common law is liable to plug any gap with something that may be confused or ambiguous or contrary to modern lease trends. A good example of the latter is the common law provision which confers significant repairs obligations upon a landlord, the general modern practice in commercial and industrial leases being to pass these on to the tenant – a phenomenon usually known as the FRI (tenant's full repairing and insuring) lease. Therefore, if a tenant is to be responsible for all repairs, this must be clearly stated in the lease, or much of the repairs obligation will revert back to the landlord. This is not the sort of thing likely to make a large financial institution investing in property very happy with its legal advisers: if the rent has been fixed

---

20 See ch 13 below.
 1 See ch 4, pt 2 below.

on the basis that the tenant does the repairs, the amount of money at stake might be quite considerable.

The early part of this book will therefore be mainly devoted to a consideration of the Scottish common law of landlord and tenant. Then, since it **is** so often contracted out of, we will take a brief look at the sort of lease terms we are likely to encounter in practice. Slightly longer consideration will be given to two somewhat problematical clauses, those relating to rent reviews and service charges; rent reviews in particular pose a number of complex problems in modern lease law. Finally we will consider the main areas of statutory control of lease contracts.

2 Basic Legal Requirements

1. FORM OF LEASE

In Scotland, contracts relating to heritable property belong to a category known as the *Obligationes Literis*[1]. This means that they must be entered into in writing, they must be signed by the parties concerned and, in addition, certain formalities must be observed. In the case of leases there is an exception where the term is for a year or less, but all other leases should take one of the following three alternative forms:

(1) *An attested document.* This is a formal deed, which is signed by both landlord and tenant on the last page, each before two witnesses, who sign opposite the main party's signature. If both parties sign at the same time, the same two witnesses will suffice. An attested deed is known as a **probative document,** ie one which proves itself. If a lease is one of importance (either because of its duration or rental value) it would normally take this form. It is sometimes signed in duplicate, so that both landlord and tenant will have their own principal copy. Alternatively, the landlord may keep the original and issue the tenant either with an unsigned copy or with a photocopy. A third possibility is for the lease to be registered with the Books of Council and Session for preservation; the original will then be retained and, for the appropriate fee, the parties can each be issued with an extract (official photocopy) which is legally equivalent to the original deed[2]. The Books of Council and Session

---

1 See Gloag *The Law of Contract* (2nd edn, 1929) pp 162-179; Walker *The Law of Contracts and Related Obligations in Scotland* (2nd edn, 1985) para 13.23 et seq; Halliday *Conveyancing Law and Practice* (1985) vol I, ch 3; McBryde *The Law of Contract in Scotland* (1987) ch 27; Woolman *An Introduction to the Scots Law of Contract* (1987) pp 53-64.
2 *Halliday* para 4.53.

may also be used in connection with the landlord's remedy of summary diligence and are discussed further in chapter 4[3].

(2) *A holograph document*. This is written entirely in the handwriting of the party concerned and signed by him. A holograph lease, therefore, might consist of an offer handwritten and signed by the landlord followed by an acceptance handwritten and signed by the tenant. Such a lease would be perfectly valid but, for obvious reasons, professionally drawn up lease documents do not normally take this form; a landlord or tenant who was asked by his lawyer to sit in a corner and copy out a long legal document by hand would probably soon be looking for another agent. However, in cases where people attempt to draw up legal documents without a solicitor (as they are sometimes foolish enough to do), the privilege awarded to holograph writings sometimes saves them from disaster.

(3) *A document adopted as holograph*. This is a variant of (2). The document is not in the handwriting of the party concerned, but is handwritten by someone else or, more commonly, printed or typewritten. The party signs it, writing above his signature the words 'adopted as holograph'. This means that he is accepting the document as if it were in his own handwriting and, as a result, it has the same legal effect as a holograph document. This method is commonly used for short leases and, in the case of leases for longer periods, as a means of holding the parties contractually bound until such time as a formal document can be drawn up. An offer and acceptance in such form would normally be known as **missives of let**.

   A lease for more than a year that fails to observe **one** of these three **alternative** forms will technically be defective in form. Under the common law of contract, a contract so entered is said to be voidable, ie one which is initially valid, but which may be successfully challenged by either party. In *Goldston v Young*[4], both offer and acceptance for the sale of a shop were handwritten by Young, the seller. Goldston, the buyer, signed the offer and Young signed the acceptance. The acceptance was therefore holograph, but the offer was not: although signed by Goldston, it was not in his handwriting, nor was his signature witnessed, nor had he adopted the document as holograph. It was held that the contract was defective in form and

---

3 See ch 4, pt 2 below.
4 (1868) 7 M 188.

Young was entitled to resile from the contract. Although this case related to a sale rather than a lease, we are dealing with the same basic principle, ie the formalities required for a contract relating to heritable property.

This may seem to be a cautionary tale about the need for professional legal advice. However, fortunately for the authors (both inside and outwith the legal profession) of sloppily-drafted leases, *Goldston v Young*[4] does not tell the full story. Certainly, a lease that is defective in form may be set aside by either party, but usually only if he takes immediate action. Otherwise, the parties are liable by their actions to have demonstrated that they intend the contract to continue; this means that either of them, under the principle of **personal bar** (the equivalent of the English principle of estoppel), may be legally prevented from backing out of the contract of lease. For example, if a tenant moves into a property without objection from the landlord and pays his rent regularly, or makes improvements to the property on the strength of the lease, either party is likely to be personally barred from backing out later, on the pretext of the informality of the lease document. Personal bar is an equitable doctrine and it is not difficult to see why it is right for it to operate in such a case: if the parties, by their behaviour, clearly demonstrate their commitment to the contract, it is unfair that one of them should afterwards be able to wriggle out on a technicality.

The relevant aspects of personal bar are **rei interventus** (actings by the party loyal to the contract) and **homologation** (actings by the party wishing to withdraw)[5]. The actings relied on must be known to the other party to prevent him from backing out[6].

A lease, or other contract, may be validated by *rei interventus* or homologation in cases where there is even more informality than in *Goldston v Young*. For example, in *Wight v Newton*[7] a draft lease of a farm, approved by both parties but unsigned, was held to constitute a valid lease because the tenant had entered into possession. In *Forbes v Wilson*[8], an offer by the tenant which was not accepted in writing by the landlord was held to be sufficient, having been followed by actings of the tenant that amounted to *rei interventus*. But without some kind of writing, however informal, no amount of actings will constitute a lease for more than a year. And no lease at all

---

5 *Gloag* pp 167-175; *Walker* paras 13.32-13.36; *McBryde* paras 27.37-27.56; *Woolman* pp 56-62.
6 *Danish Dairy Co Ltd v Gillespie* 1922 SC 656, 1922 SLT 487.
7 1911 SC 762, 1911 1 SLT 335.
8 (1873) 11 M 454, 45 Sc Jur 276.

can be created by actings if there is no evidence of the parties having agreed to a lease at all; for example, in *Pickard v Ritchie*[9] the original tenant had died and the landlord had continued to accept rent from the tenant's son and the son's wife. It was held that there was no lease, as there was no evidence that the landlord had entered into even an informal agreement with the son or his wife, or even that she knew of the original tenant's death.

Once a lease has been completed by a document observing the proper formalities, it is not normally possible (unless there has been fraud or error) to depart from its terms by using parole evidence (ie word of mouth) or by referring to any less formal writing[10].

A lease for a year or less is in a privileged position and may be entered into either verbally or by an informal document[11]. However, it need hardly be said that one should make sure that the proper legal formalities **are** observed, even in the case of leases for a year or less. In practice, however, the principle of personal bar sees to it that many otherwise invalid leases become binding and enforceable.

2. ESSENTIAL ELEMENTS IN LEASES

Having seen the form that a lease should take, let us now look briefly at its content. A modern lease is typically a complex and lengthy document, almost as formidable to the lawyer as to the layman. In order to constitute a valid lease at common law, however, only four essential elements are required[12]. These are (1) the parties; (2) the subjects; (3) the rent, and (4) the duration, and are implicit in the very concept of a lease. It is difficult to think of a lease, as we have described it, without all of these basic ingredients; without the first two (the people involved and the subject matter), it is difficult to envisage having any kind of contract at all:

(1) *The parties.* It is so fundamental as to be self-evident that a lease must have both a landlord and a tenant. Not only must they both be named, but they also must be designed, ie properly identified, usually by the addition of an address. Either landlord or tenant may

---

9 1986 SLT 466.
10 *Perdikou v Pattison* 1958 SLT 153.
11 Rankine *Leases* (3rd edn, 1916) pp 116-119; Paton & Cameron *Landlord & Tenant* pp 19-21.
12 *Rankine* pp 114-116; *Paton & Cameron* pp 5-8.

be an individual or two or more individuals acting jointly, eg where a husband and wife are joint tenants. Also, either a landlord or tenant may be a group of people having separate legal identity, eg a limited company or other corporate body.

The landlord must have a legal right to grant a lease. The most obvious and common example of a person with this right is the owner of the property. However, other parties can have a right to grant leases, such as a tenant who grants a sublease. Another example is the right of a heritable creditor under a standard security, when his debtor is in default, to enter into possession of the security subjects and lease them out, as a method of recouping part of his loss[13].

(2) *The subjects.* It is equally fundamental that there must be some property that is being leased. Furthermore, the subjects of let must be properly identified. Sometimes the postal address may be all that is necessary, except in the case of flatted properties where several subjects may share the same address. It is usually better, however, to describe the property at greater length and to provide a plan. This is particularly desirable in the case of a long lease, if it is to be recorded in the Register of Sasines or Land Register of Scotland[14].

If the subjects of let are not properly identified, this is not necessarily fatal, as it is possible that they can be established by other evidence of what the parties have agreed or, if the tenant is already in occupation, by the extent of his possession[15]. However, this should not be relied upon as a method of identification. Finally, as we saw in the previous section, where the formal document **is** clear about the extent of the subjects, it would not normally be possible to use extrinsic evidence to alter it.

(3) *Rent.* Without the above two elements, we would arguably have nothing that could be called a contract at all. However, it is possible to create a legally binding contract allowing a person to occupy a property rent free. Unfortunately, as well as appealing only to philanthropists and tenants, such a contract would not be a lease, but merely a licence[16]. This means that it would not enjoy the

---

13 Conveyancing and Feudal Reform (Scotland) Act 1970, Sch 3, para 10(3) & (4).
14 See ch 6 pt 2 below.
15 *Piggott v Piggott* 1981 SLT 269; see also *Andert Ltd v J & J Johnston* 1987 SLT 268, where not only the subjects but also the rent and duration were allegedly uncertain.
16 *Mann v Houston* 1957 SLT 89.

benefits of any of the special legal rules relating to leases, notably the provisions of the Leases Act 1449[17].

(4) *Duration*. The period of the lease should be stated. However, if it is omitted for any reason (usually by accident), this may not be fatal. Provided that there is agreement on the other three essential elements mentioned above, a duration of one year will be implied[18]. Thereafter, if neither party takes steps to terminate the lease, it can be continued indefinitely on a year to year basis by the principle of **tacit relocation** (silent renewal)[19]. Since both landlords and tenants frequently want the other to be committed to a period of more than one year, it is, needless to say, desirable to include the duration rather than to rely upon this legal safety net.

3. OTHER REQUIREMENTS UNDER THE LAW OF CONTRACT

It naturally follows from the fact that a lease is a contract that its validity depends on the same common law rules as any other contract. There must be *consensus in idem* (agreement as to the same thing), and for a contract to be valid there must be no circumstances, when it was entered into, indicating that this consent was not present.

For example, the parties must have **contractual capacity**. A contract by a pupil (boy under fourteen, girl under twelve) can only be entered by the pupil's tutor (usually a parent). A contract by a minor (under eighteen) requires the consent of his or her curator (usually also a parent). A contract may likewise be challenged if either party, at the time of entering it, was drunk, insane or was a corporate body acting *ultra vires* (beyond its powers). Also, neither party must have entered into the contract under duress, or confused by an error as to what was agreed, either because of accident or induced by the other party's fraud or negligence. All these factors undermine the consent of the parties that is fundamental to the validity of a lease, or any other contract. For a full account of the general requirements for contractual validity, the reader is referred to the standard authorities[20].

17 See pt 4 below.
18 *Gray v Edinburgh University* 1962 SC 157, 1962 SLT 173.
19 *Cinema Bingo Club v Ward* 1976 SLT (Sh Ct) 90.
20 *Gloag* ch 5 and pt III; *Walker* ch 5 etc; *McBryde* chs 8-12; *Woolman* pp 48-49, ch 5.

4. ACQUISITION OF A REAL RIGHT BY A TENANT

Having seen some implications of the general law of contract upon leases, we will now examine one notable respect in which a lease confers rights beyond those enjoyed under a normal contract. This derives from an important early enactment, the Leases Act 1449. Perhaps English law has since gone far beyond Scots law in the statutory regulation of leases; but Scotland must surely have been first off the mark with this enlightened piece of legislation, a significant beacon in our country's emergence from the Dark Ages. Compared with most modern statutes, the 1449 Act is admirably concise, and is worth quoting in full:

> 'Of Takis of Landis for Termes
> Item it is ordanit for the sauftie and fauour of the pure pepil that labouris the grunde that thai and al vtheris that has takyn or sal tak landis in tym to cum fra lordis and has termes and yeris thereof that suppose the lordis sel or analy thai landis that the takeris sal remayn with thare tackis on to the ische of thare termes quhais handis at euer thai landis cum to for sik lik male as thai tuk thaim of befoir.'

In case the meaning of the above is not immediately self-evident, let us attempt to clarify. 'Analy' means 'alienate' (transfer ownership). A 'tack' is the old Scottish term for a lease. 'Ische' (or 'ish') means 'expiry date'. 'Male' (or 'Maill') means 'rent'.

It may also help to look at the underlying theory. By its very nature, a contract usually creates only **personal** rights and obligations, ie ones which affect only the parties entering into it and not third parties. We would therefore expect the landlord and the tenant to be the only people bound by a lease; after all why should someone else be obliged to observe an agreement that he did not enter into? However, in the context of leases, the application of this theory could have unfortunate consequences. If a landlord granted a lease for (say) five years, then sold the property after two years, there would be no reason in theory why the new owner could not evict the tenant immediately, without waiting until the expiry of the lease; since he was not a party to the original lease agreement, he would not be bound by it. The tenant would be entitled to sue the original owner for damages for breach of contract, but he would have no right to remain in occupation of the property.

This may be the theory, but the practice has been averted by the 1449 Act. The Act's effect is that, where a property subject to a sitting tenancy changes hands, the new owner will require to recognise the lease and allow the tenant, not only to remain in possession until his expiry date, but to do so at the original rent. Thanks to the Act, the tenant has obtained, not just a **personal** right, enforceable against the original landlord, but a **real** right, enforceable against the original landlord's **singular successors**. A singular successor is someone who becomes the owner of heritable property by any means other than inheritance, the most obvious example being that of a purchaser. Another example of a singular successor is a creditor with a right in security over heritable property which he is forced to realise to repay the debt owing to him. Someone who inherited the property on the landlord's death, although not classed as a singular successor, would also be bound to recognise the rights of sitting tenants, by virtue of the 1449 Act, and probably under the law of contract as well[21].

In the centuries since the 1449 Act was passed, it has naturally come before the courts for interpretation on many occasions. As a result, it has been established that several conditions, implicit in the Act's wording, must be fulfilled before it applies and a real right is conferred upon the tenant:[1]

(1) *The lease, if for more than a year, must be in writing.* This is, in fact, the same as the common law rule applying to all leases.

(2) *The subjects of the lease must be land.* This has been extended to include all kinds of heritable property, including buildings. There are a few exceptions, eg leases of shootings and trout fishings[2].

(3) *There must be a specific, continuing rent.* As we saw above, this is also a basic common law requirement for all leases. It makes no difference, as long as there is a rent, if a capital sum (grassum) is also payable; however where a grassum is payable, but there is no rent, the Act does not apply[3].

(4) *There must be an ish.* ie a term of expiry of the lease.

(5) *The tenant must have entered into possession.* This condition is satisfied not only if the tenant physically occupies the property himself (natural possession), but also where someone else legitimately occupies it instead of him (civil possession). For

---

21 *McBryde* para 24.01 etc.
1 *Rankine* ch 5; *Paton & Cameron* ch 7.
2 See *Palmer's Tr v Brown* 1989 SLT 128.
3 *Mann v Houston* 1957 SLT 89.

example, where a property has been sublet, it is not necessary for a tenant to be in physical occupation, provided that the subtenant is. However, in a case where an owner granted a lease and then sold the property prior to the date of entry, it was held that the new owner was not bound to recognise the lease, even though the tenant had been allowed to occupy part of the property a week before the entry date[4].

(6) *The landlord, if he is the owner of the property, must be infeft.* For a landlord to be infeft (ie for the property to be legally vested in him as owner), a title deed in his favour (eg a feu charter or disposition) must have been recorded in the Register of Sasines or, where applicable, the new Land Register of Scotland. Under this rule, the landlord should be infeft at the time the lease was granted, although if a deed in the landlord's favour is recorded after the lease has begun, the lease will be validated retrospectively under the principle of **accretion**. The requirement for infeftment does not apply where the landlord is not the owner, the most obvious case being where he is himself a tenant who has sublet the property.

A real right is also conferred upon a tenant where a lease has been recorded in the Register of Sasines or in the Land Register of Scotland, which is gradually superseding the Register of Sasines under the new system of registration of title. In such a case, therefore, it is not essential for the conditions of the 1449 Act to be complied with. In particular, recording a lease in the Register of Sasines or Land Register is legally equivalent to possession (see condition (5) above). This means, for example, that a creditor who has a security right over a lease need not take physical possession of the property but will acquire a real right provided that the lease and the standard security (the deed securing the loan granted by the creditor) have both been recorded in the Register of Sasines or Land Register. For a lease to be recorded in the Register of Sasines or Land Register, it must be in probative form and be for a period of twenty years or more[5].

In those areas where registration of title is now operational and the lease is of twenty years or more, recording in the Land Register is now the only way for a tenant to acquire a real right[6]. In such

4 *Millar v M'Robbie* 1949 SC 1, 1949 SLT 2.
5 Registration of Leases (Scotland) Act 1857 (as amended by the Conveyancing (Scotland) Act 1924, s 24, the Long Leases (Scotland) Act 1954, s 26, and the Land Tenure Reform (Scotland) Act 1974, Sch 6).
6 Land Registration (Scotland) Act 1979, s 3(3).

cases, therefore, the 1449 Act has been superseded. The areas which have so far become operational are the counties of Renfrew, Dunbarton, Lanark and Glasgow, and over the next few years the Land Register will gradually replace the Register of Sasines, area by area, over the rest of Scotland. In due course, therefore, the 1449 Act will cease to apply in respect of all recordable leases[7].

When the 1449 Act has operated to confer a real right enforceable against the landlord's singular successors, the obligations of the lease will generally transmit as well. In other words, they will become real conditions and will run with the land, ie they will apply not only to the original landlord and tenant but to their successors under the same lease. However, for this to be so, the obligations must be of the sort normally found in a lease. If they are personal in nature, they will not transmit and will bind only the original parties. Examples of such personal obligations include the right of a farm tenant to take peat from a moss in another part of his landlord's estate, a rent abatement in return for personal sevices by the tenant to the landlord, and a right by the tenant of a 999 year lease at any time to demand a feu charter of the property from his landlord (ie to be granted ownership)[8].

---

7 For more on registration of leases, see ch 6, pt 2 below.
8 *Paton & Cameron* pp 95–97; see also *Bisset v Magistrates of Aberdeen* (1898) 1 F87.

3 Rights and Obligations of the Parties

At common law, the landlord and tenant under a lease each owe the other a number of implied obligations[1]. All of these automatically apply, unless the lease document specifically states otherwise. Some of them are commonly reinforced by inclusion in the lease document, whereas others are often contracted out of. The obligations of the tenant, of course, correspond to the rights of the landlord and vice versa.

1. OBLIGATIONS OF THE TENANT

(1) To enter into possession, to occupy and use the subjects

One might have thought that a tenant would have no reason to pay rent for a property which he is not going to occupy, but in the case of *Graham and Black v Stevenson*[2] the tenant of a hotel took the lease of another nearby hotel purely with the object of closing it down and eliminating competition. It was held that he was not entitled to do this. Likewise, one might ask why the landlord would object to non-occupation, provided that the rent was still being paid; the answer is that an empty property is likely to be neglected and fall into disrepair. In the case of *Blair Trust Co v Gilbert*[3] the tenant of a farm was sent to prison for three years for culpable homicide. It was held that his resulting non-occupation of the property was a material breach of contract which entitled the landlord to rescind, ie back out of the contract. In that particular case, the obligation was actually written into the lease, which is quite common with this obligation.

---

1 Rankine *Leases* (3rd edn 1916), chs 10 & 11; Paton & Cameron *Landlord and Tenant* (1967), ch 9.
2 (1792) Hume 781.
3 1940 SLT 322, 1941 SN 2.

The tenant will also be liable for any damage to the property caused by his non-occupation[4].

(2) To use the property only for the purpose for which it was let

If the tenant uses the property for a purpose other than the purpose for which it was let, he is said to **invert the possession**, and the landlord may raise an action of interdict to have the unauthorised use stopped. For example, in *Leck v Merryflats Patent Brick Co*[5] a tenant who had been leased a property for making bricks was stopped from using part of it as a private railway unconnected with the brickwork. And in *Bayley v Addison*[6], the tenant of a meal mill was interdicted from using it as a mill for grinding sawdust.

Although implied at common law, this obligation of the tenant is invariably written into leases in a clause known as the **use clause** (or user clause, as it is generally called in England)[7].

(3) To take reasonable care of the property

Irrespective of whether repairs are the landlord's or the tenant's responsibility under a lease, the tenant will be liable for damage caused by his own negligence. In the case of *Mickel v M'Coard*[8], where a tenant left a house empty during the winter without turning off the water or giving notice to the landlord of his intentions, it was held that he was liable for damage caused by burst pipes.

(4) To pay the rent when it becomes due

Although implied, the obligation to pay the rent when it becomes due is also invariably written into the lease. If a rent is **not** stated, the onus will be on the tenant to prove that no payment of rent was intended, otherwise he will be obliged to pay what the property is worth[9]. Invariably, the lease will also state the date when the rent is due; this is called the conventional term, ie the term of payment which the parties have agreed to. It is common for leases to state that

4 *Smith v Henderson* (1897) 24 R 1102, (1897) 5 SLT 96; *Mickel v M'Coard* 1913 SC 896, 1913 1 SLT 463.
5 (1868) 5 SLR 619.
6 (1901) 8 SLT 379; see also *Duke of Argyle v M'Arthur* (1861) 23 D 1236.
7 See ch 9 below.
8 1913 SC 896, 1913 1 SLT 463.
9 *Glen v Roy* (1882) 10 R 239, (1882) 20 SLR 165.

rent will be payable in advance, either monthly or quarterly. If no conventional term of payment is stipulated in the lease, a term of payment is implied (the legal term). When this would be depends on the type of lease involved and the relevant common law rules are somewhat complex. It is a matter of minor practical importance, since leases invariably state a conventional term of payment, and it would take more space than is available here to explain the legal terms of payment in a comprehensible fashion; however, readers of a masochistic tendency are referred to the authorities cited[10].

(5) To plenish the subjects

The tenant is obliged to stock the subjects of let with sufficient moveable property to provide security for the rent[11]. This is to enable the landlord, if required, to exercise his right of hypothec, which gives him the right to sell off moveable property on the subjects of let in order to recover the rent[12]. The landlord can enforce this obligation by applying to the court for a plenishing order; this is a precautionary measure, which may be taken irrespective of whether or not the tenant is actually in rent arrears. A plenishing order is competent even if it is required only because the tenant's moveables have just been sold off in order to recover rent arrears[13]. In fact, when a landlord raises an action of sequestration for rent (the court action used to enforce the landlord's right of hypothec) it is usual for the initial writ to include a request for a plenishing order, to follow after the sale of the seized property.

The obligation to plenish does not apply to agricultural subjects, as they are not subject to the right of hypothec[14].

2. RIGHTS OF THE TENANT

(1) To be placed in full possession of the subjects let and to be allowed to remain there for the duration of the lease[15]

The tenant must not only be given possession of the property, but possession of **all** of the property. It must also be given at the agreed

---

10 *Rankine* pp 341 et seq; *Paton & Cameron* pp 139-141.
11 *Rankine* pp 399-401; *Paton & Cameron* pp 212-213.
12 See ch 4, pt 2 below.
13 *Macdonald v Mackessack* (1888) 16 R 168; (1888) 26 SLR 124.
14 Hypothec Abolition (Scotland) Act 1880, s 1.
15 *Rankine* p 200 et seq; *Paton & Cameron* pp 127-130.

date of entry and not later. If, therefore, there is someone else already in occupation (eg a prior tenant) it is up to the landlord to have him removed in good time. If the landlord fails in this obligation to a material extent, the tenant may be able to rescind from the lease; otherwise, he will be entitled to damages in the form of an abatement of rent.

Once the tenant is in the property, the landlord must not do anything that would deprive, or partially deprive, the tenant of possession; to do so would be to derogate from his grant to the tenant[16]. However, a landlord can be liable in damages for derogation of his grant only as a result of deliberate or voluntary behaviour on his part. In *Chevron Petroleum (UK) Ltd v Post Office*[17], because of the negligence of contractors, the subtenants of a basement suffered flooding from an escape of water from their landlords' premises above. It was held that the landlords (ie the principal tenants) had not derogated from their grant and were not liable in damages.

(2) To be given subjects that are reasonably fit for the purpose for which they are let

The property should be in a reasonable condition, but not necessarily fit for a particular kind of business; as to the latter, the tenant must satisfy himself. For example, in the case of *Glebe Sugar Refining Co v Paterson*[18] a warehouse was let to a sugar refining company who used it to store sugar. A month after they took entry the warehouse collapsed, and the tenants sued the landlords claiming that, because of insecure foundations, the building was unsuitable for the purpose of the let. It was held that, within the practice in their own trade, the tenants had overloaded the warehouse. They had therefore failed to ascertain for themselves the suitability of the subjects for their business, and **they** were held liable to the **landlords** in damages. It was in fact a case of the tenants failing in **their** implied obligation to take reasonable care of the property.

If the condition of the property makes it substantially unsuitable, this will be a material breach of contract, entitling the tenant to

---

16 *Huber v Ross* 1912 SC 898, 1912 1 SLT 399; *Lomond Roads Cycling Club v Dunbarton County Council* 1967 SLT (Sh Ct) 35.
17 1987 SLT 588, 1987 SCLR 97.
18 (1900) 2 F 615, (1900) 7 SLT 374.

rescind. Rankine quotes the case of *Kippen v Oppenheim*[19]. 'Thus, where on entry to a dwelling-house the tenant found it to be overrun to a great extent and in every part with cockroaches; to be infested with bugs; to have an offensive smell; and one of the bedrooms to be too damp to be safely used, the Court held that the condition of the house was such as to render a tenant's life "substantially uncomfortable".' In that case, the tenant was entitled to rescind (or, as they quaintly put it in those days, to 'throw up' the lease).

The landlord's implied obligation to provide suitable subjects applies only to buildings and other artificial structures (as opposed to land), and in any case applies only to urban rather than rural leases, ie in leases where buildings are the main subjects of let. However, in rural leases to which the Agricultural Holdings Acts apply, the landlord has certain statutory obligations regarding farm buildings and other equipment provided by him[20].

(3) To have repairs carried out by the landlord

The right to have repairs carried out by the landlord is really the corollary of (2). Once the tenant has moved into premises that are reasonably fit for the purpose of the let, he is entitled to stay on in premises that remain so. The landlord's obligation in urban leases is to uphold the property in a tenantable and habitable condition during the currency of the lease[1]. This includes, but is not confined to, an obligation on the landlord's part to keep the premises wind and water tight so as to be proof against the ordinary attacks of the elements[2]. This has been interpreted quite narrowly to include water penetration through the roof and walls, but not through the floor. In the case of *M'Gonigal v Pickard*[3], the floor of the premises collapsed as a result of deterioration caused by dampness, precipitating the tenant and the bed on which she was lying into the basement. The landlord was held not to be liable, as it was an exceptional encroachment of water due to a cause other than the ordinary attacks of the elements. This decision seems rather strange in view of the landlord's broader obligation, a view reinforced by the more recent case of *Gunn v National Coal Board*[4], where rising damp had caused dampness and mould in the house concerned. The

19 (1847) 10 D 242; *Rankine* p 245.
20 See ch 12, pt 2 below.
 1 *Rankine* p 241; *Paton & Cameron* p 131.
 2 *Wolfson v Forrester* 1910 SC 675, 1910 1 SLT 318.
 3 1954 SLT (Notes) 62.
 4 1982 SLT 526.

tenant was held to be entitled to damages because the landlord was in breach of his general obligation to keep the premises in a habitable condition.

There are two major exceptions to the landlord's repairing obligation, ie (a) where the damage is caused by *damnum fatale* (Act of God), eg a flood or hurricane[5], and (b) where it is caused by the action of a third party or parties. The latter point is illustrated by the case of *Allan v Roberton's Trs*[6], where subsidence rendered a house uninhabitable because of mineral workings by a coal company which had encroached without permission upon the landlord's minerals. It was held that the landlord was not liable either to restore the house or to pay damages to the tenant, because the house had been destroyed by the fault of others for whom he was not responsible.

Also, the landlord is not liable for damage to the leased premises caused by a defect in nearby premises owned by him. In *Golden Casket (Greenock) Ltd v BRS (Pickfords) Ltd*[7], the subjects of let were flooded because of a blocked drain on the landlords' adjoining premises. It was held that the landlords were not liable. A fault in property other than the leased subjects did not give rise to a breach of the lease contract and the landlords had not been negligent in any way that would have founded a claim under delict.

It should be noted that such absence of liability on the landlord's part does not automatically mean that the tenant will be liable instead. In the dase of *damnum fatale*, no-one is liable and in the case of third party damage, the third party may be liable, either to the tenant or to the landlord, or to both. A wise landlord, of course, may be well advised to repair the property in order to protect the value of his investment; he will probably also arrange for such disastrous eventualities to be covered by insurance. However, at common law he is not legally obliged to do any of this. This illustrates how the common law may often be inadequate. It shows the need for a well-drawn lease agreement covering all foreseeable possibilities; a common solution, of course, is to pass all liability for repairs on to the tenant.

Another exception to the landlord's obligation is where the damage has been caused by the tenant's own negligence. Here, of course, the tenant **is** liable, as we saw earlier in this chapter when looking at the tenant's duty to take reasonable care of the property.

5   *Rankine* p 242; *Sandeman v Duncan's Trs* (1897) 4 SLT 336, 5 SLT 21.
6   (1891) 18 R 932, (1891) 28 SLR 726; see also *North British Storage & Transit Co v Steele's Trs* 1920 SC 194, 1920 1 SLT 115.
7   1972 SLT 146.

A final point about the landlord's common law repairing obliga-tion is that it does not amount to a warranty; in other words, the landlord is not guaranteeing against the property falling into disrepair. This means in effect that the landlord's obligation does not arise until the tenant has drawn the need for the repair to his attention; the landlord is not therefore in breach of contract merely because the repair has become necessary, but only after he has been notified and has failed to act[8]. This point may explain the decision in *M'Gonigal v Pickard*, as the tenant in that case had not reported the need for repairs to the landlord; however, that does not emerge as a reason for the decision in the rather truncated case report.

Once a need for repairs **has** been intimated to the landlord, he will be in breach of contract if he fails to carry them out, or does not carry them out within a reasonable time. In the case of *Scottish Heritable Security Co Ltd v Granger*[9], the landlord took a little over two months to repair drains after the defects had been pointed out by the tenant. In the meantime, the tenant had moved out. It was held that the landlord had committed a material breach entitling the tenant to rescind.

In the case of dwellinghouses, the landlord's repairing obligation has been extended by statute under the Housing (Scotland) Act 1987[10]. Also, as already noted, the repairing obligation we have been discussing refers only to urban leases. In the case of rural leases, where buildings are a subsidiary part of the subjects, there is no corresponding repairing obligation on the landlord at common law; however, in subjects where the Agricultural Holdings Acts apply, certain repairing obligations are imposed on both parties by statute[11].

If the leased premises are rendered dangerous by the landlord's failure in his repairing obligation, he may be liable in damages to anyone who is injured or whose property is damaged as a result. This liability extends, not only to the tenant, but also to anyone else who comes on to the property, possibly even a trespasser[12]. This responsibility for dangerous premises normally falls upon an occupier, but extends to a landlord where his failure in his duty to repair has caused the problem.

The landlord's common law repairing obligation is one which is very often contracted out of, particularly in commercial and

8 *Wolfson v Forrester* 1910 SC 675, 1910 1 SLT 318.
9 (1881) 8 R 459, (1881) 18 SLR 280.
10 Housing (Scotland) Act 1987 s 113 & Sch 10; see ch 14, pt 2.
11 See ch 12, pt 2 below.
12 Occupiers' Liability (Scotland) Act 1960, s 3.

industrial leases where the FRI lease (tenant's full repairing and insuring lease) is so common. From the landlord's point of view, therefore, the moral is quite obvious: if the parties have negotiated a full repairing lease, it is essential that the lease document makes the tenant's obligation clear. Otherwise, the common law may fill in the gap and make the landlord partially responsible for repairs. That is something he may not have intended, and something he may not thank his legal advisers for landing him with.

4 Legal Remedies of the Parties

In any kind of contract, where one party is in breach of his obligations, the other party will want some kind of legal redress either by forcing compliance or, in extreme cases, by backing out of the contract altogether. In either case he may also seek some kind of monetary compensation for any loss he has incurred as a result of the breach. This is true of all contracts, including leases, and there are standard breach of contract remedies designed to achieve the above ends; these remedies, and the extent to which they are relevant to the relationship of landlord and tenant, we will consider first. However, a landlord has certain additional powers, especially for the collection of rent arrears; these special remedies, which include the most powerful legal weapons at the landlord's disposal, we will afterwards consider separately.

1. STANDARD BREACH OF CONTRACT REMEDIES[1]

The standard breach of contract remedies are: (1) specific implement and interdict; (2) court action for debt; (3) rescission; (4) damages, and (5) defensive measures (lien and retention). Some of these have already been mentioned in chapter 3, and we will refer back there from time to time by way of illustration.

(1) Specific implement and interdict[2]

A party suffering from a breach of contract can seek a court decree that will force the other party to comply with his legal obligation. There are two types of court decree that will achieve this, a positive

---

1 See Gloag *The Law of Contract* (2nd edn, 1929) Part IV; Walker *The Law of Contracts and Related Obligations in Scotland* (2nd edn, 1985) ch 33; McBryde *The Law of Contract in Scotland* (1987) chs 14, 20, 21; Woolman *An Introduction to the Scots Law of Contract* (1987) pp 122-135.
2 *Gloag* ch 36; *Walker* paras 33.20-33.22; *McBryde* ch 21; *Woolman* pp 125-126.

one (specific implement) and a negative one (interdict). The first applies where the offending party has failed in some positive obligation under the contract, eg to carry out repairs. This could therefore be available either to the landlord or the tenant, depending on who was responsible for repairs. Specific implement is enforced by a decree *ad factum praestandum* (for the performance of an act). Interdict applies where a party is carrying out some action prohibited under the contract. In chapter 3 examples were given of instances when the landlord used the remedy of interdict to stop the tenant from inverting the possession, ie using the property for a purpose other than that for which it was let.

If a party fails to obey either of these types of court order, he is guilty of contempt of court and liable to a fine or imprisonment. This is the only practical way of enforcing such a decree, but it means that specific implement and interdict are rather roundabout and clumsy remedies, and in many cases there are better alternatives. For example, many leases give the landlord the power, if a tenant fails in a repairing obligation, to do the repairs himself and charge them to the tenant; this is particularly useful at the end of a lease, allowing the landlord, after the tenant has vacated the property, to carry out all necessary dilapidations and then forward the bill to the tenant. Note, however, that this right is **not** implied by law, but must be expressly reserved in the lease contract. A tenant will also normally have a better remedy than specific implement. If his landlord fails to execute repairs, or carry out any other obligation for which he is liable, there is no need for the tenant to go to the trouble and expense of raising a court action; it is far easier for him simply to retain his rent (see below).

There are certain situations where specific implement cannot be used, notably for recovery of a liquid debt. It is **not** therefore possible for a landlord to seek a decree *ad factum praestandum* to recover his rent. The reason for this is quite simply that there is little point in threatening someone with jail for not paying his rent when, as we will see below, it is much quicker and easier to legally seize his assets.

A recent case illustrates the scope of specific implement in a landlord and tenant context. In *Grosvenor Developments (Scotland) plc v Argyll Stores Ltd*[3] the tenants of a supermarket were bound under the terms of their lease to continue to occupy the premises and use them as a supermarket until the lease's expiry in 2016. The tenants gave the landlords notice of their intention to cease trading,

3 1987 SLT 738.

in response to which the landlords raised an action seeking an interdict against the tenants 'from ceasing to continue to occupy and use the supermarket premises . . . for the purposes of' trading as a supermarket. It was held that an interdict was incompetent because the obligation which the landlords wanted to enforce was a positive one, ie the obligation to occupy the shop and trade as a supermarket, and it could not be made the subject of an interdict by framing the decree in the form of a double negative. This was enough to make the action incompetent, but the court made it clear that they would not have granted a decree *ad factum praestandum* either, had it been sought. The granting of specific implement is always at the discretion of the court, and it will not be granted in respect of obligations that are insufficiently precise or in any other way impossible to enforce. In the words of Lord Kincraig:

> 'The obligation is to occupy and use the supermarket premises for the purpose of the retail sale of foodstuffs and all hardware, electrical goods and non-foods, commonly sold in super-markets and discount stores and partly as an off licence until the year 2016. To occupy and use premises and carrying on a business therein involves continuous acts of management in which multifarious actions are required as, for example, engaging and dismissing staff, ordering, taking delivery of and paying for goods etc. An order to use the premises for the purpose of retail sale of inter alia "non-foods, commonly sold in supermarkets" for a period of 42 years requires for its obedience under pain of penalty a determination by the defenders as to what at any one time is commonly sold in supermarkets. This is far too general an obligation in my opinion to be enforced by specific implement. It is one which the defenders would have difficulty in deciding at any one time whether they were acting in breach of it or not. . . . An order from the court must be precise and specific so that the defenders know throughout the period when the order is in force exactly what they are required to do and what they are prohibited from doing[4].'

The court confirmed, however, that the tenant was indeed in breach of contract by failing to occupy the premises, and that the landlords would have been entitled to damages, had they sought that remedy.

4 1987 SLT 738 at p 741.

It is worth noting in passing that interdict is more than just a breach of contract remedy. It can be used under the civil law to force a person to refrain from any unlawful act, whether or not the unlawfulness results from breach of a contractual obligation. For example, interdict is commonly used under the law of delict (in England, tort) in cases of nuisance or trespass. The English equivalent of an interdict is an injunction.

(2) Court action for debt[5]

A court action for debt is appropriate for a contractual obligation to pay a liquid sum of money and it is the standard remedy open to any creditor. It is much easier to enforce than a specific implement action: instead of the clumsy method of threatening the debtor with contempt of court unless he pays, a court decree for debt is enforced by diligence. By this means a creditor may legally seize the property of his debtor. The two most common forms of diligence are **poinding** and **arrestment**. Poinding is the attachment of the debtor's moveable property, which may be followed by a warrant sale if he still fails to pay. Arrestment is the attachment of property belonging to the debtor (usually money) which is held by a third party; the two most common situations where it is encountered are arrestment of funds in the debtor's bank account and arrestment of his wages in the hands of his employer. Another type of diligence is **sequestration for rent**, a form exclusively available to a landlord to enforce his right of hypothec; this, however, requires a special kind of court action[6].

In a landlord and tenant situation, the most obvious relevance of a court action for debt is for recovery of rent. However, this is not usually the best method available to a landlord: he would be competing with other creditors on an equal footing, instead of enjoying the advantages conferred by the landlord's hypothec or by using summary diligence. These remedies will be considered in detail later in the chapter. However, there could be cases where court action is the only appropriate method: hypothec only covers the current year's rent, and so the right to enforce it may be lost if there is any substantial backlog of arrears; and summary diligence can be used only if a clause consenting to its use has been included in the lease document.

---

5 *Walker* paras 33.15-33.19; *Woolman* p 125.
6 See pt 2 below.

In other words, as a method of collecting rent arrears, court action for debt should not be necessary for a landlord who does not delay in pursuing his arrears and whose lease document has been professionally drafted. Otherwise, it may be used as a last resort.

There can of course be debts other than rent which a tenant may owe to a landlord, or a landlord to a tenant, and for these a court action for debt would be the appropriate remedy. An example would be the one mentioned above where the lease document allows the landlord to do repairs and charge them to the tenant. It might also be the appropriate way of recovering service charges, if they appear in the lease as a separate item from the rent; only if they are included as part of the rent will the landlord's hypothec be available[7].

(3) Rescission[8]

Rescission is the right of a party to back out of a contract altogether, and is available only if the other party's action is sufficiently serious to constitute a **material breach** of the contract. What amounts to a material breach justifying rescission is a matter of degree and it will be for the court to decide in any particular case. However, there are precedents concerning certain types of breach. In chapter 3[8], we have already seen examples of material breaches in a landlord and tenant situation, eg the right of a landlord to rescind if the tenant does not occupy the property, or the right of a tenant to rescind if the landlord does not provide premises reasonably fit for the purpose of the let. Either party could probably rescind for breach of a repairing obligation, if the breach was serious and had gone on long enough. In *Couper v M'Guiness*[9] it was held that a tenant's failure to observe lease conditions obliging him to keep the garden ground of the property in a clean and cultivated condition and to maintain a boundary fence were not material breaches entitling the landlord to rescind.

In the case of a landlord, irritancy (where applicable) would usually be preferable to rescission, since its outcome is more certain[10].

---

7 See ch 11 below.
8 *Gloag* p 602 etc; *Walker* paras 33.41-33.45; *McBryde* paras 14.49-14.84; *Woolman* pp 122-124.
9 (1948) 64 Sh Ct Rep 249.
10 See pt 2 below.

(4) Damages[11]

Damages is a monetary payment that may be claimed in a court action as compensation for any loss resulting from a breach of contract. The measure of damages is the amount of the loss, so far as that can be quantified in money terms. Damages can be claimed in addition to any other breach of contract remedy, provided a loss has occurred as a result of the breach.

There are obviously cases where either a landlord or a tenant would be entitled to claim damages, some of which we saw in chapter 3. For example, where a tenant's neglect caused the landlord to suffer a loss in the value of his property (*Mickel v M'Coard*)[12], or where a landlord failed in his repairing obligation and the tenant suffered the effects of water penetration (*Gunn v National Coal Board*)[13].

(5) Defensive measures[14]

Defensive measures are extra-judicial measures which a party suffering from a breach of contract may take to protect his position. The first of these is **lien**, which is the right to hold in security some piece of property belonging to the other party, eg the right of a tradesman to hold on to goods he has been repairing until his bill is paid. There is no obvious application of the right of lien within the landlord and tenant situation, though no doubt circumstances could arise where it was appropriate.

Much more relevant in the present context is the other defensive measure, that of **retention**. This is the right of the party suffering from the breach to withhold money which he owes the other party. Retention is not always available, but only in certain specific circumstances, one of them being where the debt arises under the same contract as the broken obligation.

It follows, therefore, that a tenant will be entitled to retain his rent if the landlord is in breach of any of his obligations under the lease contract. Retention of rent is, in fact, a long established tenant's remedy and is an extremely useful one[15]. Instead of going to the

---

11 *Gloag* ch 38; *Walker* paras 33.23-33.40; *McBryde* ch 20; *Woolman* pp 126-133.
12 1913 SC 896, 1913 1 SLT 463.
13 1982 SLT 526.
14 *Gloag* ch 25; *Walker* paras 33.4-33.8; *McBryde* paras 14.33-14.48; *Woolman* p 124.
15 Rankine *Leases* (3rd edn, 1916) pp 326-335; Paton & Cameron *Landlord and Tenant* (1967) pp 141-142.

trouble and expense of raising a court action, the tenant need only do nothing and wait for the landlord to respond. If the landlord takes him to court for the rent, then he can lodge a valid defence based on the landlord's breach of contract[16].

It is important to note that, like lien, retention is merely a right in security. It does not extinguish the rental debt, but only entitles the tenant to postpone payment until the landlord's breach has been remedied, after which he will have to pay the arrears in full. It is true that the tenant may be entitled to damages if the landlord's breach has caused him any loss; however, this is a separate issue and the right to damages and their amount would normally have to be separately established in court. If a tenant is awarded damages, that exhausts his monetary remedy in respect of the breach concerned, and he will lose his right to retention unless a new breach occurs[17].

This common law right of a tenant to retain his rent may be contracted out of by an express stipulation in the lease[18]. A tenant may also, by his actions, bar himself from the right to retain his rent; for example, in a case where a tenant endured the landlord's breach and continued to pay the rent over a period of time without complaint, it was held that he had lost the right to retain his rent for that particular breach[19].

2. LANDLORD'S ADDITIONAL REMEDIES

Having examined those breach of contract remedies which apply to all contracts, we will now look at certain additional remedies which exist by virtue of the special nature of the lease contract. These are available to landlords, but **not** to tenants. They are: (1) irritancy; (2) hypothec, and (3) summary diligence.

It is not strictly correct to say that these arise only in landlord and tenant situations: irritancy and hypothec have their counterparts in feudal contracts as remedies available to superiors, and summary diligence is available under other deeds which contain acknowledgments of a liquid debt, eg standard securities. However, it **is** true to say that they are not generally available to all creditors, or other parties suffering from a breach of contract.

---

16 *M'Donald v Kydd* (1901) 3 F 923, (1901) 9 SLT 114; *Haig & Co Ltd v Boswall-Preston* 1915 SC 339, 1915 1 SLT 26; *Fingland & Mitchell v Howie* 1926 SC 319, 1926 SLT 283.
17 *Christie v Wilson* 1915 SC 645, 1915 1 SLT 265.
18 *Skene v Cameron* 1942 SC 393, 1942 SLT 210.
19 *British Railways Board v Roccio* 1970 SLT (Sh Ct) 11.

(1) Irritancy[20]

Irritancy means forfeiture and refers to a landlord's right to terminate a lease prematurely because of the tenant's breach of contract. There are two types of irritancy: (a) legal irritancy and (b) conventional irritancy.

(a) *Legal irritancy.* A legal irritancy is one which is implied by law, and is therefore available to any landlord, whether or not there is any mention of irritancy in the lease document. There is only one ground of legal irritancy, ie non-payment of rent for two years. If a legal irritancy has been incurred and the landlord has begun legal proceedings to evict the tenant, the latter has the right to **purge** the irritancy. The tenant may do this at any time before the landlord's irritancy action has been concluded and the landlord has obtained an extract decree from the court. This means that, at any time before the landlord has reached the stage where he is legally entitled to instruct an eviction, the tenant may pay off all the rent arrears; if he does so, the landlord will be forced to accept the money and his irritancy proceedings will be nullified[1].

Common law legal irritancies are rarely encountered nowadays as very few landlords will be willing to allow rent arrears to accumulate for as long as two years, when there are so many other legal steps that could be taken at a much earlier date.

There is another legal irritancy, imposed by statute, which allows agricultural tenants to be removed for six months rent arrears[2].

(b) *Conventional irritancy.* Conventional irritancies are much more common and have been the subject of controversy in recent years.

A conventional irritancy is so called because it exists by convention, or agreement. In other words, unlike a legal irritancy, it is not implied under the common law, but only exists if specifically provided for in the lease document. The grounds of conventional irritancy are unlimited, and in each case they will consist of those which have been written into the lease in question; bankruptcy or liquidation of the tenant are common grounds of conventional irritancy and so are unauthorised assignation or subletting. Most importantly of all, rent arrears is also a standard ground of conventional irritancy, though usually for a much shorter period of

---

20 *Rankine* p 532 et seq, *Paton & Cameron* ch 15.
 1 *Rankine* pp 538-539, *Paton & Cameron* p 230.
 2 Agricultural Holdings (Scotland) Act 1949, s 19; see also ch 12 pt 2 below.

arrears than the two years implied by law, eg one month or even twenty-one or fourteen days. It is also common for irritancy clauses, after giving a list of specific breaches, to finish with a general statement that any other breach of the lease will also be a ground of irritancy.

If a landlord successfully ends a lease by irritancy, he cannot also claim damages for premature termination of the lease: it has to be one or the other[3]. However, he will probably not be precluded from claiming damages for some other breach of the lease contract.

It should also be emphasised that irritancy is always a **landlord's** option. If a landlord is in breach of contract, his tenant has only the normal remedies (eg rescission for a material breach), and a tenant cannot use irritancy as a pretext for ending a lease because of his own breach[4].

The most controversial aspect of conventional irritancies was that, until recently, the tenant had no right to purge the irritancy unless the landlord agreed to let him do so[5]. In this way they differed from legal irritancies. Once the ground of irritancy had been incurred, the tenant might seek to remedy the breach, but the landlord was entitled to reject his offer and proceed with eviction. The tenant's only defence was to establish that the landlord was using the irritancy oppressively, ie misusing his powers of irritancy. This had been the law for very many years, and such irritancy clauses were virtually standard in all commercial, industrial and agricultural leases. (They also often appear in residential leases, but in such a case their effect will generally be nullified as an attempt to contract out of statutory security of tenure provisions and will be superseded by statutory grounds of removal[6].)

It is doubtful whether many tenants, when signing their leases, used to understand what draconian powers they were handing to their landlords, but they (or at least their agents) were given a sharp reminder by the leading modern case on the subject. In *Dorchester Studios (Glasgow) Ltd v Stone*[7] the tenants under a sublease incurred an irritancy by neglecting to pay their rent within the twenty-one day period stated in the lease's irritancy clause. Eleven days after the expiry of this period, the landlords informed the

3 *Walker's Trs v Manson* (1886) 13 R 1198, (1886) 23 SLR 864; *Buttercase & Geddie's Tr v Geddie* (1897) 24 R 1128, (1897) 5 SLT 108.
4 *Bidoulac v Sinclair's Tr* (1889) 17 R 144, (1889) 27 SLR 93.
5 *Rankine* pp 547-548; *Paton & Cameron* p 232; *McDouall's Trs v MacLeod* 1949 SC 593, 1949 SLT 449; *Lucas's Exors v Demarco* 1968 SLT 89.
6 See chs 13 and 14 below.
7 1975 SC (HL) 56, 1975 SLT 153.

tenants of their intention to evict them. The tenants immediately offered payment of the rent, but the landlords refused to accept it and raised an action in the sheriff court to enforce the irritancy. The court decided in the landlords' favour and the tenants appealed all the way to the House of Lords, who upheld the original decision, rejecting the tenants' defence that the irritancy had been used oppressively.

The effect of that case has now been modified by statute. However, the common law has not been completely superseded and *Dorchester Studios*, furthermore, raises some interesting issues about the concept of Scottish leases, so it is worth looking at in a little more detail. One point mentioned was the contrast between irritancy and the English concept of forfeiture. Another was the fact that, in the analogous case of conventional irritancy of a feu, the vassal **did** have a right to purge the irritancy; the reason for this apparent anomaly is that, in theory, a tenant only stands to lose a temporary right to occupy someone else's property, whereas a vassal may forfeit a perpetual right of ownership. As Lord Kilbrandon put it:

'The cases make it plain that the law of Scotland in this matter stands on a different footing from that concerned with the relief from a forfeiture for non-payment of rent forming a condition in an English lease. In the latter contract the provision for forfeiture is inserted in order to secure payment of the rent; the rent having been tendered and accepted before judgment the purpose has been served. The debt having been paid the security cannot be enforced, and, it is presumed, goes into cold storage until next quarter-day. In Scotland the irritancy . . . is regarded as a means by which a landlord can rid himself of an unsatisfactory tenant who pays his rent, not on the date on which he promised to do so, but only after the landlord has been to the trouble of appealing to the court. . . .

Whether in modern times that doctrine fairly reflects social policy may be another matter. The distinction between the feu contract and the lease has become unsubstantial since the former took to its death-bed. Moreover, the old view that the lease, unlike the feu contract, does not convey a right of property, wears today an air of unreality. Statutes governing successively dwellinghouses, agricultural subjects and business premises, have gone far to confer on tenants interests more easily classified as proprietorial than ephemeral. And the long investment lease has in recent years become a feature in Scottish cities. All these considerations point, in my opinion, to the need for the Scottish doctrine to be re-examined from the policy point of view . . . .[8]'

After a pause for the implications of *Dorchester Studios* to sink in, a small outbreak of irritancy cases hit the casebooks, probably indicative of a much larger epidemic that did not reach the courts, or went unreported. All of them followed the decision in *Dorchester Studios*. In *HMV Fields Properties Ltd v Skirt 'n' Slack Centre of London Ltd*[9], it was again claimed that the landlords had misused their power of irritancy by using it oppressively. At the time the action was raised, the landlords had only recently bought the property, a shop in Hamilton, subject to the sitting tenancy. Moreover, according to the tenants, the new landlords' directors were all directors of another company which was not only a trade competitor of the tenants throughout Scotland, but which also had a shop in Hamilton directly opposite the one leased to the tenants. The tenants also alleged that the first notice they had been given of the change of landlords was two days before the rent was due, when an invoice was sent unobtrusively to the Hamilton shop in a plain brown envelope. By the time it had been forwarded to the tenants' head office in London and been paid, nearly a month had passed and the landlords proceeded to raise an action of irritancy because the rent had been paid outwith the twenty-one day period stated in the lease. All this led the tenants to suspect that the irritancy action, rather than being merely an exercise in efficient estate management, might just have been prompted by an ulterior motive. However, the court held that a defence of oppression will only succeed where there has been a clear abuse of rights or impropriety of conduct by the landlords. The landlords' motive, or alleged motive, fell short of such impropriety, and so the tenants' averments with regard to motive were held to be irrelevant. In other words the landlord has to **do** something oppressive, not just be suspected, with however much justification, of having an ulterior motive.

After an irritancy has been incurred, if the tenant stays on in the property pending the outcome of the court action to remove him, the landlord is entitled to be paid a reasonable rent for the extra period of occupation. This was established in a follow-up action

---

8 *Dorchester Studios (Glasgow) Ltd v Stone*, 1975 SC (HL) 56 at 67 per Lord Kilbrandon.
9 1982 SLT 477; see also *HMV Fields Properties Ltd v Tandem Shoes Ltd* 1983 SLT 114 and *What Every Woman Wants (1971) Ltd v Wholesale Paint & Wallpaper Co Ltd* 1984 SLT 133.

between the parties in *HMV Fields Properties Ltd*[10]. The court fixed a rent at the rate that had been payable under the lease at its premature termination; the landlords wanted to have the rent reviewed up to the market value as at the date of irritancy, but the court spared the tenants this final indignity.

It was clear from the *Dorchester Studios* case alone that the law was in need of reform. After ten years of discussion and controversy, the situation was somewhat remedied by the Law Reform (Miscellaneous Provisions) (Scotland) Act 1985. This provides that, in the case of monetary irritancies, the landlord must, after the irritancy has been incurred, give the tenant a further fourteen days written notice to pay the arrears; only on the lapse of that further period without payment may he proceed to enforce the irritancy[11]. The landlord's notice has to be sent by recorded delivery. It should be noted that s 4 of the 1985 Act applies not just to irritancies for non-payment of rent, but also to other monetary breaches, eg failure to pay a service charge or other sum owed by the tenant.

In the case of non-monetary breaches (eg insolvency, unauthorised assignation or other ground stated in the irritancy clause), the court may only enforce the irritancy in cases where it feels that a fair and reasonable landlord would do so[12]. Where the breach is one that could be remedied within a reasonable time (eg a tenant's failure to carry out repairs), the court is to take into account, when exercising its discretion, whether the tenant has been offered a reasonable opportunity to remedy the breach.

An interesting point to note is that these provisions apply, not just to conventional irritancies, but to circumstances where a landlord is attempting to rescind from a lease on the grounds of a material breach of contract[13]. Presumably this is to prevent a landlord from switching his tactics from irritancy to rescission as a means of getting round the 1985 Act.

It would render this statutory reform fairly useless if the terms of a lease could contract out of the 1985 Act's effect, and so this is expressly forbidden[14]. Also, the Act applies equally to leases that were entered before and after it came into force, and even expressly applies in cases where the actual breach occurred before the Act, provided the landlord had not already sent the tenant a written notice exercising his powers. Finally, the Act applies only to

10 *HMV Fields Properties Ltd v Skirt 'n' Slack Centre of London Ltd* 1987 SLT 2.
11 Law Reform (Miscellaneous Provisions) (Scotland) Act 1985, s 4.
12 Ibid s 5.
13 Ibid ss 4(1)(b), 5(1)(b).
14 Ibid s 6(1).

commercial and industrial leases; residential leases, agricultural leases and leases of crofts and small landholdings are specifically excluded, presumably because the existing statutory protection in these cases is thought to be sufficient[15].

While the 1985 Act takes some of the sting out of conventional irritancies, it is arguable that it does not go far enough. The fourteen day notice provision is somewhat short, and it remains to be seen how the courts will exercise their discretion in the case of non-monetary irritancies; their attitude to defences of oppression does not give tenants grounds for optimism. It is probably therefore still advisable for a tenant to resist the inclusion of an irritancy clause in his lease, or at least try to have concessions included that go a little further than the Act. Whether or not a landlord agrees to this will, of course, depend upon the strength of his negotiating position in the transaction in question; if he is finding it difficult to get tenants, there is no saying what he will agree to.

(2) Landlord's hypothec[16]

Nature of hypothec. The landlord's right of hypothec is probably his most effective remedy for ensuring the payment of rent. Hypothec is a right of security enjoyed by a landlord over any moveable items which his tenant keeps on the leased premises. It is a 'tacit' or 'legal' right, ie, like a legal irritancy, it is implied by law and does not need to be specifically provided for in the lease contract. If the tenant is in arrears with his rent, the landlord may, after applying to the court (in an action known as a sequestration for rent), sell off enough of the tenant's moveables to pay the rent. The landlord has the right to insist upon the tenant keeping moveables on the premises of sufficient value to cover the current rent; in other words, the tenant has a duty to plenish the property[17]. If the tenant fails in this obligation, the landlord can apply to the court for a plenishing order, requiring the tenant to restock the premises. This can be done even if the reason for the lack of moveables is that the landlord has just carried out a sale to enforce his right of hypothec[18].

Items covered by hypothec[19]. The items covered by the landlord's right of hypothec are known as the *invecta et illata* ('things brought

---

15 Ibid s 7.
16 *Rankine* pp 366-411; *Paton & Cameron* ch 13.
17 See above ch 3 pt 1.
18 *Macdonald v Mackessack* (1888) 16 R 168, (1888) 26 SLR 124.
19 *Rankine* pp 373-383; *Paton & Cameron* pp 202-206.

in and carried in'). This generally includes all moveable items on the leased premises, eg furniture in the case of a house let, stock-in-trade in the case of a shop lease or machinery where the lease is of a factory. Certain items are specifically excluded, eg money, or the tenant's clothes.

With a few exceptions, hypothec also covers goods on the premises that do not belong to the tenant. In particular, items which the tenant has merely hired or is acquiring by hire purchase can be sold as if they were the tenant's own property. The owner of such an item is presumed to know about the landlord's right of hypothec, and to have consented to his property being included under it when he allowed the tenant to keep the item on the leased premises. For example, in the case of *Dundee Corpn v Marr*[20], landlords were held entitled to sell a jukebox that had been hired to the tenants by a third party. In *Ryan v Little*[1] the premises of a furniture dealer were the subject of a sequestration for rent action to enforce his landlord's hypothec. The landlord included in his sequestration articles of furniture which had been sold to a customer and paid for, but had not yet left the dealer's possession. It was held that these were covered by the right of hypothec. The property of a sub-tenant can be sold to cover his own arrears to the principal tenant and, where the landlord has not consented to the sublet, to pay off the principal tenant's rent arrears also, even when his own rent is up to date[2]. An article on loan to the tenant may also be included, provided that it was in the tenant's possession in the ordinary course of his business[3].

However, goods belonging to a lodger or to a member of the tenant's family (eg a piano belonging to the tenant's daughter) are not subject to hypothec[4]. Also, the right of hypothec has tradition-ally not been thought to cover goods belonging to third parties which are only on the premises temporarily, such as items that have been handed in for repair or for exhibition[5]. Some doubt must be cast on this principle, however, after the case of *Scottish & Newcastle Breweries Ltd v City of Edinburgh District Council*[6] where the rented premises were a pub and the landlords were held entitled

---

20 1971 SC 96, also reported as *Ditchburn Organisation (Sales) Ltd v Dundee Corpn* 1971 SLT 218.
 1 1910 SC 219, *sub nom Little v M'Connell* 1909 2 SLT 476.
 2 *Steuart v Stables* (1878) 5 R 1024, (1878) 15 SLR 689.
 3 *DH Industries Ltd v RE Spence & Co Ltd* 1973 SLT (Sh Ct) 26.
 4 *Bell v Andrews* (1885) 12 R 961, (1885) 22 SLR 640.
 5 *Pulsometer Engineering Co Ltd v Gracie* (1887) 14 R 316, (1887) 24 SLR 239.
 6 1979 SLT (Notes) 11.

to sell empty beer kegs awaiting collection by the brewers, whose property they were. This case suggests that the goods of third parties would have to be on the premises **very** temporarily not to be subject to the landlord's hypothec.

Because of this rule about the property of third parties, it has become common for the hirers of expensive moveables (such as factory machinery) not to hire to a tenant unless the landlord agrees to waive his right of hypothec with regard to their property. A reasonable landlord will probably agree to this, provided that the remaining moveables in the premises are sufficient to cover his rent. Since his refusal would probably cause the hire company to back off, he has nothing to gain by it, and there is no point in throwing obstacles in the way of his good tenants in order to take excessive measures against a few potential defaulters. In any case, prior intimation to the landlord by the owner of the item, at least in the case of single items where the whole of the landlord's security is not affected, is probably enough to exclude it from hypothec, as this would rebut the presumption that the owner consented to its inclusion[7]. However, if the landlord has already begun to enforce his right of hypothec by raising an action of sequestration for rent, the third party's only remedy is to approach the court with the request that his property be left to the last, and only sold if the tenant's own goods are insufficient to cover the rent[8].

Finally, it must be acknowledged that the law is not absolutely clear on the subject of which items are included in hypothec. Much of it depends on very old authorities, not all of which are entirely consistent. The most recent case law seemed to be pointing towards the view that the landlord is entitled to step in and grab virtually anything that happens to be on the leased premises, with few exceptions. However, the most recent case, on the surface at least, seems to go against this trend. In *Rossleigh Ltd v Leader Cars Ltd*[9], the tenants of garage premises transferred their business to an associate company and later went into voluntary liquidation, owing the landlords rent. In a reparation action by the landlords against the new occupants of the premises, the question arose as to whether the stock on the premises was covered by the landlord's hypothec. It was held that it was not because, although it was on the leased premises, it was in the possession, not of the tenants, but of a third party, ie the tenants' associate company. It did not matter that the associate company, rather than the tenants, were the ones in

7 *Dundee Corpn v Marr* 1971 SC 96 at 101-102, per Lord President Clyde.
8 *M'Intosh v Potts* (1905) 7 F 765, (1905) 13 SLT 108.
9 1987 SLT 355.

occupation of the premises. The court acknowledged that the stock might have been included in the landlord's hypothec if the status of the associate company had been that of subtenant, but that was not the case.

Where does this leave us with regard to the goods of third parties? In a slightly grey area perhaps, but the above case must be seen in perspective. Its rather unusual circumstances make it seem more exceptional than it really is. The *ratio* is that goods on the premises, not in the tenant's possession, are not included in hypothec. In most cases this would apply where the tenant himself is still in the premises, but the items are in the possession of another occupant, other than a subtenant. Examples of this would be the property of the tenant's lodger or a member of his family; and, as we saw above, these have long been recognised as excluded cases.

It might be thought that the *Rossleigh* case opens the door to limited companies evading their landlord's right of hypothec by a little judicious company re-organisation. However, it should be pointed out that the reparation claim in that case (against the tenants' associate company for inducing breach of contract) failed because the defenders had acted in good faith, without any intention of defrauding the landlords and unaware that their actions were causing the tenant to be in breach of the lease contract.

Rent covered by hypothec[10]. The landlord's hypothec secures only the current year's rent and not prior arrears. The current rental year in any lease runs from the anniversary of the date of entry. An action to enforce the right of hypothec, for any part of the year's rent, must be raised within three months of the last payment term of the year, or the right will be lost in respect of that year's rent. The traditional quarterly terms are Candlemas (2 February), Whitsunday (15 May), Lammas (1 August) and Martinmas (11 November). This means that, depending at what stage of the rental year the tenant goes into arrears, the landlord can have as long as a year or as little as three months to enforce his right of hypothec before the right is lost. If a landlord fails to raise his action in time, this does not mean that he has lost all right to such prior rent, but only to the right of security conferred by hypothec: other remedies will still be open to him, such as summary diligence or a court action for debt.

Enforcement of hypothec[11]. The court action which a landlord must raise to enforce his right of hypothec is called an action of

10 *Rankine* p 384; *Paton & Cameron* pp 206-208.
11 *Rankine* p 401 et seq, *Paton & Cameron* p 215 et seq.

sequestration for rent (not to be confused with sequestration in bankruptcy). The landlord applies to the sheriff court for a warrant to sequestrate, which the sheriff usually grants automatically. Then, instead of serving the court summons on the tenant by post in the usual manner, he gives the warrant to the sheriff officer who goes to the leased premises and serves the summons personally, at the same time making an inventory of sufficient items to cover the rent that is owing. After that the sequestrated items are said to be *in manibus curiae* ('in the hands of the court'), ie they cannot be removed from the premises until after the judicial process has been completed. If the tenant removes them he will be in contempt of court and will be penalised (possibly even by imprisonment) if he does not restore them. If anyone else takes items away (eg another creditor, or someone who has purchased the items from the tenant), that person will have to pay the landlord the value of the goods taken. If they have been taken in bad faith (ie in the knowledge that the goods are the subject of a sequestration action), the person taking them may be held liable for the whole rent owing. After the court process has been completed, the landlord can instruct the sheriff officer to hold an auction of the sequestrated items, unless the tenant has since paid the rent plus all legal expenses incurred.

Leases subject to hypothec. The right of landlord's hypothec used to apply to all types of lease, but since the Hypothec Abolition (Scotland) Act 1880, it does not apply to ground let for agriculture or pasture exceeding two acres[12]. This effectively means that most agricultural leases are not subject to hypothec. There was formerly also an exception in respect of certain small dwellinghouses, but this exclusion no longer applies[13]. In cases where hypothec no longer applies the landlord (apart from his right in some cases to summary diligence – see below) has no real advantage over other creditors, or preference in the tenant's bankruptcy[14]. Hypothec applies to all other kinds of lease, but since sequestration for rent is a rather expensive action, involving the sheriff officer from a very early stage, it is not widely used for leases of low value, such as residential lets; otherwise the landlord might often find, when selling the tenant's moveables, that he was lucky to cover the legal expenses, let alone pay off his rent. In the case of commercial and industrial leases, however, hypothec is a very useful and frequently used remedy.

---

12 Hypothec Abolition (Scotland) Act 1880, s 1.
13 Houseletting and Rating Act 1911 (now repealed).
14 *M'Gavin v Sturrock's Tr* (1891) 18 R 576, (1891) 28 SLR 414.

Advantages of hypothec. The landlord's hypothec has several important advantages over other remedies of the landlord for collection of rent arrears. First of all, it can be enforced very quickly. If a landlord sues a tenant in an ordinary debt action, he may eventually be able to sell off the tenant's moveables, but only after the completion of the court process. By this time, if the tenant is in financial trouble, he may have removed the moveables from the premises, or other creditors may have already seized them. A sequestration action can be served at a few days' notice, after which the moveables are reserved for the landlord and cannot be removed by the tenant or anyone else.

Another important feature of hypothec is that it confers an advantage in the tenant's bankruptcy. As mentioned earlier, the two main forms of diligence available to ordinary creditors are poinding and arrestment. However, if a tenant (or any other type of debtor) is sequestrated for bankruptcy (or is wound up, in the case of a limited company), any arrestments or poindings carried out within sixty days previously will cease to have effect[15]. This is called 'equalisation of diligences', and is to prevent creditors who are quick off the mark gaining an unfair advantage over the others. However, the landlord's sequestration for rent action to enforce his hypothec is not included in these provisions. And so, provided that the landlord has raised his sequestration action, his right of hypothec will not be affected by the tenant's bankruptcy or liquidation. This means that he will have a preferred claim for his rent up to the value of the moveables sequestrated, ie he will be paid his rent in full out of whatever assets the tenant has on the premises before the ordinary creditors get anything at all. The landlord's claim, however, is postponed to those of certain other creditors, notably the Inland Revenue and local rating authorities[16]. Where the tenant is a limited company, the landlord's position in relation to floating charge holders is controversial[17].

The right of hypothec is also particularly useful in its ability to raise more money than other remedies. In a poinding, only items which are owned by the debtor can be attached. In many cases such

---

15 Companies Act 1985, s 623; Bankruptcy (Scotland) Act 1985, s 37.
16 Taxes Management Act 1970, s 64; Local Government (Scotland) Act 1947, s 248 (as amended).
17 *Cumbernauld Development Corpn v Mustone Ltd* 1983 SLT (Sh Ct) 55; 'Receivership and Sequestration for rent', by George L Gretton 1983 SLT 277; 'A Legal "Black Hole"' by William G Simmons (1983) 28 JLS 352. The Companies (Floating Charges & Receivers) (Scotland) Act 1972, s 5, to which these references relate, has now been replaced, in identical terms, by the Companies Act 1985, s 464.

items may well be in the minority, so the landlord's right to take property belonging to third parties can be extremely valuable.

Finally, hypothec is a useful deterrent. If a tenant is not in financial difficulty, but is the type who is habitually reluctant to part with his rent at the correct time, an unexpected visit from the sheriff officer can be very persuasive in bringing about future punctuality. The traumatic effect of such a visit, combined with the high legal expenses, makes sequestration for rent an experience most tenants will not be anxious to repeat in a hurry. However, in the case of tenants who are thought to be financially secure, it is probably in the interests of a good landlord/tenant relationship to keep such a tactic in reserve as a last resort.

(3) Summary diligence[18]

We saw earlier in the present chapter that diligence is the process by which a court decree is legally enforced; in particular, it provides a way by which a creditor may legally seize the property of his debtor, two of the most common forms of diligence being poinding (attachment of the debtor's personal moveables) and arrestment (attachment of property in the hands of a third party). It is not usually possible to carry out these forms of diligence until the debt has been proved in court, as it would not quite be in accordance with justice to allow a creditor to seize another's property merely on the strength of his own word that he is owed the money. When a sheriff officer carries out an arrestment or a poinding, therefore, he will usually require to have an extract of a court decree as his legal authorisation.

However, there is one situation where the court process can be bypassed and a creditor can go ahead with a poinding or an arrestment without first having to prove his debt. This is by a procedure known as summary diligence. The theory behind this rather surprising power is that, where it applies, the party concerned has consented in advance to the possibility of summary diligence being carried out against him. This is because he has signed a legal deed (in the present context, a lease) which contains an acknowledgment of an obligation (in this case the undertaking to pay a specific amount of rent at certain intervals). The deed must also contain the party's consent to its being registered for execution,

---

18 *Rankine* pp 357-60; *Paton & Cameron* p 145; Halliday *Conveyancing Law and Practice*, Vol I, para 4.61.

and this (whether he knows it or not) means that he has given his consent to summary diligence.

Before we go any further, some explanation is perhaps required of the phrase 'registration for execution'. The Keeper of the Registers of Scotland has under his charge a number of public registers. The best known of these is the Register of Sasines, in which title deeds of heritable property have to be recorded before they become effective. Another important register is the Books of Council and Session. This has two functions, preservation and execution.

The function of execution is the one we are concerned with here, but it will be better understood if we explain the function of preservation first. Any valuable legal document – it may be a title deed, or a lease, or a will – may be sent to the Books of Council and Session as a precaution against its being lost. This does not need to be done immediately after the deed has been signed, but can be done at any time thereafter. For a fee, the Keeper will keep the document in the safety of his vaults and issue in its place an official photocopy (called an 'extract'). This extract is legally equivalent to the original deed and can be used in court or for any other legal purpose as if it were the original. Also, provided the requisite fee is paid, any number of extracts may be obtained, which can often be very useful.

Preservation of documents is the principal function of the Books of Council and Session. However, if the document contains a consent to registration for execution, this process can be carried out at the same time as registration for preservation. The Keeper keeps the document in the usual way and issues an extract, but in this case he adds to the extract a warrant for all necessary action to enforce payment of any sums payable in terms of the deed, ie to proceed with diligence. Such an extract for execution has the force and effect of a decree of the Court of Session, which is why a court action is rendered unnecessary.

In respect of certain types of deed (including leases) registration for preservation and execution is also competent in the books of the appropriate sheriff court[19].

Summary diligence, therefore, can greatly speed up the debt collection process. Obtaining a court decree takes time, at the very least a few weeks. If the debtor lodges a defence to the action, a court hearing will have to be fixed and it may take months. If it is a simple case of rent arrears, the tenant will probably not have a valid defence; however, by the time this can be established in court, he

---

19 *Halliday* Vol I, para 4.61.

may well have bought himself enough time to disappear from the scene. But where a lease contains a consent to registration for execution, the landlord need only take the relatively short time necessary to obtain an extract from the Books of Council and Session, and then pass it to the sheriff officer to proceed with a charge followed by a poinding or an arrestment. The procedure will be the same as if a court decree had first been obtained. However, instead of an extract court decree, the sheriff officer will use as his auhorisation the extract lease wth the Keeper's warrant.

Summary diligence is therefore a better remedy than court action, because it is much quicker, and may help a landlord to jump a few places in a queue of creditors. It is not as good as hypothec, because it does not have the bankruptcy preference and other advantages mentioned above: whether or not it proceeds from a court decree or an extract lease, an arrestment or poinding has the disadvantages mentioned in the last section (equalisation of diligences, being restricted to property in the debtor's ownership). Summary diligence may be useful, however, for collecting arrears that are outwith the current rental year and for which the right of hypothec has been lost.

It is doubtful whether many tenants realise, when they sign a lease containing the words, 'And I consent to registration for execution', quite what a formidable power they are putting in their landlord's hands. However, summary diligence does not seem to be used very often. Perhaps it is because there is usually a better remedy, or maybe landlords do not know about it either!

5 Assignation and Subletting; Interposed Leases

1. ASSIGNATION AND SUBLETTING[1]

An assignation is where a tenant transfers his interest in a lease to another person (called the assignee), who thereafter takes his place as tenant under the original contract. The assignee becomes directly liable to the landlord for the rent and other obligations of the lease, and the original tenant (usually called the 'cedent') is relieved of all such liability for the future, his involvement with the lease having entirely ended. This is in marked contrast to the situation in England where, after an assignation (there called an assignment), the original tenant remains potentially liable and may be called upon to underwrite the obligations of his assignee or any other future tenants under the same lease[2].

In the case of a sublease, the tenant creates a second lease between him and the subtenant, but his relationship with the landlord is unchanged and he remains directly liable to him for payment of the rent and performance of all other obligations under the original lease. There is no legal relationship between the landlord and the subtenant; the subtenant's landlord is the original tenant, usually in this context described as the principal (or head) tenant.

It may be wondered why a tenant would want to sublet, thereby leaving himself involved with a property he no longer occupies when, by assigning, he could be rid of it entirely. The reason is that subletting could be to his advantage in certain situations. He may be making a profit by charging the subtenant a higher rent than he is paying to his landlord. If the lease is a fairly long one, it may suit him to sublet for a temporary period, while retaining the right to resume occupation at some future date before the term of the principal lease has expired. Or he may only want to sublet part of the property,

---

1 Rankine *Leases* (3rd edn, 1916) ch 9; Paton & Cameron *Landlord & Tenant* (1967) ch 10.
2 *Halsbury's Laws of England* (4th edn, 1981) vol 27, para 389.

remaining in occupation of the remainder; this could be useful if he is forced to contract his business temporarily, but hopes to expand it again in the future.

A point we have yet to consider is the role of the landlord in all of this. Does he have to be involved in an assignation or subletting?

In the great majority of cases in fact he does, for the very simple reason that there is a standard clause in virtually all leases (often called the 'alienation clause') requiring the landlord's consent to any assignations or sublets. It has been held that such a clause is effective[3]. However, if it were to be omitted, the common law would determine the position, and here the situation is much less clear cut. We have to look to the general law of contract, at the principles governing the assignation of contracts generally.

First of all it depends upon whether the contract in question is classified as an 'executed' contract (ie one where all that remains is for one party to transfer property or pay money), or an 'executory' contract (where there is a continuing obligation or obligations requiring performance). Clearly a lease falls into the latter category. Any executory contract may be assigned by one party without the other's consent **except** where there is an element of *delectus personae* ('choice of person'), ie where the party wishing to assign was chosen for the contract because of some personal quality or professional skill[4]. Partnerships and employment contracts are obvious examples of contracts with this element present: a person will naturally want to have control over the choice of his partner or employee.

The common law position with regard to leases, therefore, is that a lease can be assigned without the landlord's consent only when there is no element of *delectus personae*. The same principle applies to sublets. In another type of contract, this would be determined by examining the circumstances of the particular case, to see if the person wishing to assign his interest had been chosen for his personal qualities or skills. This may at one time have also been the appropriate approach for leases, but is no longer so. Over a long period of time it has been established in the courts that the nature of certain types of lease creates a presumption of *delectus personae*, whereas with some other kinds of lease it is presumed to be absent. Whether or not a lease can be assigned without the landlord's

---

3 *Marquis of Breadalbane v Whitehead & Sons* (1893) 21 R 138, (1893) 1 SLT 320.
4 See Gloag *The Law of Contract* (2nd edn, 1929) pp 416 et seq; Walker *The Law of Contracts and Related Obligations in Scotland* (2nd edn, 1985) para 29.18 et seq, esp para 29.25; McBryde *The Law of Contract in Scotland* (1987) paras 17.36-17.54; Woolman *An Introduction to the Scots Law of Contract* (1987) pp 140-141.

consent, therefore, depends, not on the circumstances of the individual case, but on the type of lease involved. In some of these cases the original reasoning is still relevant, though in others the reasons are largely historical. The following rules cover most common categories of lease[5]:

(1) *Delectus personae* is presumed to be present in agricultural leases of ordinary duration. The landlord, in other words, is presumed to have an interest in the skill of the person who farms his land. This means that here the landlord's consent **is** required for an assignation. There is no hard and fast rule regarding what constitutes an agricultural lease of ordinary duration and what amounts to one of unusual duration. Twenty-one years has been held to be usual and thirty-eight years unusual; if the period of let falls somewhere in between, there is no case law to guide us[6].

(2) It is also presumed in furnished house lets, and so they too will require the landlord's permission. Again, there is some logic to this, as a landlord may well want to control the choice of person who will use his furniture, especially if he intends to return to the house himself at some future date.

(3) *Delectus personae* is **not** presumed in agricultural leases of unusual duration, and so the landlord's consent is not required at common law. Presumably the reasoning is that the landlord's personal choice of tenant would require unusual longevity to survive a lease term of (say) 99 years.

(4) It is **not** presumed in unfurnished lets of urban subjects, which therefore do **not** require the landlord's consent. This is undoubtedly the most important rule of all, because this category includes a wide variety of leases, including all commercial and industrial leases and unfurnished house lets.

It will be seen that the common law position is somewhat unsatisfactory. While it may be interesting to speculate about the historical reasons for the above rules, the fact of the matter is that in **all** kinds of leases – not least in commercial and industrial lets – the landlord has an interest in retaining some control over the choice of tenant. This is a basic principle of sound estate management. Not only does the landlord want to make sure that he has a tenant who will look after his property, but he also needs someone who is financially secure and able to pay the rent. Particularly in commer-

---

5 *Rankine* pp 173-176; *Paton & Cameron* pp 149-151.
6 See *Rankine* p 173 and cases cited there.

cial and industrial leases, the landlord will generally make financial and other inquiries about a tenant before agreeing to take him on; the point of this would be somewhat lost if the tenant could then transfer the tenancy, without consent, to someone who had not been vetted in this way.

In all cases therefore it is in the landlord's interest to contract out of the common law situation by including in the lease the standard provision requiring his consent to any assignation or sublet. Since such a clause **is** standard, the above rules are, in practical terms, of secondary importance; however, it is important to be aware of the common law position, if only in order to appreciate the need to clearly contract out of it.

Form of assignation. An assignation would normally take the form of a formal probative deed signed by the tenant, though there is no particular wording laid down. Where the landlord's consent is required, the easiest way to achieve this is to have him sign the deed as well. Where his consent is not required, the assignation, to be effective, must be intimated to the landlord by the tenant who is assigning; it is also of course in the latter's interest to do this, as he will not want the rent notices to continue to be sent to him. It has recently been held that, provided intimation has been given to the landlord, there is no need for the deed of assignation to have been delivered to the assignee for the assignation to take effect[7].

Transfer of tenancy of matrimonial home. It will be convenient to consider here a situation which is a kind of assignation, though not of the type considered above. It is not a voluntary assignation, but a compulsory one, which can be imposed by the court without the consent of either the landlord or the existing tenant. The Matrimonial Homes (Family Protection) (Scotland) Act 1981 was passed to protect the interest of a spouse (usually the wife) who might have no legal title to the matrimonial home either as joint owner or tenant. The Act gives the 'non-entitled' spouse (the one who is not the owner or tenant) occupancy rights to the home and also provides for the 'entitled spouse' to be excluded from the home in certain circumstances, eg where there is a history of domestic violence. In the case of leased property the court also has the power, in appropriate circumstances, to transfer the tenancy from the entitled to the non-entitled spouse[8]. The new tenant takes on all the

7 *Smith v Place D'Or 101 Ltd* 1988 SLT (Sh Ct) 5.
8 Matrimonial Homes (Family Protection) (Scotland) Act 1981, s 13.

liabilities of the tenancy, apart from any existing rent arrears, which remain the responsibility of the spouse who was the original tenant. If there is a joint tenancy, the court has the power to vest the tenancy in one party only. The landlord must be notified and be given an opportunity to object. Certain categories of lease are excluded from the provision, eg houses attached to agricultural holdings or houses let in connection with the tenant's employment.

Transfer of landlord's interest. We have seen that a tenant is generally not permitted to assign or sublet his interest without his landlord's consent. But what of the opposite situation? Does a tenant have a corresponding right to object to a change of landlord? The answer is no. He can have a new landlord imposed on him without having any say in the matter. The landlord is the owner of the property, any leases are incidents of ownership and so, if he sells the property, the new owner will automatically become the new landlord. This assumes that the conditions of the Leases Act 1449 have been fulfilled, conferring on the tenant a real right valid against the original landlord's singular successors[9]. If not, the tenant will be in an even worse position: the new owner will not be bound to recognise his lease at all.

2. INTERPOSED LEASES

Sale of the property by the landlord is the most obvious way by which a new landlord can be imposed upon a tenant, but it is not the only way. If a landlord creates an interposed lease, the tenant will end up with a new landlord, even though the original landlord has not sold the property. This is a back door method of creating a subtenancy. It occurs where a landlord under an existing lease grants a lease of his interest (the 'reversion') to a new tenant, the result being to interpose the new tenant between him and the original tenant. The latter is thereby degraded to the status of a subtenant without his consent. Interposed leases have always been valid in England; however, until 1974, they were thought to be illegal in Scotland[10]. The law of the two countries was brought into line by the Land Tenure Reform (Scotland) Act 1974, which made interposed leases legal, and extended this validity retrospectively to any interposed leases that had been created prior to the Act[11].

---

9 See ch 2, pt 4 above.
10 For a consideration of the law prior to 1974, see *Paton & Cameron* pp 170-171.
11 Land Tenure Reform (Scotland) Act 1974, s 17.

There was a good reason for this change in the law, which otherwise might have seemed a little odd, if not a retrograde step. To understand why, we must first realise that an interposed lease situation can arise in circumstances other than those described above. It can arise accidentally, as an unintended by-product of a transaction designed to achieve some quite different purpose. In particular, an interposed lease or leases can come into being as a result of a sale and leaseback transaction.

Sale and leaseback is a method of raising capital by which an owner sells his property to an investor and then takes a lease of it back from the investor. The sale price will provide him with the lump sum he requires as capital, and, as with a conventional loan, he will thereafter pay a periodical sum to the person or institution who financed him; however, instead of instalments of interest, or of capital and interest, the payments will be rent under the new lease. In times of high interest rates, this can be a better method of raising capital than a conventional loan, as the rent payable by the former owner might well work out lower than the loan repayments would have been. It is also advantageous to the investor, as he gains a capital asset that he would not otherwise have had.

What has this to do with interposed leases? It may be that, prior to the sale and leaseback, part of the property has already been leased. The effect of the sale and leaseback will be to demote these existing tenants to subtenants. A hypothetical example may make this easier to follow.

A company, Freshfood Stores Ltd, owns a supermarket and three office suites on the upper floors of the same building. Freshfood occupy the supermarket themselves, but have leased the offices to three tenants. Freshfood want to raise money for their business, so they sell the property to Shylock Holdings and then lease it back from Shylock. This happens in two stages: (a) the sale, after which the landlord of the three office tenants ceases to be Freshfood and becomes Shylock, and (b) the leaseback, whereby Freshfood is interposed between Shylock and the office tenants. The nature of the transaction is such that the office tenants end up with Freshfood as their immediate landlord once more. However, their status has nevertheless been changed to that of subtenant without their consent. In any case, the second stage of the transaction (the leaseback) definitely creates an interposed lease, which would probably have been illegal in Scotland prior to 1974.

It was felt that this incidental and quite unintentional illegality was perhaps discouraging the use in Scotland of a useful commercial practice. Moreover, those transactions which **had** taken place were tainted with the suspicion of illegality if they involved the creation of an interposed lease. The effect of the 1974 Act, by making interposed leases legal both for the future and retrospectively, was to facilitate sale and leaseback transactions by removing any possibility of illegality, even where the transaction took place prior to 1974.

In any case, quite apart from sale and leaseback situations, the practice of interposing leases can be justified in its own right. With commercial and industrial property it is commercially convenient and very common to have subtenancies, eg a landowner may lease land to a developer, who builds (say) an office block and then sublets the individual offices. There can also be situations where it will be convenient to create a subtenancy by interposing a lease. A development company which has completed a project (either on land which they own or hold on lease) may, after leasing out the various units, want to retain the development as an investment without having the trouble of day to day management. They could achieve this by interposing a lease to a management company between them and the tenants of the individual units. The legalising of interposed leases, therefore, adds flexibility to lease practice, giving Scottish commercial and industrial leases even more scope to be influenced by their English counterparts.

6 Long Leases

1. GENERAL

There is no prescribed length of time that determines whether or not a lease should be regarded as a 'long lease'. As we saw in the last chapter, the common law is rather vague about the dividing line between leases of 'ordinary' and 'unusual' duration. The statutory provisions considered below mainly apply to leases of more than twenty years. However, much longer leases are very common, ground leases in particular often extending to 99 years or more, in some cases even to 999 years. Perhaps the main point to note is that, the longer its term, the less a lease continues to resemble the basic concept that we have been considering so far, ie a temporary right of occupancy. A lease of (say) 99 years confers upon the tenant something that is much more like a right of ownership. The rent may be relatively low, particularly in ground leases where the tenant has built or paid for the buildings himself. Also, a lease with a long unexpired term has a market value, and a tenant wanting to sell his interest would normally be able to receive a capital sum (or 'grassum') in return for granting an assignation. If the unexpired term of the lease is long enough, the amount he receives may be comparable to the market price in an outright sale.

Long leases of commercial and industrial subjects are in fact much more common than outright sales of such property. This is partly due to the influence of the English business lease on its Scottish counterpart: as we saw in chapter 1, leasehold tenure has always been more prevalent south of the Border. This trend was reinforced by the provisions of the Land Tenure Reform (Scotland) Act 1974, which continued the process of reforming feudal tenure in Scotland by setting up the machinery to abolish feuduties. As a result, while it is still possible for a landowner to dispose of land feudally, reserving to himself a right of superiority in the process, it is no longer possible to create new feuduties[1]. This means that,

1 Land Tenure Reform (Scotland) Act 1974, s 1.

when disposing of land for commercial or industrial development, there is much more incentive for the landowner to grant a long lease which (in addition to any capital sum which the parties agree to) will give him a periodic return in the form of rent. As we will see below, this is no longer possible with residential property.

There are a number of statutory provisions relating to long leases, which will be our main concern in this chapter.

2. RECORDED LEASES

We saw in chapter 1 that, although writing is normally required for the creation of leases, they can be relatively informal, and any defects can often be cured by the actings of the parties. However, it is desirable for longer leases that have a capital value to be completed with greater formality. If a tenancy is a marketable asset, it is all the more important for the tenant to have a proper document of title. This is particularly so if he wants to borrow money on the security of his interest as a tenant; the creditor requires something of legal substance to which he can attach his right of security. This is the reason why, under the Registration of Leases (Scotland) Act 1857, it became possible to record a lease in the Register of Sasines.

The Register of Sasines is a public register in which title deeds have to be recorded in order to become effective. As well as long leases, it records, among other things, the deeds that create and transfer feudal rights of ownership and those that create rights in security over heritable property. It has no exact equivalent in England. Under the Land Registration (Scotland) Act 1979, the Register of Sasines is gradually being replaced by a new Land Register of Scotland, the purpose being to introduce a system of registration of title. This is a modern, computer-based system which identifies individual properties with reference to a series of Ordnance Survey plans and is backed by a government guarantee of title. In time this will greatly simplify the conveyancing system in Scotland. However, the change is necessarily a slow one, involving a separate transfer between the registers for each individual property, usually carried out when the property changes hands. The registration process is therefore being introduced in a piecemeal fashion, and to date the operational counties are Renfrew, Dunbarton, Lanark and Glasgow. In those areas, therefore, and eventually throughout Scotland, a lease can no longer be recorded in the Register of Sasines, but may, subject to the same conditions, be registered in the Land Register instead.

Under the 1857 Act, a lease may be recorded in the Register of

Sasines if (a) it is probative, and (b) its duration exceeds twenty years[2]. 'Probative' is used here in its strictest sense, ie a formal attested deed. The same conditions apply for registration in the Land Register[3]. A lease that is merely holograph or adopted as holograph may be valid at common law, but such a document cannot be recorded in the Register of Sasines or registered in the Land Register, nor can an informal document that has been validated by *rei interventus* or homologation[4].

The recording of a lease in the Register of Sasines is equivalent to possession of the property by the tenant, and also renders unnecessary the other conditions of the Leases Act 1449[5]. One of the effects of recording, therefore, is to create a real right valid against the landlord's singular successors.

In the case of long leases registrable in the Land Register, this principle has been taken a stage further: the 1449 Act has been superseded and registration is now the **only** way of obtaining such a real right[6]. This should have the effect of making the registration of long leases virtually standard under the new system. In the past, leases of more than twenty years that were not recorded in the Register of Sasines would still have been protected by the 1449 Act. However, in those areas where the 1979 Act has come into operation, the tenant will have to register a long lease in the Land Register, or he will not obtain a real right valid against the landlord's singular successors.

Recording (or registering) a lease helps to make it a marketable commodity, which may be used as security for a loan. Prior to 1970, the method of achieving such a security was for the tenant to assign the lease to his creditor. This meant that the creditor would nominally be the tenant, but that the original tenant remained in possession; thus the condition of possession required by the Leases Act 1449 would not be fulfilled, and the creditor would not be given a real right valid against the landlord's singular successors. The effect of this would have been to nullify the creditor's security if the ownership of the property changed. By making the recording of a lease equivalent to possession, the creditor was given a means of avoiding this pitfall.

2 Registration of Leases (Scotland) Act 1857, s 1 (as amended by the Land Tenure Reform (Scotland) Act 1974, Sch 6, para 1).
3 Land Registration (Scotland) Act 1979, s 29(1).
4 See ch 2, pt 2 above.
5 Registration of Leases (Scotland) Act 1857, s 16(1) (as amended by the Land Tenure Reform (Scotland) Act 1974, Sch 6, para 3); see also ch 2, pt 4 above.
6 Land Registration (Scotland) Act 1979, s 3(3); see also ch 2, pt 4 above.

Since 1970, the reason for recording leases is slightly different. The Conveyancing and Feudal Reform (Scotland) Act 1970 created a new form of heritable security called the standard security[7]. This deed is now the only valid method of creating rights in security over interests in heritable property, whether they be feudal interests (ie perpetual ownership rights) or leasehold interests. To be effective, a standard security must be recorded in the Register of Sasines or Land Register. It is therefore necessary that the legal interest over which the security is granted should already appear in the relevant register. A standard security, therefore, can only be granted over a leasehold interest if the lease itself has been recorded.

A lease can be recorded at any time after the date of entry.

3. CREATION AND VARIATION OF LEASE OBLIGATIONS

We saw in chapter 2 that the effect of the Leases Act 1449 was to create a real right valid against the landlord's singular successors, and we have just seen above that a similar result is obtained by recording a lease in the Register of Sasines or Land Register. A further consequence is that the lease obligations, so far as they are not of a personal nature, can be enforced against the tenant by the landlord's singular successor. Furthermore, when the tenant's interest in a lease is assigned, the new tenant automatically takes over all the original tenant's obligations under the lease. This effectively means that the obligations in a lease run with the land, ie they are effective not only against the original parties to the contract, but also to the successors in title of both landlord and tenant. When we also consider the fact that there are many leases with very long terms, and that long leases can be recorded in the Register of Sasines or Land Register, then lease conditions begin to acquire very similar characteristics to the real burdens and conditions that appear in feudal titles.

A recent statutory provision has made the parallel with feudal titles even more marked. When a feudal interest is being disposed of, it has always been possible to create real burdens and conditions, not only in a feu charter or feu contract granted by a superior, but also in a disposition (the deed granted by a vassal when he is disposing of a property outright to a new owner)[8]. This is very

---

7 Conveyancing and Feudal Reform (Scotland) Act 1970, s 9.
8 Halliday *Conveyancing Law and Practice* (1985), Vol II, para 19.13 et seq.

useful when the property is being subdivided; for example, with housing estates or blocks of flats, one way of imposing common repairs provisions, or other mutual obligations, is to include them in the dispositions to individual proprietors. The same can be done with industrial estates, office blocks or shopping centres. An alternative method is to include the obligations in a deed of conditions, applicable to the whole area and incorporated by reference into the individual dispositions, thus avoiding the need for the repetition of much similar material[9].

However, until recently, there was no parallel facility for leases. At common law, there was no authority to suggest that it was competent for a tenant to give an assignation incorporating new conditions that would be valid not only against the assignee but also against the assignee's singular successors. Moreover, it was extremely doubtful whether a tenant, even under a recorded lease, was entitled to grant a deed of conditions[9].

A way round this was to sublet, imposing new conditions in the sublease. However, as we will see below, leases (and subleases) of residential property for a period of more than twenty years have been prohibited since 1974; this exclusion also prohibits subleases, granted after 1974, of leases which were granted before that date.

Section 3 of the Law Reform (Miscellaneous Provisions) (Scotland) Act 1985 has now made it possible for the assignor of a recorded lease to impose conditions which, when the assignation is recorded in the Register of Sasines or Land Register, will be effectual against the assignee's singular successors[10]. The obligation cannot be a monetary one, unless it is (a) rent or an apportionment of rent; (b) a continuing expense (eg a service charge), or (c) is imposed under a heritable security. The 1985 Act also made it possible to grant a deed of conditions in relation to leasehold property and for its terms to be incorporated by reference into an assignation.

The main difficulty that s 3 was designed to resolve related to residential property. This makes it, to some extent, of minor importance, as long residential leases are now fairly rare, for reasons explained more fully below. However, it adds a new flexibility into lease practice which will be useful in other areas. For example, it can be employed in commercial and industrial leases as an alternative to subletting, if a proliferation of subleases is thought undesirable. In such cases, of course, subletting is used, not just to impose new

---

9 Conveyancing (Scotland) Act 1874, s 32.
10 Registration of Leases (Scotland) Act 1857, s 3(2)-(5) (added by Law Reform (Miscellaneous Provisions) (Scotland) Act 1985, s 3).

obligations on the various subtenants, but also to earn a profit by subletting at a higher total rent than that paid by the principal tenant to his landlord. The wording of the 1985 Act suggests that this might now be possible with an assignation[11].

Variation or discharge of lease obligations. Another important stage in the reform of Scottish land tenure came with the provision in the Conveyancing and Feudal Reform (Scotland) Act 1970 for the variation or discharge of land obligations by the Lands Tribunal for Scotland. The main reason for this was that conditions in feudal titles were often very old and, as a result, not only irrelevant but often very restrictive regarding the uses to which an owner could put his property; for example, a large town house which was feued towards the end of the last century solely as a dwellinghouse, might today enjoy a market only for commercial uses. Prior to 1970, the only way to get round this was to apply to the superior for a minute of waiver, for which he would usually charge a sizeable sum of money, if he were willing to grant a waiver at all. If a lease is of considerable length, a similar situation could easily arise in relation to lease obligations, and so the 1970 Act included land obligations under a recorded lease among those which could be varied or discharged by the Lands Tribunal[12].

The Lands Tribunal's powers do not extend to all obligations in a recorded lease, only to those that are 'land obligations' within the meaning of the 1970 Act. In *George T Fraser Ltd v Aberdeen Harbour Board*[13], it was held that the Tribunal had no power to qualify the alienation clause (ie the prohibition of assignation and subletting). The reason was that the obligation related to the tenant rather than to the land itself: it created a continuing *delectus personae*.

The Lands Tribunal may either vary or completely discharge a land obligation. Its criteria are: (1) the obligation has become unreasonable or inappropriate by reason of changes in the character of the land or the neighbourhood; (2) the obligation is unduly burdensome compared with any benefit resulting from its performance, or (3) the existence of the obligation impedes some reasonable use of the land[14]. The Tribunal has power to award

---

11 Law Reform (Miscellaneous Provisions) (Scotland) Act 1985, s 3(3)(a).
12 Conveyancing and Feudal Reform (Scotland) Act 1970, s 1(2) and s 2(6); Land Registration (Scotland) Act 1979, s 29(2); see also *McQuiban v Eagle Star Insurance Co* 1972 SLT (Lands Tr) 39.
13 1985 SLT 384.
14 Conveyancing and Feudal Reform (Scotland) Act 1970, s 1(3).

compensation to persons who would have benefited from the continuance of the obligation (benefited proprietors), eg if the obligation is designed to protect the amenity of the area. In the case of a lease, a benefited proprietor would be either the landlord, or neighbouring landowners. Such an award is at the Lands Tribunal's discretion, and they have the power to decide who are benefited proprietors entitled to compensation[15]. No application can be made for the variation or discharge of a land obligation within two years of its creation; in the present context that would mean within two years of the granting of the lease that contained the obligation.

4. LONG RESIDENTIAL LEASES

As has already been mentioned, long leases of residential property are a special case. The Land Tenure Reform (Scotland) Act 1974 prohibits the creation of long leases of dwellinghouses for a period in excess of twenty years[16]. This is in marked contrast to the situation in England, where long leases of residential property are a common alternative to freehold ownership.

The reason for this Scottish provision is historical and requires some explanation. Traditionally in Scotland most heritable property, including dwellinghouses, was held on feudal titles. Long leases of residential property were possible, but relatively uncommon. This was largely because, under the feudal system, it was possible to create an annual feuduty, which was to be paid in perpetuity by the owner (or vassal) to the feudal superior. When land was being disposed of for development, therefore, there was no need for the owner to grant a long lease if he wanted to receive a periodic payment in addition to a capital sum; he could dispose of the property feudally and collect an annual feuduty instead of a rent.

In modern times, the imposition of feuduties was considered unfair and was much resented by property owners, particularly householders. The main purpose of the 1974 Act, therefore, was to prohibit the creation of new feuduties and set up machinery for the redemption of existing ones. It was feared, however, that this might cause a massive switch to leasehold tenure by developers, thus perpetuating the system in another form by imposing rents instead of feuduties. As we have already seen, such long leases are already

---

15 *Smith v Taylor* 1972 SLT (Lands Tr) 34.
16 Land Tenure Reform (Scotland) Act 1974, s 8.

common for commercial and industrial properties. The purpose of this provision in the 1974 Act was to plug this potential loophole in relation to dwellinghouses. Because a lease has to be for over twenty years to be recorded in the Register of Sasines or registered in the Land Register, this effectively means that there cannot be any new recorded leases of residential property.

If a property, or part of it, subject to a lease of over twenty years, is used as a dwellinghouse without the landlord's consent, the landlord may give the tenant twenty-eight days' notice to stop the residential use, failing which he may have the lease terminated[17]. If it is proved that the residential use has the landlord's knowledge and consent, the tenant may not be removed, but the remaining duration of his lease will be restricted to twenty years[18]. Normally, of course, a landlord will know what kind of use a building is designed for; however, conversions or other adaptations could be made by tenants, or a landlord might have granted a ground lease, unaware of what type of building the tenant intended to erect.

There still exist some long residential leases that were created prior to 1974, and their validity is not affected by the 1974 Act. Some of these may contain an obligation on the landlord, at the lease's expiry, to grant a renewal for a period in excess of twenty years. It was initially uncertain whether such renewals could still be granted in the light of the 1974 Act. The Law Reform (Miscellaneous Provisions) (Scotland) Act 1985 has now made it clear that they can[19].

For the historical reasons mentioned above, such long residential leases were always comparatively rare. They were made even rarer by the provisions of the Long Leases (Scotland) Act 1954[20]. This allowed long leases of dwellinghouses, granted prior to 10 August 1914 for a period of not less than fifty years, to be converted into feus by the tenant serving notice upon the landlord. The notice had to be served within five years of the 1954 Act coming into force, ie before 1 September 1959. This means, of course, that the provision is no longer effective; however, while it was in force, the number of tenants taking up this option to acquire ownership had the effect of making long residential leases even less common than they were before. Nevertheless, there are still a few of them around.

17 Land Tenure Reform (Scotland) Act 1974, s 9.
18 Ibid s 9(4).
19 Law Reform (Miscellaneous Provisions) (Scotland) Act 1985, s 1.
20 Long Leases (Scotland) Act 1954, Part I.

5. RENEWAL OF LONG LEASES[1]

A long lease (either of residential or any other kind of property) sometimes contains an obligation upon the landlord to grant a renewal of the lease at its expiry. As we saw above, the 1985 Act made it clear that such a renewal was valid in respect of residential leases. However, the situation may arise, for any kind of property, where the landlord fails to grant a renewal. In the case of very long leases, the identity of the present landlord may be unknown. Accordingly, the 1985 Act made it possible for a tenant in such a situation to apply to the sheriff, who has power to grant a renewal of the lease as if he were the landlord. Where the landlord's identity is known, he must have been given three months' notice of the tenant's desire for a renewal before an application to the sheriff can be made.

For the purpose of this section, a long lease is again defined as a probative one for more than twenty years[2].

1 Land Registration (Scotland) Act 1979, s 22A (added by the Law Reform (Miscellaneous Provisions) (Scotland) Act 1985, s 2).
2 Land Registration (Scotland) Act 1979, s 28(1).

7 Termination of Leases

1. METHODS OF TERMINATION

There are a number of ways by which a lease may come to an end. Of those considered below, all except the last are situations where it may end prematurely, ie at some point prior to the contracted date of expiry. In some cases the termination occurs in accordance with the lease terms, in others it comes about quite independently of them.

The following are the main types of termination: (1) break; (2) renunciation; (3) irritancy; (4) rescission; (5) frustration; (6) bankruptcy of tenant; (7) death of tenant, and (8) notice to quit.

(1) Break

A break can occur when there is an appropriate break clause in the lease. There are three types of break clause: (a) 'landlord only' breaks; (b) 'tenant only' breaks, and (c) mutual breaks. A 'landlord only' break is where the lease allows the landlord, by notice to the tenant, to terminate the lease at some intermediate point prior to its expiry date, but where there is no corresponding right given to the tenant. A 'tenant only' break is where only the tenant has an option to break and a mutual break is where either party may exercise such an option. The lease may state one or more dates for the occurrence of a break, eg halfway through its duration, or every five years. Where there is a mutual break at (say) year ten of a twenty year lease, this is really no different from a ten year lease with an option to renew it for a further ten year period.

(2) Renunciation

Since the purpose of all contracts, including leases, is to legally bind the parties, neither party to a lease may renounce it unilaterally, unless of course there is some legal ground of termination. In *Salaried Staff London Loan Co Ltd v Swears and Wells Ltd*[1], where a tenant repudiated a lease without the landlords' consent, it was held that the landlords were not limited to a claim of damages for the breach of contract; they were entitled to enforce all of the tenants' obligations, including the continued payment of the rent.

However, there is no reason why both parties, if they want, cannot agree to a premature termination. Sometimes a tenant may want to renounce for reasons that suit the landlord, eg if he wants to lease larger premises from him. Even where the landlord does not have such a motive, he may not want to hold to a lease a tenant in financial difficulty, if there is a more sound tenant in the offing who could take his place.

(3) Irritancy

Irritancy has been considered fully in chapter 4 and need not further concern us here.

(4) Rescission

We have already seen, in chapter 4 and elsewhere, that either party may rescind a lease contract if the other is guilty of a material breach of contract[2]. Where there is an irritancy clause in the lease, a landlord would probably be better to rely upon it as the surer method but, since the modification to the common law by the Law Reform (Miscellaneous Provisions) (Scotland) Act 1985, the outcome of an irritancy action is now less certain. However, as we saw in chapter 4, the provisions of the 1985 Act apply, not only to irritancy, but also to rescission on the ground of a material breach of contract. This means that an irritancy action will still have the comparative advantage, because a landlord will not have to establish in court that the tenant has committed a material breach of contract. Nevertheless, he has still to satisfy the court, in the case of a non-monetary irritancy, that the situation is one where a fair and reasonable landlord would insist on termination.

1 1985 SLT 326.
2 See ch 4, pt 2 above.

(5) Frustration

Any contract of a continuing nature may end prematurely if its purpose is frustrated[3]. One of the ways this can happen is by supervening impossibility, ie where the contract becomes impossible to perform because of something that occurs after it has been entered into. There are two types of supervening impossibility which can particularly apply in leases: (a) *rei interitus*, or total destruction of the contract's subject matter, and (b) constructive total destruction, which is damage falling short of total destruction, but nevertheless so severe as to render the subject matter no longer fit for the purpose of the contract. Provided that the cause of the damage is accidental and not the fault of one of the parties, the effect is to terminate the contract without liability of either party. Thus a lease may be terminated prior to its expiry date if the leased property is accidentally destroyed or severely damaged (most commonly as a result of fire)[4].

Frustration can also occur in circumstances where there is no actual physical damage to the property but something else happens that makes it impossible for the lease to continue. In *Mackeson v Boyd*[5], a nineteen year tenancy of a furnished mansion house was interrupted during the 1939-45 war, when the property was requisitioned by the military authorities and the tenant was ejected. The court held that it had become impossible for the tenancy to continue and that the tenant was entitled to abandon the lease.

The doctrine of frustration is common to the law of contract in both Scotland and England. In theory, therefore, it should be possible for an English lease to be terminated by frustration; however, the English courts have not applied the doctrine to leases in the way that the Scottish courts have done, and the circumstances where an English lease may be terminated by frustration are extremely rare[6].

---

3 Gloag *The Law of Contract* (2nd edn, 1929), ch 19, esp pp 347-349; Walker *The Law of Contracts and Related Obligations in Scotland* (2nd edn, 1985), 31.49 to 31.57; McBryde *The Law of Contract in Scotland* (1987), ch 15; Woolman *An Introduction to the Scots Law of Contract* (1987) pp 168-176.

4 *Duff v Fleming* (1870) 8 M 769, (1870) 7 SLR 480; *Cantors Properties (Scotland) Ltd v Swears & Wells Ltd* 1978 SC 310, 1980 SLT 165, affirming 1977 SLT (Notes) 30.

5 1942 SC 56, 1942 SLT 106; see also *Tay Salmon Fisheries Co Ltd v Speedie* 1929 SC 593, 1929 SLT 484.

6 *National Carriers Ltd v Panalpina (Northern) Ltd* [1981] AC 675, [1981] 1 All ER 161.

(6) Bankruptcy of tenant[7]

At common law the bankruptcy of the tenant does not automatically bring a lease to an end. Instead the tenancy passes to the tenant's trustee in bankruptcy, who is the person appointed to ingather the tenant's estate and distribute it among his creditors.

However, there is a standard provision in many leases prohibiting the transmission of a lease to a trustee in bankruptcy. Also, most conventional irritancy clauses list bankruptcy as a ground of irritancy.

Even if a lease does not contain such provisions (and it usually will), a trustee will become a tenant only if he agrees to adopt the lease; since this would make him liable for all future rent and past rent arrears, there is not much incentive for him to do so.

And so, although in theory it is possible for a lease to continue after a tenant's bankruptcy, in practice it will usually come to an end. A reasonable landlord will probably allow the trustee a temporary period of occupation to sort out the tenant's affairs, provided of course that his rent is secure.

If the tenant is a limited company, the lease will automatically come to an end when the company is wound up, as the tenant will then no longer be in existence. However, the lease will probably prohibit the transmission of the tenancy to a liquidator or receiver, and receivership or liquidation are standard grounds of conventional irritancy. The lease will probably therefore be terminable by the landlord at an earlier stage.

If the lease is to a partnership, the bankruptcy of one of the partners will dissolve the partnership, unless the partnership agreement provides otherwise[8]. If the partnership does end, this will naturally terminate the lease.

Alternatively, the lease may continue if the trustee (or liquidator or receiver) finds a new tenant for the premises and the landlord gives his consent to the assignation.

(7) Death of tenant[9]

If a tenant dies, the lease passes to his executor[10]. The executor then has the power to transfer the tenancy to the person, or one of the

---

7 Rankine *Leases* (3rd edn, 1916), p 693 et seq; Paton & Cameron *Landlord and Tenant* (1967), ch 12.
8 Partnership Act 1890, s 33(1).
9 *Paton & Cameron* ch 11.
10 Succession (Scotland) Act 1964, s 16.

persons, due to inherit the deceased's estate. However, this can be done only with the landlord's consent, so in practice the result may be that the lease comes to an end.

The above assumes that the deceased tenant has either not left a will (ie died intestate), or that his will makes no provision for the disposal of the lease. However, a tenant may actually bequeath his tenancy, and here the landlord's consent will not be required unless the lease contains an express prohibition against assignation or against a bequest of the lease.

Usually, of course, a lease will at the very least contain a prohibition against assignation without the landlord's consent. And so, in practice, the death of the tenant will also usually bring the lease to an end. This also illustrates the need for a landlord to make sure he inserts the appropriate clause in the lease; it is as much in his interest to keep control over bequests as it is with assignations.

A lease to a partnership will end on the death of one of the partners, unless the partnership agreement provides otherwise. However, if the partnership agreement makes it clear that the death of a partner will **not** dissolve the partnership, the lease will continue[11].

The above mainly applies in the case of commercial and industrial leases. In agricultural and residential lets, there is often a statutory right of transmission on the death of a tenant[12].

(8) Notice to quit

So far we have been looking at various ways in which a lease may end prematurely. It remains to look at the procedure for bringing it to an end at the contracted termination date.

One could be forgiven for thinking that the answer was obvious: if both parties have signed a contract providing that the lease is to last for a stated period, surely it will come to an end when that period expires?

Unfortunately, it is not as simple as that. Even though the specified termination date may have arrived, the lease does not automatically come to an end at that time. This only happens if either the landlord or the tenant intimates that he wishes the lease to end by sending the other a notice to quit. If neither sends such a notice, the law presumes that both want the lease to continue and it

11 Partnership Act 1890, s 33(1); *Gordon & Co v Thomson Partnership* 1985 SLT 122.
12 See ch 12 pt 6, ch 13 and ch 14 below.

is automatically extended for a further period by a principle called
tacit relocation (silent renewal)[13]. If the original lease duration
was less than a year, the extension will be for the same period, eg a
six month lease will be extended for a further six months, a three
month lease for another three months etc. If the original lease
duration was a year or more, the period of extension will be one year.
If either party wants to end the lease at the expiry of the extended
period, he will require to send a notice to quit, or else a further
extension of the same amount will take place. Furthermore, until
such time as either party takes the necessary steps to end it at the
current termination date, the lease will continue to be renewed
indefinitely.

For example, suppose A leases a property to B for a period of five
years, the period of notice required being forty days. If the lease is to
end at the stated period, either the landlord or the tenant must send
to the other a notice to quit at least forty days before the end of year
five. Otherwise the lease will continue by tacit relocation for another
year, and the earliest date it can be terminated will be the end of year
six. If neither party sends to the other notice to quit at least forty
days prior to the end of year six, it will not be terminable before the
end of year seven, and so on *ad infinitum*.

A lease on tacit relocation continues on exactly the same terms
and conditions as the original lease contract. It is because of this
factor that the principle of tacit relocation is of such practical
importance, particularly for landlords, as we shall see below. The
only exception to this rule is the duration: as we saw above, a lease
for more than a year will be extended for one year only. Nor will the
extended lease incorporate any terms that are inconsistent with a
lease from year to year. In *Commercial Union Assurance Co*[14], the
leases in question contained options to renew on the same terms, but
the expiry date passed without the tenant exercising the options, or
either party taking steps to terminate the leases. It was held that the
lease had continued for a year on tacit relocation, but that the option
rights were no longer enforceable.

The period of notice to quit is often laid down in the lease
contract, but, in any case, statutory minimum periods are provided
in the Removal Terms (Scotland) Act 1886 and the Sheriff Courts
(Scotland) Act 1907[15]; these provisions are fairly complex, but may
be summarised as follows:

---

13 *Rankine* p 598 et seq; *Paton & Cameron* ch 14.
14 *Commercial Union Assurance Co* 1964 SC 84, 1964 SLT 62.
15 Sheriff Courts (Scotland) Act 1907, ss 34–38.

Leases of lands exceeding two acres. The period of notice must be not less than one year and not more than two years prior to the date of expiry. There is an exception in the case of leases for less than three years, where the minimum period of notice is reduced to six months. This provision includes most agricultural lets and is reinforced by the provisions of the Agricultural Holdings Acts, which lay down a minimum period of notice of one year for all agricultural holdings[16]; this means that the six months' notice provision mentioned above will take effect only in cases where the Agricultural Holdings Acts do **not** apply.

Other leases of more than four months. The period of notice is forty days.

Other leases of less than four months. The period of notice is one third of the duration of the let. In the case of dwellinghouses, this is subject to a statutory minimum period of twenty-eight days[17].

Under the 1886 Act, where a lease is due to end at Whitsunday or Martinmas, notice to quit must be given at least forty days prior to 15 May or 11 November respectively; however, if the tenant is to be removed, unless the lease expressly stipulates otherwise, he need not do so until noon on the 28th day of the month concerned[18]. Although that Act, on the face of it, applies only to houses, a house is defined very widely as a 'dwelling-house, shop, or other building and their appurtenances', as well as houses let with agricultural land[19]. At least some commercial leases, therefore, would appear to fall within its scope. In *Campbell's Trustees v O'Neill*[20], it was held that a notice requiring a tenant to remove 'at the term of Whitsunday 1910' without specifying whether Whitsunday meant 15 or 28 May was valid, as the tenant had suffered no prejudice. A notice specifying the date of removal as the 29th, the 28th being Sunday, has also been held to be valid[1]. However, a notice to quit specifying the date of removal as the 15th of the month has been held to be invalid[2]; obviously, in that case the tenant **did** suffer prejudice, as he had a right to stay on until the 28th.

---

16 Ch 12, pt 3 below.
17 Rent (Scotland) Act 1984, s 112.
18 Removal Terms (Scotland) Act 1886, s 4.
19 Ibid s 3.
20 1911 SC 188, sub nom *Watson's Trs v O'Neill* 1910 2 SLT 392.
 1 *Temperance Permanent Building Society v Kominek* 1951 SLT (Sh Ct) 58, 67 Sh Ct Rep 154.
 2 *Grant v Moran* 1948 SLT (Sh Ct) 8, 64 Sh Ct Rep 133.

Notices to quit must be in writing, though there is some authority for informal notice being sufficient in short urban lets[3]. However, in the latter case, the simplified removal procedure introduced by the 1907 Act would not be available. A landlord may invalidate his notice by his later actions, eg if he accepts rent after the date of the expiry of the notice[4].

The 1907 Act provides various forms of notice which must be strictly adhered to if the removing procedures laid down by the Act are to be followed[5]. Such notices should be posted by registered mail, by the landlord or his agent, or delivered personally by the sheriff officer[6].

Quite apart from the statutory provisions, it is good practice to clearly specify in a lease both the period of notice and that such notice should be in writing.

We saw above that when a lease continues on tacit relocation, it does so on the same terms and conditions as the original lease. One of these conditions will be the amount of rent payable, and this is why it is so important for landlords or their agents to be aware of the law here. When a tenant's lease is due to end, the landlord will probably not want to evict him, but he will certainly want to put up the rent. He can achieve this only by terminating the existing lease and negotiating a new one at a revised rent. If he fails to send a notice to quit, or sends it late, the tenant will be able to insist that the lease continues for a further year at the old rent, and since this might by now be several years behind the current market rental, the landlord's negligence on this point could lose him quite a lot of money, particularly at the rent levels charged for commercial and industrial property.

Because of this danger, it is a common practice for landlords to arrange for all their leases to expire at particular times in the year, eg at Whitsunday or Martinmas. In this way it becomes a fairly simple twice yearly administrative exercise to check which leases are due to expire, send out notices to quit at the required time and then negotiate renewals. However, it is not usually convenient for the date of entry to be at one of these terms: tenants are generally anxious to commence business as soon as possible and would not take kindly to a suggestion that, for administrative convenience, they should wait a few months until the next term of Whitsunday or

---

3 See *Paton & Cameron* pp 223 et seq and pp 272-273.
4 *Coatbridge Town Council v Tamburrino* 1958 SLT (Sh Ct) 4, (1958) 74 Sh Ct Rep 16; *Milner's Curator Bonis v Mason* 1965 SLT (Sh Ct) 56.
5 Sheriff Courts (Scotland) Act 1907, Sch 1, Rules 110-114 and Forms H, I and J.
6 Sheriff Courts (Scotland) Act 1907, Sch 1, Rule 113.

Martinmas; landlords, in any case, will be equally anxious to start collecting their rent. As a result of this, many leases are not for a round period, such as exactly three years, five years, twenty years etc. Instead there will be an irregular period from the date of entry until the first term of Whitsunday or Martinmas, and the five years, or whatever is the agreed duration, will run from then.

2. REMOVINGS

We saw above that, if a lease is terminated at the expiry date by a notice to quit, the parties often agree to a new lease, usually at a higher rent. However, this of course need not be the case. The parties may not be able to agree the terms of a renewal, or the landlord may simply want the tenant out. But what happens if the landlord gives notice, for the proper period and in the proper form, but the tenant does not move out when the expiry date arrives?

The first and most important point to note is that the landlord cannot take the law into his own hands. He has to abide by the due process of law by raising a court action to have the tenant removed. This will give the tenant the opportunity to lodge a defence, and only if the court eventually grants a decree of removing will the landlord be in a position to instruct the sheriff officer to proceed with an eviction. In the case of lets of dwellinghouses, this principle is reinforced by statute[7]; however, the necessity for court action to remove a tenant at the end of his lease is also a common law principle and applies to all leases[8].

If a landlord attempts to remove a tenant without raising a court action, he may, at common law, be liable to the tenant in damages[9]. Furthermore, in the case of residential accommodation, the common law has been considerably reinforced by statute: any coercion or harassment of a residential occupier by his landlord, or anyone else, may make the person who is responsible for the coercion or harassment not only liable in damages, but also subject to criminal proceedings[10].

There is a partial exception to the rule requiring court action before a tenant can be removed. In the case of leased subjects of more than two acres, if the lease is in probative form and specifies a term of endurance, or the tenant has signed a separate formal letter

---

7 See ch 13 below.
8 *Fairbairn v Miller (Cockburn's Tr)* (1878) 15 SLR 705.
9 *Rankine* p 592; *Paton & Cameron* p 249.
10 See ch 13 below.

of removal, the tenant can be removed without any court proceedings[11]. However, this rather drastic procedure does not seem to be used very often.

The various processes of removal are regulated by the Sheriff Courts (Scotland) Act 1907[12]. If the tenant's lease has come to an end, the appropriate court process is an action of removing. If the tenant is being removed prematurely (eg as a result of irritancy, rescission or a landlord's break) the process is known as an extraordinary removing. An action of removing should be distinguished from an action of ejection, which strictly speaking is the process for evicting a squatter, ie someone who never had any right to occupy the property at all, as opposed to someone whose right of occupancy has ended. However, the matter is somewhat confused, as the 1907 Act uses the term 'ejection' in connection with certain removings. The term 'summary removings' is used for the process for removing tenants of property let for less than a year.[13].

Violent profits[14]. At common law a payment known as violent profits may be due to an owner of heritable property from anyone (not just a former tenant) who occupies his property illegally. Violent profits are a form of penal damages designed to act as a deterrent against illegal occupancy and to compensate the owner for being deprived of the benefits of possession. They may therefore be payable by a tenant who continues to occupy a property after his lease has been legally terminated[15]. However, they may not be payable by a tenant who remains on in the property with the landlord's consent while negotiating a new lease, even if the negotiations fall through[16].

The measure of violent profits derives from very old authority and custom, and varies according to the area concerned. In burghs it is estimated at double the rent. Elsewhere, it is based on the greatest profit that the landlord could have made, either by possessing the property himself or by letting it to others, together with compensation for any damage caused to it by the illegal possessor.

If a tenant lodges a defence to an action of removing, the sheriff has discretion to demand caution (ie security) from him for violent

---

11 Sheriff Courts (Scotland) Act 1907, ss 34 and 35.
12 Ibid ss 34-38 and Sch I, Rules 110-122; for a detailed consideration of removings see also *Paton & Cameron*, ch 17.
13 Sheriff Courts (Scotland) Act 1907, s 38.
14 *Rankine* pp 580-586; *Paton & Cameron* pp 279-283.
15 *Jute Industries Ltd v Wilson & Graham Ltd* 1955 SLT (Sh Ct) 46; (1955) 71 Sh Ct Rep 158.
16 *Hyams v Brechin* 1979 SLT (Sh Ct) 47.

profits[17]. This does not mean that the tenant will necessarily end up having to pay violent profits; that will depend on the outcome of the action. In an extraordinary removing, such as irritancy, caution for violent profits cannot be demanded because the tenant cannot be branded as a violent possessor until the irritancy or other termination ground has been proved[18]. The position is similar if the owner is seeking to eject the occupant as a squatter, but he claims to be a tenant[19].

3. TENANT'S FIXTURES AND IMPROVEMENTS

It may be that, during the currency of the lease, the tenant will make some additions to the property at his own expense. These may have the effect of improving the property and increasing its value. But what happens when the lease comes to an end? Can the tenant take away any items he has added or will he have to leave them on the property? If the latter is the case, can he claim any compensation from the landlord?

We will see in chapter 12 that, under the Agricultural Holdings Acts, a farm tenant is entitled to compensation for any improvements he has made to the holding[20]. Alternatively, he may remove fixtures at the end of the lease, after first giving the landlord an opportunity to purchase them[1]. In a dwellinghouse leased by a public sector landlord, a tenant may be reimbursed at the end of his lease for improvements he has made with the landlord's consent[2]; this is not a right, but is made at the discretion of the landlord. In other leases, the position regarding additions by the tenant will often be regulated by the lease document[3]. Here we will consider the position at common law.

If an item added to the property is sufficiently attached to the property, eg a building or something attached to a building, it will become part of the property. In other words, it will be a heritable fixture[4]. Since the heritable property that is being leased belongs to

---

17 Sheriff Courts (Scotland) Act 1907, Sch I, Rules 110 and 121 (as amended by the Sheriff Courts (Scotland) Act 1913).
18 *Simpson v Goswami* 1976 SLT (Sh Ct) 94.
19 *Middleton v Booth* 1986 SLT 450.
20 Ch 12, pt 4 below.
1 Ch 12, pt 2 below.
2 Housing (Scotland) Act 1987, s 58; see also ch 14 below.
3 See ch 9 below.
4 For a brief discussion of the law of fixtures, see Gloag and Henderson *Introduction to the Law of Scotland* (9th edn, 1987) para 36.5.

the landlord this means that, in theory, any fixture added to that property will also belong to him, even though the fixture might have been added or paid for by the tenant.

However, there are two exceptions to this rule which have long been recognised at common law. **Trade fixtures** added by the tenant may be removed by him at the end of his lease, provided they can be removed without any substantial damage to the property. A trade fixture is something that has been attached to the property for the purpose of the tenant's trade or business, eg heavy factory machinery that may be bolted to the floor. In *Syme v Harvey*[5], the tenants of a nursery garden were held entitled, at the end of their lease, to remove greenhouses, forcing pits and hotbed frames added by them for the purpose of their trade.

A similar rule applies to **ornamental fixtures**, which are things that have been attached for the better enjoyment of the articles themselves, rather than with the purpose of improving the property. In the English case of *Spyer v Phillipson*[6], the tenant of a flat installed valuable antique panelling, ornamental chimney pieces and 'period' fireplaces, the last two requiring a small amount of structural alteration. After the tenant's death, his executor was held entitled to remove the additions: they had been installed, not in order to benefit the property, but for the enjoyment of the articles themselves, and they could be removed without irreparable damage to the property.

---

5 *Syme v Harvey* (1861) 24 D 202, 34 Sol Jo 98; see also *Lloyds Bowmaker Ltd v William Cook Engineering (Evanton) Ltd* 1988 SCLR 676.
6 *Spyer v Phillipson* [1931] 2 Ch 183, [1930] All ER 457, CA.

8 Tenancy of Shops

We saw in chapter 1 that a major difference between the law of Scotland and England was the lack of statutory control of commercial and industrial leases in Scotland. There is, however, a minor exception to this in the form of the Tenancy of Shops (Scotland) Acts, which give limited rights of security of tenure to shop tenants[1]. The original Tenancy of Shops (Scotland) Act was introduced in 1949 as a temporary measure to protect the rights of shopkeepers, but after a number of yearly extensions was made permanent in 1964.

A shop is defined for the purposes of the Acts as, 'Any premises where any retail trade or business is carried on'. Retail trade or business is stated to include the business of a barber or hairdresser, the sale of refreshments or intoxicating liquors, the business of lending books or periodicals when carried on for purposes of gain, and retail sales by auction. It does not include the sale of programmes and catalogues and other similar sales at theatres and places of amusement[2]. The Acts would therefore appear to apply to hairdressers shops, cafes, pubs, profit-making libraries and auction salerooms, but not to theatres or other places of activity where retail sales are incidental.

The above definition has been further clarified by a number of court decisions. The principle emerging seems to be that premises which are not exclusively retail may still come within the definition of a shop as long as the retail element is substantial. Properties held to come within the definition include a sub post office[3], opticians' premises[4], premises used for the repair of boots and shoes where a minor but substantial part of the tenant's income came from articles for sale[5], and garage premises where the tenant's profits derived

---

1 Tenancy of Shops (Scotland) Act 1949 (as amended by the Tenancy of Shops (Scotland) Act 1964 and the Sheriff Courts (Scotland) Act 1971).
2 Shops Act 1950, s 74(1).
3 *King v Cross Fisher Properties Ltd* 1956 SLT (Sh Ct) 79, 72 Sh Ct Rep 203.
4 *Craig v Saunders & Connor Ltd* 1962 SLT (Sh Ct) 85, (1962) 78 Sh Ct Rep 154.
5 *Oakes v Knowles* 1966 SLT (Sh Ct) 33.

equally from retail activities and repair work, even though a larger area was used for repairs[6]. Among those properties excluded from the definition of a shop, and hence from the application of the Acts, are a blacksmith's premises[7], a travel agent's[8] and a dry cleaner's[9]. Also held to be excluded from the definition was a builder's yard because not only was the retail element subsidiary, but the property was mainly open space which was not, in the court's opinion, the type of property the Acts were intended to protect[10].

The Acts can be invoked when a shop lease is due to expire and the landlord has sent the tenant a notice to quit. If the tenant is unable to obtain a renewal on satisfactory terms, he may, within twenty-one days, apply to the Sheriff Court for a renewal of the lease. The sheriff has the power to renew the lease for a period not exceeding one year on such conditions as he thinks reasonable. The parties will thereafter be considered to have entered a new lease for that period. If the landlord wants to remove the tenant at the end of the extended period, he will require to send a fresh notice to quit[11]. A further application may be made by the tenant at the end of the renewed term, and at the end of any future periods of renewal which may be granted. Each application should be regarded on its own merits, without the court being influenced by any arguments that might have been put forward at earlier applications[12].

It has been held that the Acts do not extend to applications by subtenants for a renewal of subleases from the principal tenants[13].

The Acts lay down the following grounds upon which the sheriff may refuse a renewal:

(1) That the tenant is in breach of a material tenancy condition. Where the use clause in a lease provided that the shop should be used exclusively as a newsagent's and stationer's, the tenant was held to be in material breach of a tenancy provision for selling cigarettes and tobacco[14].

---

6 *Thom v British Transport Commission* 1954 SLT (Sh Ct) 21; see also *Grosvenor Garages (Glasgow) Ltd v St Mungo Property Co Ltd* (1955) 71 Sh Ct Rep 155.
7 *Golder v Thomas Johnston's (Bakers) Ltd* 1950 SLT (Sh Ct) 50.
8 *Wright v St Mungo Property Co Ltd* (1955) 71 Sh Ct Rep 152.
9 *Boyd v Bell & Sons Ltd* 1970 JC 1, 1969 SLT 156.
10 *Green v M'Glughan* 1949 SLT (Sh Ct) 59, (1949) 65 Sh Ct Rep 155.
11 *White v Paton* (1953) 69 Sh Ct Rep 176; *Scottish Gas Board v Kerr's Trs* 1956 SLT (Sh Ct) 69, (1956) 72 Sh Ct Rep 139.
12 *Wallace v Bute Gift Co Ltd* 1954 SLT (Sh Ct) 55.
13 *Ashley Wallpaper Co Ltd v Morrisons Associated Companies Ltd* 1952 SLT (Sh Ct) 25, 68 Sh Ct Rep 94.
14 *McCallum v Glasgow Corpn* (1955) 71 Sh Ct Rep 178.

(2) That the tenant is bankrupt.

(3) That the landlord has offered to sell the tenant the premises at a price, failing agreement, to be fixed by arbitration[15].

(4) That the landlord has offered the tenant suitable alternative premises on reasonable terms. Premises where the tenant would have suffered a loss in passing trade have been held unsuitable[16].

(5) That the tenant has given the landlord notice to quit and the landlord has contracted to sell or let the premises, or has committed himself in some other way, as a result of receiving the notice.

(6) That greater hardship would be caused by renewing the lease than by refusing the application. There have been a number of cases on this ground. An example is the case of *Skelton v Paterson*[17], where a tenant who had invested his savings in the shop was granted a renewal as the landlord was considered to be suffering less hardship from being denied the opportunity to expand his business. On the other hand, in *Anderson v National Bank of Scotland Ltd*[18], it was held that a bank which was the landlord of a shop and, to the tenant's knowledge, had for some years desired possession of the shop in order to rebuild its premises would suffer greater hardship than the tenant, and accordingly a renewal of the tenancy was refused. The rather strange concept of a bank suffering hardship suggests that the application of this criterion does not always lead to an obvious outcome. It has been suggested in more than one case, though none seem to have been decided directly on this point, that the imposition of several successive yearly renewals on him could eventually amount to greater hardship for the landlord[19].

The sheriff has a great deal of discretion in the matter and his decision is final.

It will be seen, therefore, that these measures fall very far short of the comprehensive provisions which apply to business leases in England under the Landlord and Tenant Act 1954. In any case, unlike the Landlord and Tenant Act 1954, the Tenancy of Shops Acts apply only to shops and not to factories or office premises, which remain virtually free of statutory control in Scotland.

---

15 *J Bartholomew & Son v Robertson* (1960) 76 Sh Ct Rep 64.
16 *Hurry v M'Lauchlan* (1953) 69 Sh Ct Rep 305.
17 (1954) 70 Sh Ct Rep 287.
18 (1957) 73 Sh Ct Rep 10.
19 *Wallace v Bute Gift Co Ltd* 1954 SLT (Sh Ct) 55; *White v Paisley Co-operative Manufacturing Society Ltd* 1956 SLT (Sh Ct) 95, 72 Sh Ct Rep 289.

9 Common Lease Terms

We saw in chapter 1 that, at common law, the minimum requirements for a lease are a landlord, a tenant, subjects of let, a rent and a duration. However, the sort of lease normally encountered nowadays usually goes far beyond these basics and can be a very lengthy, complex and forbidding document. The purpose of this book is to give a general introduction to the law of leases, and so it is outwith our scope to provide styles of documents[1]. However, to adhere rigidly to an exposition of the common law and statute law would leave the reader with something missing from an overall picture of leases. The common law in particular is so frequently contracted out of that to look at it in isolation would give a misleading impression of what actually happens in practice.

The purpose of the present chapter, therefore, is to draw attention to some of the more important provisions that are commonly found in a modern lease. Our main point of reference will be a commercial or industrial lease, although many of the clauses can be found in other types of lease as well. However, in leases of dwellinghouses, and to a lesser extent in agricultural leases, the lease terms take second place to the statutory framework, since the frequent prohibition against contracting out nullifies anything inconsistent with the statutory provisions. For example, a conventional irritancy clause in a lease of a dwellinghouse subject to protection by the Rent (Scotland) Act 1984 would be superseded by the security of tenure provisions and the statutory grounds of removal[2]. And so the realm of commercial and industrial leases, where the lease terms reign supreme, will be our main point of focus. These leases are also likely to be the longest and most complicated; they are the ones where there is often most money at stake, and where landlords and tenants have the most to gain by

---

1 For modern styles of the various types of leases see Halliday *Conveyancing Law and Practice*, Vol III (1987), Part 1.
2 See ch 13 below.

going to great lengths to protect themselves and/or bamboozle the other.

This brief survey is not intended to be comprehensive, but merely to help the beginner to chart his way through the horrendous jungle of verbiage he is likely to encounter, and to enable him to establish some basic landmarks. Two of the more important clauses, those relating to rent reviews and service charges, will be dealt with in chapters ten and eleven, as each deserves a chapter on its own.

(1) Alienation

The alienation clause will include the standard provision prohibiting the tenant from assigning or subletting the lease without the landlord's permission. It will also have the effect of preventing the lease transmitting to one of the tenant's heirs after his death. It is common also to include a prohibition against creditors or managers of creditors, which will prevent the lease, without the landlord's consent, from transmitting to the tenant's liquidator or trustee in bankruptcy.

These provisions are important for the landlord if he wants to retain control over the choice of tenant who occupies his property. As we saw above, the omission of this clause would allow the tenant of a commercial or industrial lease to assign or sublet without the landlord's consent, that being the position at common law[3].

A tenant would normally want the clause modified by the addition of a qualification that the landlord's consent 'will not be unreasonably withheld'. Unfortunately, the addition of this phrase adds an element of ambiguity. Who decides what is reasonable and what is unreasonable? The landlord and tenant may well have different views, so the court (or possibly an arbiter) would have to decide, and the door has thus been opened to unwelcome litigation. However, it is a qualification that is difficult to escape from. It is in the tenant's interest to have some defence against the stranglehold of an unreasonable landlord and, as we will see in chapter 10, too tight a control by a landlord over assignations can limit the amount of rent he is able to charge at rent review.

In England, the landlord's reasonableness is imposed by statute[4]. The same statutory provision declares it to be unreasonable for a landlord to demand a money payment in exchange for his consent, and reasonable for him to refuse consent if the change of tenant would diminish the value of the property or neighbouring premises

3 See ch 5 below.
4 Landlord and Tenant Act 1927, s 19.

belonging to the landlord. These statutory provisions do not apply in Scotland, but it is likely that a court would find their principles persuasive when interpreting a similar provision in a Scottish lease. It has been held in England that the onus is on the tenant to establish that the landlord is being unreasonable[5].

In the recent Scottish case of *Renfrew District Council v AB Leisure (Renfrew) Ltd (In Liquidation)*[6], the clause in question provided that the landlord's consent to an assignation would not be unreasonably withheld, and in particular would not be withheld where the assignee's resources were adequate. As a condition of granting an assignation, the landlords wanted the arrears of rent to be paid, and the court agreed that this was reasonable. However, the landlords also wanted to make their consent to an assignation conditional upon an immediate rent review taking place, a full repairing and insuring clause being added to the lease and rent reviews being reduced from five yearly to three yearly intervals. The court held that the landlord was not entitled to impose these last three conditions, which effectively would have created a new lease in different terms.

(2) Payment of rent

The dates when the rent is payable will depend upon what is stated in the lease. The commonest provision in commercial and industrial leases is for it to be paid quarterly in advance at the four Scottish quarter days, ie Candlemas (2 February), Whitsunday (15 May), Lammas (1 August) and Martinmas (11 November). There will usually also be a provision for interest to be paid to the landlord in the event of late payment of rent or of any other sum of money due under the lease. Since this provision could be invoked at any time over the period of the lease, during which time interest rates will probably fluctuate, it is probably better not to state a specific rate in the lease, but to relate it to a current bank rate, eg 3-4 per cent above the base rate of a specified bank. The landlord should be careful not to state a rate that is too high, otherwise a court might declare it to be a penalty (ie an attempt to punish the tenant rather than a reasonable pre-estimate of the landlord's loss); if this happened, the clause would be unenforceable[7].

5 *Mills v Cannon Brewery Co* [1920] 2 Ch 38 at 46, 89, LJ Ch 354.
6 1988 SLT 635.
7 See Gloag *The Law of Contract* (2nd edn, 1929) pp 673-679; Walker *The Law of Contracts and Related Obligations in Scotland* (2nd edn 1985), paras 20.22 to 20.34; McBryde *The Law of Contract in Scotland*, paras 20.125-20.159; Woolman *An Introduction to the Scots Law of Contract* (1987), pp 135-137.

(3) Use of premises

The clause dealing with the use of the premises is generally referred to as the 'use clause' (or in England the 'user clause'). It reinforces the common law provision that the tenant may only use the property for the purpose for which it was let, not only by stating the general purpose of the property (eg shop, office, factory or dwellinghouse) but also, in the case of commercial and industrial leases, laying down the type of business that has to be carried on. The latter is particularly important in shop leases, where the landlord may want to control the trade mix and ensure that there are not too many shops of the same type in one area; he may also be able to charge a shop tenant a higher rent, if he can assure him of a monopoly or partial monopoly in the locality.

However, as we will see in chapter 10, keeping this degree of control, while it may be to the landlord's advantage in terms of estate management, could rebound upon him financially, by limiting the amount of rent he is able to charge at a rent review[8]. It is therefore not in the landlord's interest to tie the tenant down too tightly to a particular use of the premises. He may allow a qualification that his consent to a change of use 'will not be unreasonably withheld'. In leases of offices or factories, he may want to consider whether it is necessary to limit the tenant to a specific type of business at all, as the considerations of trade mix that apply with retail premises are not really relevant with other types of property. Another solution is to limit the tenant to a use within a particular class of the Town and Country Planning (Use Classes) (Scotland) Order 1989[9]; this could have the effect of limiting a property to a particular category of use, without specifically stating a particular kind of business.

It is common in use clauses for there also to be a prohibition of any uses of the property that would cause a nuisance to neighbouring tenants or otherwise affect the amenity of the area.

(4) Insurance

The most common type of commercial and industrial lease today is the tenant's full repairing and insuring lease (the FRI lease), in which the tenant is made entirely responsible for all repairs and for payment of insurance premiums. In the case of insurance, where the

8 See ch 10, pt 3 below.
9 SI 1989/147.

property is situated on its own (eg a factory on an isolated site) the lease may make it the tenant's responsibility to take out insurance for the full value of the property, and the landlord will safeguard his position by reserving the right to approve the choice of insurance company and the amount of the cover, as well as to inspect the insurance policy and the premium receipts. He will also want to have his insurable interest noted on the policy.

If the property is not an isolated one (eg if it is in a shopping centre, office block or industrial estate) the landlord will invariably prefer to effect the insurance himself and recover the cost of the premiums from the tenant by way of a service charge[10]. This not only has the advantage of administrative convenience, but the landlord will be making absolutely sure that his valuable property is insured to its full value. Also, by taking out a block insurance for a number of properties, he may be able to get better terms from the insurance company. In fact, so paramount is the landlord's interest in making sure that his property is adequately insured, that it might also be better for him to take over the insurance arrangements in isolated properties, unless the tenant is one who is eminently trustworthy and of good standing.

It is common in insurance clauses for the landlord to contract out of the common law doctrine of *rei interitus*. We saw in chapter 7 that a lease may be terminated prematurely by supervening impossibility if the premises are totally or almost totally destroyed by fire or otherwise[11]. If a landlord wants to ensure that he can hold a tenant for the full term of his lease (and a landlord who wants to maximise his investment generally will), he can provide in the lease that, in the event of such damage or destruction, the lease will not end but will carry on in full force and effect. The tenant, however, would normally be given the right to a rent abatement for the period during which the property was being rebuilt.

(5) Alterations and additions

It is normal for leases to provide that the tenant may not make any alterations or additions to the premises without the landlord's consent. Also, where alterations have been made, with or without consent, the landlord will hold the tenant bound, if he so requires it, to remove any alterations or additions at the end of the lease.

The landlord in this situation is not trying to prevent the tenant

10 See ch 11 below.
11 See ch 7, pt 1 above.

from making alterations, but trying only to keep control of the situation. He will want to ensure that any alterations are of a sufficiently high standard and are not damaging the property in any way. Also, he will not want the property changed too much to suit the tenant's specialist business, as this might reduce its market value in the event of a relet to another tenant.

(6) Repair and maintenance

We saw in chapter 3 that, at common law, the landlord is obliged to keep the property in a tenantable and habitable condition[12]. In FRI leases, therefore, it is necessary to contract out of this provision by specifically making the tenant responsible for all repairs. In order to best ensure that the value of his property is maintained, the landlord will usually also reserve the right, in the event of the tenant failing in his maintenance obligations, to carry out any necessary repairs himself and to charge them to the tenant. He will probably also reserve a right of access to the property to inspect its condition. In properties where there is multiple occupancy (eg office blocks or shopping centres) the landlord will normally undertake any common repairs himself and recoup a proportion of the cost from each tenant by way of a service charge[13].

It is also common for a landlord to contract out of his obligation to provide subjects that are reasonably fit for the purpose of the let. This is done by inserting a condition that the tenant accepts the property as being in good condition and repair and fit for the purpose of the let.

The combined effect of these standard provisions goes to the heart of the concept of the FRI lease. The investment landlord wants a 'clear lease', ie one where the return on his investment is maximised by passing as many of his overheads as possible on to the tenant. This is fine for the landlord, but we must also look at things from the tenant's point of view, and it is clear that an over-enthusiastic application of this principle may not only involve the latter in additional expense, but also put him in some danger. The most obvious manifestation of this is seen in the vexed question of **inherent** (or **latent**) **defects**.

The meaning of the term 'inherent defect' will depend upon how it is defined in the lease in question. However, it usually arises in leases of new buildings in relation to some fault of construction or

12 See ch 3, pt 2 above.
13 See ch 11 below.

design that was not apparent at the beginning of the lease. At a future date the defect may emerge, requiring expensive repair work, or even substantial rebuilding. It seems unfair that this should be the responsibility of the tenant. The question arising here is this: do the normal terms of an FRI lease make it so?

In England it has been held that a fairly standard tenant's repairing obligation made him responsible for rectification caused by inherent defects, provided it fell short of having to reconstruct substantially the whole of the premises[14]. It is doubtful whether a simple repairing obligation could have that effect in Scotland, unless it also contracted out of the landlord's common law obligations to provide and maintain suitable premises. Also, in extreme cases, the defect may cause sufficient damage to amount to frustration by constructive total destruction, thus relieving the tenant of responsibility. However, as we have already seen, all of these common law provisions can be contracted out of. The difference between the two countries boils down in practice to one of lease wording: provided that the lease provisions are sufficiently comprehensive in their scope, a Scottish tenant may also be made liable for damage caused by inherent defects[15].

It is accordingly in the tenant's interest to insist that his repairing obligation be modified to free him of such responsibility. A landlord will be inclined to resist this, of course, and the outcome will depend on the respective negotiating strengths of the parties, ie whether there is a greater shortage of tenants or of premises for let. It should be pointed out, however, that the landlord has other directions in which he may look for reimbursement. He may be able to insure against the defects, or he may have a claim against the contractor responsible, provided that the latter's errors have not been sufficiently prevalent to force him into bankruptcy[16].

Let us finally take a brief look at landlord's repairing obligations, which sometimes still occur. We saw earlier that the landlord's repairing obligation at common law is not a warranty, ie his obligation does not arise until the defect has been drawn to his attention. It has recently been held that, where the terms of the lease make the landlord responsible for repairs, this is not an absolute

---

14 *Ravenseft Properties Ltd v Davstone (Holdings) Ltd* [1980] QB 12, [1979] 1 All ER 929.

15 *Thorn EMI Ltd v Taylor Woodrow Industrial Estates Ltd* (1982) C of S (Outer House), 29 October (unreported).

16 For a fuller discussion of the subject of inherent defects (as well as repairing obligations generally) see Ross and McKichan *Drafting and Negotiating Commercial Leases in Scotland* (1985), ch 8.

obligation unless the lease makes this clear; otherwise the land-lord's duty is merely to take reasonable care in his maintenance obligation[17].

(7) Irritancy

Irritancy has already been fully dealt with in chapter 4[18]. Despite the modification in the law by recent legislation, a wise tenant will not accept an irritancy clause in unqualified form, but will want to reserve the right, within a reasonable period, to remedy any breach that might give rise to irritancy.

(8) Arbitration

It is common for leases to provide that any disputes between the parties should be referred to arbitration rather than decided by the court. It is arguable, however, whether this would effect any significant savings in time or money, and a case could be made for omitting such a clause[19]. An exception would be in the case of rent reviews, where a disputed rent should be fixed by an arbiter or expert (usually a surveyor) who is qualified to make valuations[20].

---

17 *John Menzies plc v Ravenseft Properties Ltd* 1987 SLT 64.
18 See ch 4, pt 2 above.
19 See *Ross and McKichan*, paras 12.18–12.21.
20 See ch 10, pt 4 below.

10 Rent Reviews

1. GENERAL

If this book had been written a dozen or so years ago, the inclusion
of a chapter on rent reviews might have appeared a little odd. It
might have seemed to be an undue concentration upon a rou-
tine aspect of lease draftsmanship in a work purporting to be
an elementary treatise on the substantive law of landlord and
tenant.

Yet today the subject of rent reviews is undoubtedly one of the
most complex and important areas of modern lease law, as well as
being the fastest growing[1]. And, though it does centre upon certain
problems of conveyancing practice, the continuing deluge of case
law on the subject makes it far more than that. Finally, even though
the bulk of this unwelcome effusion originates in England, the
Scottish lawyer does not have the option of taking refuge behind a
barrier of national chauvinism: enough strands of the web have
reached over the Border to secure him firmly in its grip!

So what has given rise to all this fuss? The answer, as we might
have suspected, is money. We are here in the realm of commercial
and industrial lets, ie leases of shops, offices and factories. Since the
1939-45 war financial institutions, such as banks, insurance companies or pension funds, have increasingly invested in this type of
property. At the same time, there has been an increasing trend for
companies and firms to rent the property they occupy rather than tie
up their capital by buying it. And the years since 1945 have also seen
an unprecedented rise in the rate of inflation, particularly in the
1970s, so that rental values never remain static for long. It is normal,
therefore, for rents to be periodically reviewed to keep up with

1 For a more detailed discussion of rent reviews from the Scottish viewpoint, see
Ross and McKichan *Drafting and Negotiating Commercial Leases in Scotland*
(1985), ch 6; see also E D Buchanan 'Rent Review Clauses in Commercial Leases',
Journal of the Law Society of Scotland (Workshop Section) April/July, 1983.

inflation. The most common period for review nowadays is five years, although periods of three years have been known.

If we have a lease of comparatively short duration (say five years), reviewing the rent is not a problem. As we have already seen, the landlord will simply serve a notice to quit prior to the end of the term, preventing the onset of tacit relocation and entitling him to remove the tenant if necessary[2]. The landlord will then inform the tenant that he may stay on, provided that he enters into a new lease at a new rent. As long as the notice to quit is sent in time, the matter is comparatively simple.

However, there has been an increasing demand, from both landlords and tenants, for leases of much longer duration. A financial institution will want its rental yield to be secure and not subject to periodic uncertainty by the need to find a new tenant: if the tenant wants out, the onus will be on him to find someone to assign to. Tenants, on the other hand, may want the legal right to stay on in the premises for a reasonably extended period. This is particularly true in Scotland, where there is no equivalent of the (English) Landlord and Tenant Act 1954, allowing tenants of business premises to apply for a renewal of their lease when it is due to end.

We thus have a situation where each party wants a binding contract for a lengthy period of time. However, the landlord will not agree to this unless there is some mechanism for changing one of the main contractual terms (ie the level of rent) at more frequent intervals. The answer is to include a rent review clause in the lease.

This may seem straightforward enough, but if we gain nothing else from the rent review case law, we will learn the folly of such a naïve outlook, as we see past clauses, again and again, being minutely scrutinised by the courts and found wanting; as drafting pitfalls, which the most able lawyer could have been forgiven for overlooking, have proved fatally expensive for either landlord or tenant. Knowledge of the law in this area is therefore essential for the lawyer who wants to avoid such mistakes in future leases. But unfortunately it does not end there. The long duration of commercial and industrial leases means that we will be atoning for the unwitting sins of the past for many years to come. Today's and tomorrow's disputes will continue to be fought over clauses drafted in an earlier age of innocence. And so, if such disputes are to be kept to a minimum, it is necessary for landlords and tenants of existing leases to have advisers who are alert to the problems.

2 See ch 7 pt 1 above.

As if all this were not enough, the Scottish lawyer is faced with additional difficulties. Almost all of the case law is English. So how much of it applies in Scotland? As we have already noted, there are considerable differences between Scottish and English lease law. On the other hand, the law of contract and principles of contractual interpretation, upon which many of the cases hinge, contain much common ground. The unhelpful answer is that some of the case law undoubtedly applies to Scotland, some does not, and the sparsity of Scottish authority makes it far from certain where the border between the two lies.

This lack of Scottish case law at first sight seems a little strange. In England there is an unending flow of rent review cases, with twenty or thirty new ones reaching the case books every year. In Scotland, the tap seems to be turned off, leaving us with the occasional drip. This is only partly explained by the difference in size of the two countries and the greater financial incentive for litigation provided by high rental values in the south of England. The main reason is probably the difference in Scottish and English arbitration law. As we will see shortly, it is common for rent review disputes to be settled by arbitration. In England either party to a dispute has the right to appeal to the court against an arbitrator's decision on points of law[3], and such appeals are the source of most rent review case law from south of the Border. The parties may agree in advance to exclude the jurisdiction of the courts, but this right has existed only since 1979, and there has been a long tradition of judicial review of arbitration in England[4]. In Scotland, a limited right of appeal on points of law by stated case to the Court of Session was introduced for the first time in 1972. From the outset this right could be contracted out of, and in practice it usually is[5]. In this way Scottish landlords and tenants are spared the distress of having their disputes unduly prolonged, but at the expense of an even greater than usual English influence in the development of the law.

The main rent review topics to be dealt with here will be the mechanism for initiating a review, including the consequences of late notice, the basis on which the new rent will be calculated, and the methods of settling disputes, by an arbiter or expert. Finally, we will briefly look at two alternative methods of calculating the rent level, by index linked or turnover rents.

3 Arbitration Act 1979, ss 1 and 2.
4 Ibid s 3.
5 Administration of Justice (Scotland) Act 1972, s 3; see also pt 4 below.

2. THE REVIEW MECHANISM

Some of the most serious problems to have arisen concern the procedure when a rent review date arrives. These difficulties may best be understood by initially asking ourselves a number of hypothetical questions. What happens if a landlord lets a rent review date pass without asking for a review? Does he lose his right to review the rent until the next review date in the lease, which may be four or five years in the future? Or can he review late? If the latter is the case, can he charge the increase retrospectively to the missed review date, or only from the later date when he began proceedings? Many leases in the past have tried to clarify matters by laying down a strict timetable for initiating a review. For example, a lease may specify a minimum period (say six months) prior to the review date for the landlord to send the tenant a 'trigger' notice, stating the proposed new rent. The tenant may be given a fixed period (often as little as twenty-one days) within which to reject the landlord's proposal, failing which he will be deemed to have accepted the landlord's figure. There may also be a time limit for referring the matter to a third party in the event of a dispute. Such timetables may superficially seem to be a good idea, but it eventually became clear that they create more problems than they solve. What happens if a landlord is late in sending a trigger notice or referring a dispute to arbitration? Will he be stuck with charging the old rent for another five years? Or what if the tenant fails to send a counter-notice within the prescribed period? Will he have to pay the landlord's proposed new rent until the next review date? Bearing in mind that the figure in the landlord's trigger notice, being his first salvo in the negotiating battle, is likely to be unrealistically high, the consequences to the tenant of such a slip could be financially disastrous. On the other hand, if such dire consequences are not to follow a failure to observe the time limits, what is the point of having a timetable at all?

The key to answering these questions is found in the leading cases of *United Scientific Holdings Ltd v Burnley Borough Council* and *Cheapside Land Development Co Ltd v Messels Service Co*[6]. These two cases, which raised basically the same principles, were heard together in the House of Lords. In each case there had been a failure on the part of the landlords to adhere to the rent review timetable and in each case the Court of Appeal upheld the tenants' view that the landlords had lost their right to review the rent until the next

6 [1978] AC 904, [1977] 2 All ER 62.

review date. However, the House of Lords reversed that judgment and found for the landlords in each case. The *ratio* of the decision is found in Lord Diplock's now famous dictum:

'So upon the question of principle which these two appeals were brought to settle, I would hold that in the absence of any contra-indications in the express words of the lease or in the inter-relation of the rent review clause itself and other clauses or in the surrounding circumstances the presumption is that the time-table specified in a rent review clause for completion of the various steps for determining the rent payable in respect of the period following the review date is not of the essence of the contract[7].'

In other words there is a presumption that time is not of the essence in the review timetable. This means that, unless there are circumstances to rebut the presumption, a landlord will not lose his right to review the rent because of a late notice and a tenant will not be stuck with a landlord's proposed rent by failing to send his counter-notice in time. And where a landlord reviews late, he will be entitled to backdate the increase to the original review date. This last point had been decided in the earlier case of *CH Bailey Ltd v Memorial Enterprises Ltd*[8], and was quoted with approval by their lordships in the *United Scientific* and *Cheapside* cases.

The decision in these cases reversed what had been thought to be the position in English law. At the core of their lordships' reasoning was the point that delay in fixing a new rent does not cause any serious detriment to a tenant. Instead, it may be to his advantage, as he will have the use of the money representing the difference between the old and new rents for a longer period before having to pay it to his landlord. This contrasts with the considerable detriment to a landlord if he is unable to increase the rent until the next review period (ten years in the *United Scientific* case). Moreover, if the tenant wants to know what the new rent is going to be he can get a fair idea of the current market level by consulting his surveyor. Alternatively, if a landlord fails to send a trigger notice in time, it is open to the tenant to send a notice specifying a period within which the landlord is required to notify the tenant if the rent review is going ahead. Such a notice, if sent by the tenant, would make time of the essence in relation to the landlord's reply.

After the decisions in *United Scientific* and *Cheapside*, a number

7 [1978] AC 904 at 930.
8 [1974] 1 All ER 1003, [1974] 1 WLR 728.

of landlords woke up to the idea that this apparent change in the law offered them the chance to put right past blunders that they had thought irreparable. After allowing for the ponderous processes of the law, a number of cases appeared in which the landlords were held entitled to review the rent retrospectively. In many of these the time that had elapsed since the review date was considerable, eg eighteen months[9], twenty-two months[10], twenty-four months[11], and even twenty-seven months[12]. In one case (*Telegraph Properties (Securities) Ltd v Courtaulds Ltd*)[13] six years was held to be an unreasonable delay, but that case was later overruled by the Court of Appeal in *Amherst v James Walker Goldsmith & Silversmith Ltd*[14].

It is perhaps worth looking at that last case a little more closely, as it represents the most extreme formulation to date of the *United Scientific* doctrine. In *Amherst* the landlords' notice, in terms of the lease, should have been served by 25 December 1974. They were a month late in serving it and the tenants refused to accept the notice as valid, their claim being upheld in court. However, in 1980, the landlords, encouraged by the *United Scientific* decision, served a fresh notice on the tenant. It was held that time was not of the essence and the landlords were entitled to review the rent retrospectively despite the fact that they had served their new notice five years after the review date. In the course of his judgment, Oliver LJ said:

'I know of no authority for the proposition that the effect of construing a time stipulation as not being of the essence is to substitute a fresh implied term that the contract shall be performed within a reasonable time . . . I would in fact go further and suggest that, despite what Lord Salmon said in the *United Scientific* case, even delay plus hardship to the tenant would not disentitle the landlord to exercise the right which he has, on the true construction of the contract, unless the combination amounted to an estoppel . . .

'In particular, I cannot, speaking for myself, see how the right can be lost by "abandonment." So far as I am aware, this is not a term of art but I take it to mean the unilateral sig-

---

9 *H West & Son v Brecht* (1981) 261 EG 156.
10 *Printing House Properties Ltd v J Winston & Co Ltd* (1982) 263 EG 725.
11 *Vince v Alps Hotel Ltd* (1980) 258 EG 330.
12 *London and Manchester Assurance Co Ltd v GA Dunn & Co* (1983) 265 EG 39, 131, CA.
13 (1980) 257 EG 1153.
14 [1983] Ch 305, [1983] 2 All ER 1067, CA.

nification of an intention not to exercise the contractual right in question. If that is right I cannot see how it could bind the landlord save as a promise (promissory estoppel) or as a representation followed by reliance (equitable estoppel) or as a consensual variation of the agreement or as a repudiation accepted by the other party[15].'

This seems to make the position clear enough. Unfortunately, it only makes it clear in England, and in Scotland the position is a little more complicated. In *Banks v Mecca Bookmakers (Scotland) Ltd*[16], one of the few Scottish rent review cases, the landlords had several leases with the tenants, whom they notified in April 1978 of their wish to review the rents. This was nearly a year after the rent review date in some of the leases, and nearly two years after it in the others. It was held that the acceptance by the landlords of rent at the old rate after the review dates, without qualification or any explanation, inferred abandonment of the landlord's right to seek review until the next review dates. Pointing out that the concept of waiver was not raised in *CH Bailey Ltd v Memorial Enterprises Ltd*[17] or in the *United Scientific* and *Cheapside* cases, Lord Grieve went on to say:

'As I understand the law of Scotland the question of "waiver" is concerned with whether or not a right under a contract has been abandoned. It is a question of fact, and, as such, the question whether or not a person has abandoned a right cannot be affected one way or the other by prejudice suffered by the person who alleges that the right has been abandoned. Accordingly in cases such as this where the issue is concerned with the alleged abandonment of a right, prejudice need not be averred, and indeed would be irrelevant if it was[18].'

Neither the concept of waiver nor the *Banks* case were referred to in *Amherst*, even though it was heard a year after the Scottish case had been reported. Nor has there so far been any further Scottish authority on the point. It is clear that the two cases are incompatible, one rejecting and the other recognising the concept of abandonment, one giving a landlord the right to backdate even where the tenant has suffered hardship, the other depriving him of

15 [1983] Ch 305 at 315-316.
16 1982 SC 7, 1982 SLT 150.
17 [1974] 1 All ER 1003, [1974] 1 WLR 728.
18 1982 SLT 150 at 153.

the right to review even without hardship. What is not clear is whether the discrepancy reflects an underlying difference in the law of the two countries or merely a different interpretation of common principles. The principle of waiver is certainly not peculiar to Scots law, and it is not immediately obvious that the English doctrine is different from the Scottish one. *Halsbury's Laws of England*[19] defines waiver as 'the abandonment of a right in such a way that the other party is entitled to plead the abandonment by way of confession and avoidance if the right is thereafter asserted, and is either express or implied from conduct'. So far, this seems in line with the *Banks* decision, but Halsbury goes on to say that, not only must there be a promise or assurance (which may be express or implied) by the party alleged to have granted the waiver, but that the other party must have acted upon it and altered his position in some way. The Scottish version, as formulated by Professor Gloag seems remarkably similar[20]. 'The party who alleges waiver must in some way have altered his position, or abstained from fulfilling the condition, in reliance on the words or conduct of the other. "The essence" of the plea of personal bar "is that owing to the action of one party the other party is put in a worse position than he would otherwise have been in".'

So now we have both Scotland and England apparently on the side of the English authority. Gloag apparently regards waiver as an aspect of personal bar, the Scottish equivalent of the English doctrine of estoppel, which was one of the possible exceptions to the rule acknowledged in *Amherst*. Also, the tenant having acted to his detriment, which was declared to be irrelevant in *Banks*, is considered an essential factor. But, unfortunately, the saga does not end there. The need for prejudice to exist in cases of waiver has been questioned as an unwarranted introduction of English principles into Scots law by Professor Gloag and his sources[1]. If that line of reasoning is followed, *Banks* must be regarded, not as a maverick decision, but as reflecting a genuine difference in the law north of the Border. But the position is not exactly settled.

And so what conclusion can we draw from all of this? It may help if we distinguish between two separate types of case. The first is where the landlord has in fact initiated the rent review process prior to the review date, but either the landlord or the tenant has not strictly conformed to the review timetable laid down in the lease, eg

19 16 *Halsbury's Laws of England* (4th edn) para 1471.
20 Gloag *The Law of Contract* (2nd edn 1929), p 281.
 1 McBryde *The Law of Contract in Scotland* (1987), paras 23.01 to 23.20; see also *Armia Ltd v Daejan Developments Ltd* 1979 SC (HL) 56, 1979 SLT (HL) 147.

where there has been late service of a landlord's trigger notice or of a tenant's counter-notice. Here it is clear that Scots and English law are in line and that the *United Scientific* principle applies in both countries: this is implied in *Banks* and has been subsequently confirmed in a growing body of Scottish cases[2]. The second situation is where the landlord has let the review date pass entirely and has continued to accept rent at the old rate before deciding (or remembering) to ask for a review. It is plain that this makes no difference in England, from the number of late reviews that were allowed there after the decision in the *United Scientific* case[3]. But in Scotland, in the light of the *Banks* case, the landlord is likely to be held to have waived his right to a review, and will be prevented from increasing the rent until the next review date. Whether future Scottish cases will follow this line and continue the divergence remains to be seen.

Let us now return from this brief excursion into comparative law and pick up the main thread of the story. That does not mean, alas, that the difficulties have gone, but only that, for the time being, we are back to ones that straddle the Border. We have seen that there is a general presumption in relation to rent review timetables that time is not of the essence. However, there are a number of situations where it has been established that the presumption has been rebutted and time **is** considered to be of the essence:

(a) *Where the lease expressly states that time is of the essence in relation to the review timetable or any part of it.* As we will see below, this is probably the only situation where the position is clear and free of controversy.

(b) *Where the tenant serves a notice on the landlord making time of the essence.* It is clear from Lord Diplock's judgment in *United Scientific* that the tenant has this option. However, it may only apply if the tenant has no other remedy available. In *Factory Holdings Group v Leboff International*[4], the tenant sent a notice to the landlord requiring the landlord to refer the dispute to arbitration within twenty-eight days and purporting to make time of the essence. In terms of the lease it was equally open to the landlord and

---

2 *Scottish Development Agency v Morrisons Holdings Ltd* 1986 SLT 59; *Yates, Petitioner* 1987 SLT 86; *Leeds Permanent Pension Scheme Trustees Ltd v William Timpson Ltd* 1987 SCLR 571; *Legal and Commercial Properties Ltd v Lothian Regional Council* 1988 SLT 463.

3 See footnotes 9-14 above.

4 [1987] 1 EGLR 135, 282 EG 1005.

the tenant to apply for the appointment of an arbitrator. It was held that the tenant was not entitled to serve a notice making time of the essence because, in the particular circumstances of the case, he did not need that remedy.

(c) *Where there is an inter-relationship between the rent review clause and a tenant's break provision.* This is the one contra-indication specifically mentioned in the *United Scientific* case as implying that time is of the essence and rebutting the presumption. The reason is quite logical. If the tenant is given the option of terminating the lease prematurely, and he is required to give notice of his intention on or shortly after the landlord's last date for sending his rent review trigger notice, the presumption is that the purpose of the break provision is to allow the tenant to get out of the lease if he thinks the new rent is too high. Time is of the essence in relation to the tenant's notice exercising the break, because the landlord needs to know whether or not he will have to look for another tenant[5]. It would therefore be grossly unfair on the tenant if he let pass his opportunity to terminate the lease only to receive a late trigger notice from the landlord demanding an unacceptably high rent. Subsequent to the *United Scientific* decision, there have been a number of English cases where an inter-related rent review and break clause has been held to make time of the essence[6]. However, there have also been cases where the presence of a break clause has not had that effect. In *Edwin Woodhouse Trustee Co v Sheffield Brick Co*[7], the tenant had a right to break at the rent review date. The tenant had to give six months' notice of his intention to exercise the break, but there was no corresponding provision for a landlord's trigger notice. It was held that time could not be of the essence in relation to a date that was not specified in the lease. In *Metrolands Investments Ltd v JH Dewhurst Ltd*[8], the rent review and break timetables, on the surface, seemed closely integrated. However, one of the events in the landlord's timetable was the actual obtaining of the arbitrator's decision (as opposed to a referral to arbitration or

5 *United Scientific Holdings Ltd v Burnley Borough Council, Cheapside Land Development Co Ltd v Messels Service Co* [1978] AC 904, [1977] 2 All ER 62 at 929, per Lord Diplock.
6 *Saloom v Shirley James Travel Service Ltd* (1981) 259 EG 420, CA; *Legal and General Assurance (Pension Management) Ltd v Cheshire County Council* (1984) 269 EG 40, CA; *Coventry City Council v J Hepworth & Sons Ltd* (1983) P & CR 170, 265 EG 608, CA; *William Hill (Southern) Ltd v Govier & Govier* (1984) 269 EG 1168.
7 (1984) 270 EG 548.
8 [1986] 3 All ER 659, CA.

applying for an arbitrator to be appointed). As this was outwith the landlord's control, it was held that time could not be of the essence in relation to the rent review timetable. The fact that the tenant would want to know the new rent before deciding whether or not to exercise his option to break was countered by the fact that, under the terms of the lease, he also had the right to begin the arbitration process if he felt there was likely to be any delay. 'For these reasons,' said Slade LJ, 'there can, in our judgment, be no doubt that the potential detriment to which the lessor under this particular lease would have exposed itself by agreeing that time should be of the essence as regards the stipulated date for the obtaining of the arbitrator's decision would have far outweighed any potential detriment to which the lessee would have exposed itself by agreeing that it should not be[9].' This is fine as far as the landlord is concerned but it is not really satisfactory from the tenant's point of view. The tenant might very well have had the right to initiate arbitration proceedings, but he had no more control than the landlord over when the arbitrator would reach his decision, and no matter how diligent he was with his referral, he might still have lost the right to exercise his option to break by the time he found out what the new rent was going to be. It is difficult to see how that particular lease could have been interpreted in a way that was entirely fair to both parties.

These and other familiar arguments cropped up in the Scottish case of *Scottish Development Agency v Morrisons Holdings Ltd*[10]. There a tenant's break clause and the rent review clause were held not sufficiently inter-related to make time of the essence because (1) there was no provision for a landlord's trigger notice, whereas notice by the tenant was required to exercise his break (2) the lease required the rent to be assessed by the Valuation Department for Scotland, and the landlord had no control over the timing of that (it took two years!) (3) the lease required the valuation to be made as at the rent review date and the valuation could not be known for certain in advance of that date and (4) it was open to the tenant to make his own enquiries about the likely rent level. Presumably the same option was open to the tenant in the *Metrolands* case, though the point was not made in that case.

(d) *Where the lease contains other contra-indications making time of the essence.* Here we are once more thrust into the jungle of

---

9 *Metrolands Investments Ltd v J H Dewhurst Ltd* [1986] 3 All ER 659 at 670-671, CA, per Slade LJ, (1986) 277 EG 1343.
10 1986 SLT 59.

apparently conflicting decisions, both north and south of the Border. It is difficult to draw general principles here because so much has depended on the individual wording of particular leases, and considerable financial consequences to both landlords and tenants have hung upon minor differences in what seem to be substantially similar clauses. 'It is highly undesirable that decisions of this type of dispute shall turn upon fine distinctions,' said Sir John Donaldson MR in one of the most problematic cases[11], and his words have been echoed by many judges, both north and south of the Border, when reaching decisions in this field. Unfortunately, this excellent sentiment is generally followed by yet another application of a finely-honed forensic scalpel, after which another legal hair has been parted lengthwise. In *Drebbond Ltd v Horsham District Council*[12], a notice by the landlord requiring arbitration had to be served within three months 'but not otherwise'. It was held that these last three words made time of the essence. On the other hand, in *Touche Ross & Co v Secretary of State for the Environment*[13], a notice had to be given 'as soon as practicable and in any event not later than' a particular period. It was held that time was **not** of the essence. (Admittedly, that case also hinged on the fact that part of the timetable – the appointment of a surveyor by the President of the Royal Institution of Chartered Surveyors – was outwith the control of the parties, the same reason given in the 'break' cases.) In *Lewis v Barnett*[14], the penalty laid down in the lease for the landlord failing to apply in time for the appointment of a surveyor was that his trigger notice would 'be void and of no effect'. Time was held to be of the essence. And in the most extreme case of all *Trustees of Henry Smith's Charity v AWADA Trading and Promotion Services Ltd*[15], the Court of Appeal was faced with a rent review timetable containing more deadlines than a news editor's diary. The landlords served their trigger notice in time, but were late in referring the matter to arbitration. It was held that if the parties had agreed to confine their movements so tightly, they must be presumed to have meant it, and time was held to be of the essence. The landlords had wanted the rent raised to £29,000 per annum, but were held to the existing rent of £8,000 per annum for another five years. This means that, if the landlords' estimate bore any

11 *Trustees of Henry Smith's Charity v AWADA Trading and Promotion Services Ltd* (1984) 47 P & CR 607, 269 EG 729, CA.
12 (1978) 37 P & CR 237, 246 EG 1013, DC.
13 (1983) 46 P & CR 187, 265 EG 982, CA.
14 (1982) 264 EG 1079, CA.
15 (1984) 47 P & CR 607, 269 EG 729, CA.

resemblance to the market rent, their failure to serve the notice in time cost them in the region of £100,000! This gives a fair idea of the amount of money at stake in some of these cases.

In *Taylor Woodrow Property Co Ltd v Lonrho Textiles Ltd*[16], the deputy judge was faced with the task of reconciling the *Henry Smith* case with the earlier case of *Mecca Leisure Ltd v Renown Investments (Holdings) Ltd*[17]. Both were Court of Appeal cases, making them both binding precedents in his court, and they appeared to contradict each other. He reached the conclusion that the distinction lay in whether the 'deeming' provisions in the timetable were one way or two way. In other words, if the tenant, by sending a counter-notice late, was deemed to have accepted the figure in the landlord's trigger notice, but there was no scope for the landlord suffering a comparable sanction, time was not of the essence. The result would be the same if a tardy landlord was in danger of being held to the existing rent, without the tenant running the risk of any comparable penalty. However, if the clause was framed in such a way (as in the *Henry Smith* case) that **either** party's delay at a crucial moment might mean their financial ruin then time **was** presumed to be of the essence and either party could be strictly held to the consequences of their mistake.

In the words of Dillon LJ in the *Touche Ross* case, 'there is no magical formula which alone achieves the result of making time of the essence of a contract'[18]. It depends upon the wording of the lease in the individual case and to some extent (one suspects) on how the judge in question wants to interpret it. Unfortunately the conflict is also present in the Scottish authority. In *Yates Petitioner*[19], Lord Davidson, following the dissenting opinion in the *Mecca* case, held that time was of the essence for service of the tenant's counter-notice. Fortunately for the tenant in that case, the trigger notice served by the landlord was too informal to be valid. Furthermore, a new angle was added. Time was also of the essence in relation to the landlord's trigger notice, and his fault was not serving it too late but too early! The reason was that, if the tenant was given the landlord's proposed new rent too far away from the review date, it made it more difficult for him to judge whether the figure was a reasonable one, as the market could change in the interim. And so the landlord was required to give 'precisely, or in

---

16 (1986) 52 P & CR 28, (1985) 275 EG 632.

17 (1985) 49 P & CR 12, (1984) 271 EG 989, CA.

18 *Touche Ross & Co v Secretary of State for the Environment* (1983) 46 P & CR 187, 265 EG 982 at 190, per Dillon LJ.

19 1987 SLT 86.

any event, substantially three months' notice prior to the relevant terms'. This was to apply even if it meant the landlord having the notice delivered by hand on a Sunday!

Fortunately, in the most recent Scottish authority, there seems to be a growing reluctance by the courts to regard time as being of the essence. In *Leeds Permanent Pension Scheme Trustees Ltd v William Timpson Ltd*[20], the landlord was three weeks late in serving his trigger notice. It was held that time was not of the essence and he was allowed to review. In *Legal and Commercial Properties Ltd v Lothian Regional Council*[1], the lease contained an elaborate time-table and the tenant failed to serve a counter-notice within the required twenty-eight days. Lord Jauncey considered the *Henry Smith* and *Yates* cases, but was reluctant nevertheless to regard time as being of the essence. He held that it was not of the essence because (1) there was no time limit imposed on the landlord's application for the appointment of a surveyor and (2) the lease expressly gave the landlord the opportunity to review at a later date if he missed the review date. In other words, there was a 'one-way' deeming provision – only the tenant and not the landlord risked the supreme penalty for delay. This gives a pretext for not following the *Henry Smith* case, but the reasons for distinguishing *Yates* seem much more elusive. And so, in this particular area, we must reluctantly conclude that the case conflict has extended to Scotland.

Let us now try, not before time, to take stock of the situation. The law regarding review machinery may not be a model of clarity, but the lessons to be learned from this horrendous muddle are much easier to formulate:

(1) When drafting a rent review clause in a new lease, **do not include a strict timetable**. If the reader has gained nothing else from the above account (apart from a headache), he may just have got the impression that, for both landlords and tenants, timetables are not a good idea! After all, the tenant has signed a lease containing rent review dates and should not have to be reminded when they are due to arrive. The landlord will probably, as a matter of practice, write informally to the tenant well in advance of the date, proposing a new rent and starting off negotiations, but there is no need for a formal requirement to send a trigger notice. If the tenant is worried about the possibility of the review date being missed and a retrospective increase being imposed on him perhaps years later, the solution is simple. A provision can be inserted allowing the

20 1987 SCLR 571.
 1 1988 SLT 463.

landlord to review late, but at some later anniversary of the review date rather than retrospectively. In such a case it is in the tenant's interest to make sure that the date of valuation is still the original review date. Otherwise the landlord might, at a time of rental stagnation, be tempted to deliberately postpone the review until rent levels have risen again.

(2) A landlord would be advised to include a disclaimer to the effect that accepting rent at the old level after the rent review date will not amount to a waiver of his right to review. Whether or not this would be effective in avoiding the disastrous outcome to the landlord in the *Banks* case has not been tested in court, but it is worth a try.

(3) In addition to the general inadvisability of having a strict timetable, the tenant in particular should resist inclusion of a provision deeming him to have agreed to the landlord's rental figure if he fails to send a timeous counter-notice. This is especially so if time is expressly declared to be of the essence for the counter-notice, as that would probably be upheld by the court. If the tenant loses the right to challenge the landlord's inevitably optimistic figure, the consequences could be financial disaster.

So much for the lessons to be learned by future lease drafters. But what about the poor lawyers and surveyors who will have to live for years to come with the timetables in existing leases, drafted before the benefit of all this hindsight was available? How are we to advise them? There are a few practical considerations that may ease their burden:

(1) In order to minimise the possibility of missing a review date, the landlord's agent should have a proper administrative system for reminding him when the rents in the various leases under his care are due for review.

(2) The landlord's agent should check the rent review terms of **each individual lease** where a review is due, and make sure that all time limits are strictly observed, whether or not time is stated to be of the essence. No matter how standard the terms of his leases, an individual check is still necessary: when the lease was drafted, many years before, the standard style might have been different, or the tenant's agent might have negotiated changes, now forgotten. Since the courts have shown how much can depend upon minor differences of wording, this is an essential precaution.

(3) The tenant's agent, for his part, should also check his lease and make sure that he observes all time limits incumbent upon him, particularly if he is required to send a counter-notice to the landlord's trigger notice.

(4) As well as meeting all deadlines laid down, both landlord and tenant should observe any requirements of the lease regarding the form of the notices involved. If no requirements are laid down, the notice should be made as formal as possible, stating the sender's intentions clearly and unambiguously. In the *Yates* case[2] the landlord's trigger notice was held to be invalid, not only because it was sent early, but also because it was couched in informal terms, included social pleasantries, and seemed more like an invitation to negotiate than a formal notice. Also, there have been many cases in England where tenants indicated in time that they were unhappy with the landlord's proposed new rent, but the wording of their communication rendered it ineffective as a counter-notice. Some examples are: 'We would hardly need add that we do not accept your revised figure'[3], 'Our client . . . contends that the open market rental value . . . is at this time less than the present rental value'[4], 'We cannot agree with your rent increase'[5], 'Will you please accept this letter as counter-notice to the effect that we consider that the rent of £50,000 is excessive and will appreciate it if you will kindly forward to us comparables on which you have based this figure'[6], 'I am writing to inform you that the Board does not accept your proposed increase of £6,500'[7], and, in a letter headed 'Without prejudice and subject to contract', '. . . I suggest it would be appropriate to make application to the RICS for an independent valuer . . . I must advise my clients accordingly'[8]. All of these were held **not** to be valid counter-notices. In all of them time was of the essence (generally because the lease expressly said so), and the tenant was held to the figure in the landlord's trigger notice.

3. VALUATION GUIDELINES

Surely, the reader will be thinking, as he casts his rent review timetable in the dustbin and moves thankfully on to the next topic, things must get easier from now on. To fix the rent level at review, surely all we need to do is simply put a provision in the lease that the parties should agree a market rent. If they can't agree, then the lease

---

2 *Yates, Petitioner* 1987 SLT 86.
3 *Bellinger v South London Stationers Ltd* (1979) 252 EG 699.
4 *Oldschool v Johns* (1980) 256 EG 381.
5 *Amalgamated Estates Ltd v Joystretch Manufacturing Ltd* (1980) 257 EG 489.
6 *Edlingham Ltd v MFI Furniture Centres* (1981) 259 EG 421.
7 *Horserace Totalisator Board v Reliance Mutual Insurance Society* (1982) 266 EG 218.
8 *Sheridan v Blaircourt Investments* (1984) 270 EG 1290.

should lay down some mechanism for an arbiter or some other independent third party to tell them what the rent is. What could be simpler?

Unfortunately, as our ever-optimistic reader will by now have guessed, there is much more to it than that. We are not yet through the minefield. The following cautionary tale will illustrate the point.

In *Ponsford v HMS Aerosols Ltd*[9], there was a lease of a factory for twenty-one years with seven yearly rent reviews. A year after the lease began, the premises burned down and were rebuilt by the landlords from the insurance money. However the tenants, with the landlords' permission, decided to take the opportunity afforded by the rebuilding process to incorporate substantial improvements in the building, which they paid for themselves at a cost of £31,780. Thus the property was increased in value at the tenant's expense. When the rent came to be reviewed, the tenants claimed that any value added to the premises by them should not be taken into account in assessing the new rent. After all, they had paid the capital cost of the improvements. If they were then asked to pay an even higher rent because this had made the property more valuable, they would in effect be paying for the improvements twice. But nothing was said about this in the lease. It merely said that the tenant should pay a 'reasonable' rent for the relevant period. The House of Lords confirmed, by a majority of three to two, that this did not mean the improvements should be disregarded in assessing the rent. The job of an arbiter or other independent party is to value the property which he sees on the ground, subject to any instructions given to him in the lease. Unless the lease tells him to disregard tenant's improvements, therefore, he is bound to include the effect of them in his valuation.

We will return later in this section to tenant's improvements, one of the most important factors to be taken into account in working out our valuation guidelines. The above story, however, should be enough to illustrate that a rent review clause, to be fair to both parties, will have to contain valuation instructions a little more subtle than a simple request to fix a market rent. The way this is normally achieved is by means of a fiction called **the hypothetical letting**. After all, if it is a market rent that is to be fixed at the review date, we must ask ourselves how that is normally determined. The answer is that it is usually fixed in quite different circumstances from those a landlord and tenant are in at a rent review date. A market rent is what a tenant will be willing to pay and a landlord willing to accept for premises that are vacant and available for let.

9 [1979] AC 63, [1978] 2 All ER 837.

Usually there will be other premises which the tenant, should he so wish, could choose instead. Likewise, the landlord will possibly have other tenants to choose from. Neither party, therefore, is under any legal or other compulsion. Moreover, the premises are as provided by the landlord, not yet altered in any way by the tenant. Nor has the property acquired any value in the way of goodwill brought about by the tenant having occupied the property over a period of time.

This is in contrast to the real situation of the parties at a rent review date. The premises are not vacant, the property is not actually on the market. It is occupied by the tenant. Without the landlord's permission the tenant is not at liberty to go elsewhere, nor is the landlord free to take another tenant. They are both bound by the contract of lease. It may be that one of them wants out but is being held to the bargain by the other. Moreover, the tenant, by having occupied the property over a period of time, may be committed to it in other ways; he may, as we have seen, have made improvements, he may have established goodwill in that particular location and, even in the absence of these, it would probably be easier for him to stay where he is rather than to move. Unlike our fictional tenant on the lookout for suitable premises, he may well have a vested interest in staying put.

The **hypothetical letting**, therefore, is a simulation of a real market situation, created for the purpose of a rent review. It is a construction to be made by the valuer in accordance with the instructions in the rent review clause. The way this is usually achieved is by stating a number of factors that should be taken into account and others that should be left out when making the rental valuation, ie the normal assumptions and disregards.

The normal assumptions

It is, of course, up to the parties to decide what these should be when drawing up the lease, but common assumptions to be found are: (1) that there is a willing lessor and a willing lessee; (2) that the premises are vacant; (3) as to the length of the term of the lease yet to run; (4) that the tenant has fulfilled his obligations under the lease, and (5) that the hypothetical let is on the same terms as the actual lease. These are not all the assumptions that are sometimes made, but are some of the more common and important ones[10]. Let us look at these one at a time.

---

10 For a more detailed consideration of valuation assumptions, see *Ross and McKichan* paras 6.21 to 6.38.

(1) *The assumption of a willing lessor and a willing lessee.* The best analysis of these fictional characters was made by Donaldson J in the case of *FR Evans (Leeds) Ltd v English Electric Co Ltd*[11]. Neither of them is the actual landlord or tenant but 'is a complete abstraction, and, like the mule, has neither pride of ancestry nor hope of posterity'.

> '(The willing lessor) is a hypothetical person with the right to dispose of the premises on an 18-year lease. As such, he is not afflicted by personal ills such as a cash-flow crisis or importunate mortgagees. Nor is he in the happy position of someone to whom it is largely a matter of indifference whether he lets in October 1976 or waits for the market to improve. He is, in short, a willing lessor. He wants to let the premises at a rent which is appropriate to all the factors which affect the marketability of these premises as industrial premises – for example, geographical location, the extent of the local labour market, the level of local rates and the market rent of competitive premises, that is to say, premises which are directly comparable or which, if not directly comparable, would be considered as viable alternatives by a potential tenant.
>
> 'Similarly, in my judgment, the willing lessee is an abstraction – a hypothetical person actively seeking premises to fulfil needs which these premises could fulfil. He will take account of similar factors, but he too will be unaffected by liquidity problems, governmental or other pressures to boost or maintain employment in the area and so on[12].'

These parties may resemble the actual landlord and tenant, but they need not do. They are a necessary invention for our market simulation.

(2) *The assumption that the premises are vacant.* In the real world, as opposed to the hypothetical let, the tenant may have sublet the property and, if this was taken into account, it might affect the rental value at review. It could have the effect of either increasing or decreasing the rental value depending on the terms of the sublease and the amount of rent payable under it, and thus could either favour the landlord or the tenant. It is generally thought fairer to

---

11 (1977) 36 P & CR 185, 245 EG 657.
12 *FR Evans (Leeds) Ltd v English Electric Co Ltd* (1977) 36 P & CR 185 at 189-190, 191, 245 EG 657.

both parties to assume vacant possession so that any distortion by subletting will not be taken into account. The assumption of vacant possession will also mean that the tenant's fixtures and fittings, which might have added to the rental value, will also not be taken into consideration. If no assumption of vacant possession is made, the other terms of the lease may imply it[13]. However, it is safer to state it explicitly.

(3) *The term of the lease still to run.* There are two possible assumptions here, either that the full term of the lease should be taken into account, or only the unexpired residue. For example, let us suppose that we are at year twenty of a twenty-five year lease with five yearly rent reviews. Depending on what assumptions are made, this can be valued either as a twenty-five year lease or a five year lease. The rent will generally be higher for the former as a tenant will be willing to pay extra for a longer period of security of tenure. It is in the tenant's interest, therefore, that a lease for the unexpired residue be assumed, as this reflects the reality of the situation. Landlords, however, may want an assumption that there is a lease for the full original term. This point is more important in Scotland than in England. In England, the fact that a tenant may have a right to renew his lease under the Landlord and Tenant Act 1954 will mitigate this effect on the rental value towards the end of a lease[14]. In Scotland, there will be no such effect, and so the discrepancy will be greater. A tenant, therefore, should resist any attempt by a landlord to include an assumption that the full term of the lease has still to run.

(4) *The assumption that the tenant has fulfilled his lease conditions.* If, for example, necessary repairs have not been carried out, this will probably have the effect of lowering the value of the property. If the lease is a full repairing one, then the tenant could potentially benefit, by way of a lower rental, from having failed in a lease obligation. This would be obviously unfair to the landlord, and so an assumption in the above terms is usually made. If not included, this assumption may be implied, but it is safer to state it in the lease[15].

(5) *The assumption that the hypothetical let is on the same terms as the original lease.* There are many terms in a lease that may affect the

---

13 *Avon County Council v Alliance Property Co Ltd* (1981) 258 EG 1181.
14 *Pivot Properties Ltd v Secretary of State for the Environment* (1980) 41 P & CR 249, 256 EG 1176, CA.
15 *Harmsworth Pension Fund Trustees v Charringtons Industrial Holdings* (1985) 49 P & CR 297.

rental value of the property. For example, if a landlord undertakes to repair or to insure the property, he will be able to charge a higher rent than if these had been the tenant's responsibility. This assumption is therefore fair as it reflects the actual position of the parties. If the terms of the lease do not indicate otherwise, this is another assumption that may be automatically implied[16]. However, so much can hang on minute differences of wording in individual leases, that once more it is best to include this assumption clearly and explicitly.

One qualification often made here is that the hypothetical let will be on the same terms as the original let 'other than those relating to rent'. The obvious reason for this is that the valuer should be free to depart from the original rent stated in the lease when fixing a new rent at review. However, the tenant should beware. There have been cases where it has been held that a qualification in these terms also excludes the rent review provisions[17]. This means that a lease with rent reviews will be valued as if there were no reviews at all, and the landlord will be able to charge a premium (as much as 20 per cent in some cases) on the untrue assumption that he will have no further opportunity to raise the rent before the end of the lease. Not all cases have favoured this interpretation[18]: as usual the infinite variety of possible wording in individual clauses allowed different decisions to be reached in superficially similar circumstances. An admirable attempt to construct some order out of the chaos was made by the Vice-Chancellor, Sir Nicolas Browne-Wilkinson in *British Gas Corpn v Universities Superannuation Scheme Ltd*[19]. Pointing out that the logical conclusion of excluding **all** provisions relating to rent would be an absurd situation in which the valuer had to ignore the tenant's obligation to pay the rent and the landlord's remedies for non-payment, he went on to produce rules of thumb to assist interpretation in such cases:

> '(a) words in a rent exclusion provision which require **all** provisions as to rent to be disregarded produce a result so manifestly contrary to commercial common sense that they cannot be given literal effect;

16 *Basingstoke and Deane Borough Council v Host Group Ltd* (1987) 284 EG 1587, CA.
17 *National Westminster Bank v Arthur Young McClelland Moores & Co* [1985] 2 All ER 817, [1985] 1 WLR 1123, CA.
18 *MFI Properties Ltd v BICC Group Pension Trust Ltd* [1986] 1 All ER 974, 277 EG 862; *Datastream International Ltd v Oakeep Ltd* [1986] 1 All ER 966, [1986] 1 WLR 404.
19 [1986] 1 All ER 978, 277 EG 980.

(b) other clear words which require the rent review provision (as opposed to all provisions as to rent) to be disregarded ... must be given effect to, however wayward the result, and

(c) subject to (b), in the absence of special circumstances it is proper to give effect to the underlying commercial purpose of a rent review clause and to construe the words so as to give effect to that purpose by requiring future rent reviews to be taken into account in fixing the open market rental under the hypothetical letting'[20].

Perhaps the study of rent review litigation makes one cynical, but the above pronouncement seems so redolent of common-sense that it almost seems bound not to last. Already there have been erosions[1]. And although in *Equity & Law Life Assurance PLC v Bodfield Ltd*[2], the Court of Appeal approved the guidelines, they did so with qualifications. The guidelines were not, said the court, mechanistic rules of construction to be applied rigidly in every case, but priority must always be given to the actual wording of the individual lease. 'Guidelines such as the Vice-Chancellor's cannot entitle the court to construe and apply, not the clause which the parties have entered into, but the different clause which they might have, or probably would have, entered into if their lawyers had thought rather more deeply about how the intricate scheme they were setting up would work in practice[3].' This seems to be saying that the rules should not be used to deprive lawyers of the right to profit from their own mistakes in later litigation! In that case, the particular wording of the review clause resulted in the rent review provisions being excluded. The Vice-Chancellor's rules, although approved of in general, were not applied on that occasion.

Another term of the lease that can have an effect on the rental value is the use (or user) clause. We have already seen that, from the point of view of estate management, it will be to the landlord's advantage to keep a tight control over the uses the property can be put to. However, in the case of *Plinth Property Investments Ltd v Mott, Hay & Anderson*[4], it was shown that this policy can rebound upon a landlord financially. In that case, a lease provided that the

---

20 *British Gas Corpn v Universities Superannuation Scheme Ltd* [1986] 1 All ER 978, 277 EG 980 at 984.

1 *General Accident Fire & Life Assurance Corpn plc v Electronic Data Processing Co plc* (1987) 53 P & CR 189, 281 EG 65.

2 [1987] 1 EGLR 124, 54 P & CR 290, CA; see also *British Home Stores plc v Ranbrook Properties Ltd* (1988) 16 EG 80, where the rules *were* applied.

3 *Equity & Law Life Assurance Society v Bodfield* [1987] 1 EGLR 124, 54 P & CR 290 at 294, CA, per Dillon LJ.

4 (1978) 38 P & CR 361, (1978) 249 EG 1167.

property could only be used as an office for the purpose of the tenant's business of consulting civil engineers. The court held that, at a rent review, the arbitrator was justified in fixing a rent considerably lower than the full market rental (£89,200 instead of £130,455). This was because the lease was theoretically only assignable to other civil engineers and therefore had a lower market value than if the use had not been thus restricted. The landlords argued that if the tenants ever wanted to assign, they would be willing to waive the restriction, but this was held to be irrelevant; the tenant was entitled to assume that the landlord would insist upon his legal rights. Alternatively, if he agreed to a change he might insist on the tenant paying some financial consideration in return.

On the other hand, if the landlord goes even further and restricts the use not just to a narrow category, but to one named person, ie the tenant himself, this cannot be exploited by the tenant to depress the rent payable at review. In *Law Land Co Ltd v Consumers Association Ltd*[5], the Court of Appeal held in these circumstances that the hypothetical lease should have a use clause in which the tenant's name had been deleted. This is in keeping with the *FR Evans* case, where it was emphasised that the hypothetical landlord and tenant were imaginary figures, not the actual parties. In any case, in the lease in question, narrowing the use to one tenant was inconsistent with references in the rent review clause to 'market rent', 'open market', and 'vacant possession'. This case, incidentally, illustrates the dangers of sloppy draftsmanship where a lease, or any other legal document for that matter, is put together from standard clauses derived from different sources, without properly checking whether they are consistent with each other: the result, in the present case, was 'a lease which, like an old sock, contains strands of different colours and textures roughly stitched together'[6].

Another point to note, following from the *Plinth* case, is that the landlord cannot get round the effect of that decision by unilaterally imposing a wider range of uses on the tenant purely to justify a rent increase at the rent review. This was tried in *C & A Pensions Trustees Ltd v British Vita Investments Ltd*[7], but the court held that the landlords were not entitled to impose upon the tenants an additional number of authorised uses which they neither requested nor wanted.

The *Plinth* decision obviously indicates a danger to the landlord.

5 (1980) 255 EG 617, CA.
6 *Law Land Co Ltd v Consumers Association Ltd* (1980) 255 EG 617 at 617, CA.
7 *C & A Pensions Trustees Ltd v British Vita Investments Ltd* (1984) 272 EG 63.

How should he react to it? There are two main possibilities. Firstly, he can qualify the assumption that the hypothetical lease should incorporate all the terms of the original lease by excluding or amending the provision relating to use of the property. Alternatively, he may allow a qualification that his consent to a change of use 'will not be unreasonably withheld', or even dispense entirely with naming the type of business involved: it is arguable whether this is really necessary, other than in shop leases, where it may be required in order to control the mix of tenants' businesses.

There is an additional Scottish dimension here which should perhaps be considered. In the *Plinth* case, the rent was depressed because of the limited range of tenants to whom the property could be assigned, and it had to be assumed that the landlord might insist upon his legal rights. It could be argued that a similar effect might result from an absolute prohibition of assignation without the landlord's consent. This issue could not really occur in England because any attempt to impose such a prohibition would be qualified by statute to the effect that the landlord's consent would not be unreasonably withheld[8]. There is no such statutory provision in Scotland, and Scottish draftsmen should perhaps take note and amend either their alienation or their rent review clauses accordingly.

The usual disregards

Unlike the assumptions, these have a statutory origin and derive from s 34 of the Landlord and Tenant Act 1954 (which does not apply to Scotland). We have already noted that, under that Act, a tenant of business premises in England may apply for a renewal of his lease when it is due to come to an end. If he is granted a renewal, the rent is fixed subject to the disregards set out in s 34. Their statutory application is therefore when leases are due to end, rather than to rent reviews in mid-term, but the same disregards are generally incorporated into rent review clauses, both in Scotland and England. They are: (1) any effect on rent of the tenant being in occupation; (2) tenant's goodwill; (3) tenant's improvements, and (4) the effect of any licence.

(1) *Effect of the tenant being in occupation.* As we have already seen, the hypothetical tenant, who is willing to pay the market rent for the property he wants, is a free agent. He is not yet in occupation of the property he needs and is not committed to any one property. Any

8 Landlord and Tenant Act 1927, s 19(1)(a).

attempt to charge him more than the market rent is liable to make him go elsewhere. The actual tenant at rent review is less fortunate. He is in all probability committed to one property, the one he is occupying, because of goodwill he has built up there, because he has gone to the bother of making improvements to it, or simply because he does not want to go to the trouble and expense of moving. In the real world he might be prepared to pay over the odds to stay where he is. It is generally felt that this is not a factor that the landlord should be entitled to take account of, hence the present disregard. Incidentally, at the end of a lease, as opposed to a mid-term rent review, there seems to be nothing to prevent a Scottish landlord from charging extra to let the tenant stay on. As we have seen, he would be prevented from doing so in England by the operation of the 1954 Act.

(2) *Effect of the tenant's goodwill.* If a tenant has been in business for a period of time, and has been operating well, he is likely to have enhanced the value of that business by the build-up of goodwill, ie the probability that clients and customers will return to him. This value is mainly personal to the tenant, rather than something that attaches to the property he occupies. However, it is possible that some of it will rub off on the property, particularly in the case of shops, if a business of a particular kind has been carried on in the same location for a long time. A new tenant, who wanted to operate the same type of business, might well be prepared to pay extra in rent to secure that particular property. This is therefore a feasible component of the market rent, but it would be unfair at rent review to charge extra to the tenant who had provided that goodwill in the first place.

(3) *Tenant's improvements.* We saw at the beginning of the section, as illustrated in the *Ponsford* case, why it was right to disregard the value of tenant's improvements: it was unfair that he should be charged for them twice, once when he paid the capital cost of them, and then again in the way of higher rent. Section 34 of the 1954 Act qualifies this by excepting the value of improvements carried out under a lease obligation to the landlord, and this exception is usually also included in rent review clauses.

The disregard of the value of tenant's improvements is probably the most important of all the valuation guidelines and should always be included in rent review clauses as an essential component of the hypothetical lease. A few supplementary points are worth noting.

If a tenant enters a new lease with the same landlord, it should be made clear in that new lease that the value of improvements made during the currency of the original lease should also be disregarded. In *Brett v Brett Essex Golf Club Ltd*[9], the tenants (ie the golf club) laid out the land as a golf course and built a clubhouse. Later they entered into a completely new lease of the property with the same landlord. As the course and clubhouse were already incorporated in the property when the new lease was entered, it was held that their considerable value could not be disregarded as a tenant's improvement when the rent came up for review. This seems less hard on the golf club company in light of the fact that, when the work was done, the company was virtually owned by the landlord, Mr Brett, who held three quarters of the shares, and that these had been sold by him prior to the new lease being entered into. However, it should be noted that this was **not** a relevant legal consideration in the case and was not taken into account in reaching the decision. A limited company is a distinct legal person from its shareholders, no matter who owns the shares: the rent review clause should provide for all the tenant's improvements to be disregarded, whether they were made during the current lease or an earlier one between the same parties.

Secondly, it is a usual provision in leases that tenants must obtain the landlord's permission before carrying out any alterations or improvements. Also, in rent review clauses it is common to qualify the disregard of improvements to the effect that the landlord's permission must have been obtained for them. Such a provision was included in the lease in *Hamish Cathie Travel England Ltd v Insight International Tours Ltd*[10]. The tenant failed to get the landlord's consent to alterations he made and it was held that their value could not be disregarded at the rent review.

Finally, it should be noted that the improvements disregard does not always work in the tenant's favour: it can be in the landlord's interest also to have it included. The reason for this is that it cannot be assumed that alterations made to the property will always add to its value. They may be to a poor standard. Or they may have the effect of adapting the premises for the specialised business of the tenant, which could lower their market value to other tenants with different types of business. It would obviously be unfair to the landlord if this had the effect of lowering the rent he could charge at review. In the light of this, it would perhaps be more accurate to refer in the disregard to 'alterations' or 'alterations and improvements' rather than merely 'improvements' carried out by

9 (1986) 52 P & CR 330, 278 EG 1476, CA; see also *Panther Shop Investments Ltd v Keith Pople Ltd* (1987) 282 EG 594.
10 [1986] 1 EGLR 244.

the tenant. This ensures a situation that is fair to both parties.

(4) *Effect of a licence*. This may refer to a betting or gaming licence, or a licence to sell alcohol. The theory is that any effect on rent caused by the fact that the tenant holds such a licence should be disregarded, presumably because this value is personal to the tenant and not an attribute of the property. This can be important, as it is a field where a lot of money may be involved. In *Cornwall Coast Country Club v Cardrange Ltd*[11], which related to a casino in Mayfair, the case hinged on, among other things, the precise effect of a lease provision for the disregard of the tenants' gaming licence. The tenants' estimate of the market rent was £180,000, whereas the landlords thought it should have been £3,000,000. Obviously this is an area where the stakes are high!

'Upwards or downwards' valuation

One important valuation guideline remains to be considered. It is normal for landlords to include in rent review clauses a provision that any rent review should be upwards only, or, at the very least, that the rent should not fall below the current level. Until a few years ago this was not something that tenants were likely to quibble about: in the mid-1970s, when inflation was soaring, the suggestion that rental levels might sometimes fall would have seemed to be firmly in the realm of fantasy. Since then, however, there have been situations where rental values have fallen in some areas. This is a timely reminder that when we are drafting a commercial or industrial lease we are producing a contract that may determine the parties' rights and obligations many decades into the future. It would be a rash person who would try to predict the economic circumstances likely to prevail over such a period. The rent review clause, as well as the rest of the lease, should be framed as flexibly as possible, so as to cope with as many different types of circumstances as possible.

With this in mind, the tenant should insist that any reviews may be either upwards **or** downwards. A corollary of this is that the tenant, as well as the landlord, should have the right to call for a review at the review date; otherwise, if rent levels were ever to fall, the landlord might conveniently 'forget' about the review. Landlords, of course, may resist the inclusion of these modifications, but tenants should do their best to insist. A future generation of tenants may be grateful.

---

11 [1987] 1 EGLR 146, 282 EG 1664; see also *Daejan Investments v Cornwall Coast Country Club* (1985) 273 EG 1122, 82 LS Gaz 3085.

4. SETTLING OF DISPUTES: ARBITER OR EXPERT

If nothing else has been gained from the preceding sections, the reader will at least be stripped of any illusion that a rent review clause could be a simple and uncomplicated matter. If we do not have valuation guidelines, for example, we are liable to produce a rent that in some sense may be a market rent, but is liable to be unfair to at least one of the parties. However, without such guidelines, we would still have a rent review clause that was operational. It would still produce a result, however inequitable. On the other hand, without some formula for deciding between the parties in the event of disagreement, we are in danger of producing a rent review clause that is totally unenforceable. The courts are liable to declare it void from uncertainty. Arguably, then, the machinery for independent determination of the rent is the single most important element in any rent review clause.

It seems incredible that there might actually have been cases where clauses provided for a rent to be 'agreed between the parties' and left it at that. Nothing is more predictable than that the landlord and tenant are liable to disagree about this, so where do they go from there? Yet there have been such cases, both in relation to options to renew and mid-term rent reviews. Unfortunately, they do not agree about the legal effect, partly because of slightly differing circumstances, but also because of differing opinions of the judges concerned. Sometimes such a provision has been held void from uncertainty[12], sometimes a workable formula has been written in to the contract by the court[13], and sometimes the rent has been left as it was[14].

Yet again we have a situation where the law may be unclear, but the moral is plain: it is absolutely essential to have some means of fixing the rent independently of the parties themselves.

In the context of a hypothetical letting this is usually achieved by providing for disputes to be referred either to an arbiter or an expert. Sometimes a lease will allow a landlord to choose either. What is the difference between them?

The first point to note is that we are not talking about different types of individual. In rent review cases, each is likely to be a chartered surveyor. The difference lies in the role that he is called upon to play. In neither case is it advisable for a lease to name a

---

12 *Kings Motors (Oxford) Ltd v Lax* [1969] 3 All ER 665, [1970] 1 WLR 426.
13 *Brown v Gould* [1972] Ch 53; *Beer v Bowden* (1975) 237 EG 41; *Thomas Bates & Son Ltd v Wyndhams (Lingerie) Ltd* (1979) 39 P & CR 517.
14 *King v King* (1980) 41 P & CR 311, 255 EG 1205.

particular individual: the person selected may have retired or died even before the first rent review, and if not will require considerable longevity to survive to the last rent review of some leases. There should therefore be some formula for selecting a person. The most common one is to provide that the parties will select an arbiter or expert and that, failing their agreement, he will be selected by the Chairman for the time being of the Scottish Branch of the Royal Institution of Chartered Surveyors.

The difference between an arbiter and an expert is that an arbiter performs a quasi-judicial function, hearing submissions and expert testimony put forward by both parties. An expert, on the other hand, is simply asked to carry out the professional task of making a valuation. Using an expert has the advantage of comparative speed and cheapness. However, there is a danger of choosing what has come to be called an 'eccentric expert', who may reach a valuation far removed from what either the landlord or the tenant contemplated. There will be no appeal against his decision, although it is possible that he could be sued for professional negligence[15]. The reason for a bad decision by an expert may be incompetence, or simply the fact that he was not sufficiently acquainted with the area in question. This may also be true of an arbiter, but at least the nature of the arbitration process is liable to ensure that he is properly informed before he reaches a decision.

This at any rate is the distinction as it is normally formulated in relation to England. It is often assumed that the position in Scotland is roughly the same. However, we must not forget about the considerable differences in the arbitration law of the two countries[16]. In England, arbitrations are almost entirely regulated by statute[17]. In Scotland, however, although there are certain areas where statutory arbitrations occur (under the Agricultural Holdings Acts, for example), it is mainly a common law matter, with some relatively minor statutory intrusions[18]. It has been suggested by some commentators that the nature of arbitration under Scots law is such that, in rent review clauses in Scottish leases, a reference to a decision by an expert is a *de facto* arbitration, unless the expert's role is limited absolutely to that of valuer, without any power to

15 *Campbell v Edwards* [1976] 1 All ER 785, [1976] 1 WLR 403, CA; regarding the liability generally of arbiter and expert, see *Ross and McKichan* paras 6.53 to 6.54.
16 See pt 1 above.
17 Arbitration Acts 1950 and 1979.
18 Arbitration (Scotland) Act 1894; Administration of Justice (Scotland) Act 1972, s 3.

decide between conflicting sets of facts or on points of law[19]. Nevertheless, the distinction between arbiter and expert appears to be recognised in practice in Scotland.

As mentioned earlier[20], there is a limited right in Scottish arbitrations to appeal by stated case to the Court of Session on points of law. However, this can only be done during the course of the arbitration, not after the arbiter's decision has been made. Moreover, this right can be contracted out of, and usually is[21]. Apart from that, an arbiter's award can sometimes be challenged on grounds other than the merits of the case, eg where the arbiter has an interest or there has been a procedural irregularity. In the recent case of *Safeway Food Stores Ltd v Scottish Provident Institution*[1], the Court of Session reduced an arbiter's award because he had misinterpreted the lease and included certain improvements that should have been disregarded.

In *Grahame House Investments Ltd v Secretary of State for the Environment*[2], a surveyor agreed to act as an arbiter in a rent review dispute having, on the same day, accepted an appointment to act as an independent expert in relation to other premises owned by the same landlord in the same office building. In a stated case, the tenants challenged the arbiter's impartiality, as he began the arbitration having already issued his decision as expert for the other premises. It was held that he was not disqualified from acting as arbiter.

5. ALTERNATIVE METHODS OF RENT REVIEW

Having now seen the scope for unforeseen complication, untoward expense and general grief inherent in the rent review procedures we have examined so far, it is tempting to look for some other method, for some magical formula that will calculate the new rent without worry or fuss, and without any room for disagreement between the parties. Is such a thing possible? If so, why has it not been adopted wholesale by landlords and tenants, abandoning the hypothetical let and all its paraphernalia to masochists and madmen? The answer is

---

19 See ED Buchanan, 'Rent Review Clauses in Commercial Leases', Journal of the Law Society of Scotland (Workshop Section) p 369 (July 1983); *Ross and McKichan* para 6.52.
20 See pt 1 above.
21 Administration of Justice (Scotland) Act 1972, s 3; see also pt 1 above.
1 1988 GWD 23-966.
2 1985 SLT 502.

that there **are** other **methods but, as usual,** they also have draw-backs. Let us look at two such alternatives, which sometimes crop up in Britain, but more often abroad.

Index linked rents

This is a method by which the rent is varied simply by reference to a published index, such as the Retail Price Index. It is therefore jacked up automatically in line with inflation, in a completely mechanistic way, without there being any scope for ambiguity or argument. What could be simpler? Gone are the complex valuation guidelines of our hypothetical let and their endless problems of interpretation; gone is the delay, worry and expense of resorting to arbiter or expert. Instead, we make a simple mathematical calculation and the job is done.

Unfortunately, if we substitute for a system involving fallible human judgment one in which there is no human judgment involved at all, the result is not necessarily better. First of all, rent increases may not always be in line with the general level of inflation: sometimes rents lag behind other prices, at other times they shoot ahead. But there is no government index that measures only property values. There are several privately produced indexes that do this, but even they are not sufficiently sophisticated to take into account, except in very broad terms, all the regional variations and other local factors that could affect the market value of a particular property. The result, therefore, may be easy to calculate, but it is probably not the market rent. Certainty has been achieved at the expense of accuracy.

Moreover, to frame a clause that works properly involves some sophistication of drafting; index linking, therefore, does not offer immunity from litigation over the meaning of clauses[3]. If there are few reported cases, it is probably because such clauses are still fairly rare.

Turnover rents

This is a method by which the rent is linked to a percentage of the tenant's gross turnover in his business. The landlord's 'cut' therefore varies according to whether the tenant is doing well or

---

3 For a brief review of some of the decided cases, see HW Wilkinson 'Rents and the Retail Price Index', New Law Journal March 27 1987, p 288.

badly. Turnover rents are common in America and are increasingly being used in Britain too.

This method can also be criticised for not necessarily achieving a market rent. It could result, for example, in an anomalous situation where there were two adjoining identical shops with quite different rents, simply because one tenant was trading more successfully than the other. The one paying more might well feel that he was being unfairly penalised for his success. On the other hand, even the most competently run business can hit bad times, and a turnover rent can cushion the effect of a difficult period by easing the rent burden when takings are down. Nor is it necessarily correct to think of the landlord's percentage as unearned income. Having a stake in their tenants' success provides landlords with an incentive to provide better services and generally be more interested in looking after their tenants' interests.

Another problem with turnover rents is the difficulty of obtaining an accurate estimate of a tenant's turnover: apart from procedural problems (what to do about returned goods, for example) the tenant has an obvious motive to falsify the figures. This problem has been resolved in some modern shopping centres, where the presence of all the tenants within one building allows their tills to be linked to a common computer, monitored by the landlord.

It has also been observed that the use of turnover rents in America can lead to the rather ruthless practice of linking the level of turnover to the landlord's right to terminate a lease prematurely: in other words, if the tenant's performance is not satisfactory, he can be replaced by one who provides the landlord with a bigger cut. It has been pointed out in England that the protection of the Landlord and Tenant Act 1954 would prevent this practice. It should no longer be necessary to add that this protection does not apply in Scotland, so perhaps tenants north of the Border should regard turnover rents with more caution.

Finally, we should note that it is not the normal practice for rents to be calculated **entirely** by reference to turnover. Usually there is a base rent which will be topped up by a percentage of the tenant's turnover. Since the base rent will probably be subject to review by the normal method, this means that turnover rents are not really an alternative method of calculation, but merely a supplementary one. They may have their attractions, but they are not going to avoid the incidence of disputes and the need to resort to arbitration, and sometimes, also to litigation.

6. CONCLUSION

The reader, if he has stayed the course so far, will probably by now be contemplating an alternative career, or will at least have retreated to some area of the law where he need never have to draft a rent review clause. Nor will he be reassured by the thought that the cases referred to in this chapter are only a fraction of those reported, and that there is no sign of the flood of new ones abating. The reader may have been forced to look into the vortex, but we have not let him be sucked entirely in: considerations of space prevailed in what is essentially an elementary work. In any event, so many of the cases concern the interpretation of drafting idiosyncrasies in individual leases, that it is sometimes difficult to draw general principles.

Fortunately, the lease drafter is not entirely without assistance. Model rent review clauses have been drawn up to assist him. In England, two such models have been provided by the Royal Institution of Chartered Surveyors (in conjunction with the English Law Society), and by the Incorporated Society of Valuers and Auctioneers respectively. However, these clauses should be regarded with some caution in Scotland: they contain much terminology that is peculiarly English, and of course they have taken no account of the significant differences in Scots law which we have noted in this chapter. Better alternatives for the Scottish lawyer would be the styles of commercial lease (including rent review provisions) produced by Messrs Ross and McKichan and by Professor Halliday[4]. If this chapter helps the reader to approach his models with understanding instead of resorting to blind adoption, then it will have served its purpose.

---

4 *Ross and McKichan*, Appendix 1; Halliday *Conveyancing Law and Practice* Volume III (1987), paras 29.41 to 29.43.

11 Service Charges

1. GENERAL

Service charges arise in properties where a number of tenants share common areas, facilities or parts of a building, and the landlord provides common services for them. The kinds of service that can be involved are extensive, but typically include things like insurance, cleaning of common parts, provision of staff, gardening, heating and air conditioning, security, fire prevention, refuse disposal, maintenance and provision of car parks, toilet facilities and administration and management[1].

Most of the above are what one might expect from the meaning of the word 'service'. However, items normally included in service charges extend some way beyond this usual meaning. We have seen that the most common type of commercial and industrial lease nowadays is the full repairing and insuring lease, one of the main reasons for this being the desire of financial institutions investing in property to keep their rental income as free as possible of overheads. Where the property is self-contained, this can be achieved simply by making the tenant responsible for repairs, insurance and any other outgoings. In the case of properties in multiple occupation, however, it would be quite impractical for the tenants to be responsible for maintaining the fabric of the property in a piecemeal fashion.

It therefore makes sense for the landlord, not only to provide common services of the type mentioned in the first paragraph, but also to undertake the maintenance and repair of the common parts of the property. Thereafter he will recover a proportion of the cost of these services and repairs from each tenant. We are not therefore dealing with a negligible item of a tenant's expenditure, and it is

1 For a more detailed consideration of service charges from the Scottish viewpoint, see Ross and McKichan *Drafting and Negotiating Commercial Leases in Scotland* (1985), ch 11.

necessary to include a properly drafted provision in the lease to regulate the situation.

Service charges can arise in different types of property. In England they occur regularly in residential property, ie in blocks of flats. In Scotland there is little tradition of long leases of residential property, and, as we have already seen, new residential leases of more than twenty years have not been possible since 1974[2]. However, we may find service charges in Scotland in residential lets of shorter duration. They also occur regularly in industrial estates and in office blocks, where services undertaken by the landlord help to provide a pleasant working environment for the tenants and their staff. However, service charges are probably most important in shopping centres. There the services are being provided, not just for the tenants and their workers, but predominantly for members of the public visiting a centre. A high standard of service is therefore required to attract the public into a centre, with the result that service charges for tenants in shopping centres tend to be relatively high.

A number of important issues need to be dealt with in drafting a service charge clause. These include the tenant's obligation (including the method of apportionment between tenants and the method of collection), the landlord's obligation and, finally, whether or not a sinking fund should be set up.

2. THE TENANT'S OBLIGATION

The clause will usually specify the types of service the tenant will have to pay for – insurance, cleaning, heating etc – and will also typically give the landlord discretion in determining the standard of service provided. They will also include a 'sweeper' clause (eg 'any other services provided by the landlord from time to time', etc), to cover any services that might have been omitted. This is reasonable, as it is often difficult to predict in advance every service that might in the future be necessary or desirable. The tenant would be advised, however, to make sure that the 'sweeper' clause is not too general in nature and is suitably qualified so as not to give the landlord unlimited discretion in extending the scope of charges. For example, the 'sweeper' clause could be limited to those services that are 'reasonably necessary' or 'in keeping with the principles of good estate management'. It is advisable for some such limitation of the

2 Land Tenure Reform (Scotland) Act 1974, s 8; see also ch 6 pt 4 above.

landlord's discretion to be included in the clause; however, if it were to be omitted, some protection may be provided by the law. In *Finchbourne Ltd v Rodrigues*[3], the court implied a term into the lease that the service charges recoverable from the tenant should be 'fair and reasonable'. 'In my opinion,' said Cairns LJ, 'the parties cannot have intended that the landlords should have an unfettered discretion to adopt the highest conceivable standard and to charge the tenant with it[4].' On the other hand, in the recent Scottish case of *WW Promotions (Scotland) Ltd v De Marco*[5], where the certificate of the landlord's surveyor was declared in the lease to be final, it was held that it was therefore up to the surveyor to decide on reasonableness, and that his certificate could not thereafter be challenged by the tenant on the ground that the charges were unreasonable. It is safer for the tenant, therefore, to try and get his protection from unreasonable charges built into the lease terms.

One of the most problematic areas concerns the method of apportioning the service charges among the various tenants in the property. One common method is to base it on the floor area occupied by each tenant, and another is to tie it to the rateable values of the various units. The former has the disadvantages that it could lead to disputes regarding measurement, and also complaints from tenants of larger units that the extra amount they pay is disproportionate to the extra benefits they receive from the provision of the services. The rateable value system caters for this in that larger units are valued proportionately less. However, a system of apportionment based upon rateable value has other drawbacks. In a new development, the rateable values will not be known at the outset and may have to be estimated. Also, they would be subject to individual appeals by tenants, which could lead to uncertainty and confusion.

Instead of including a formula in the lease for working out the proportion, the landlord may wish to avoid uncertainty by stating a fixed percentage of total services for which the tenant is liable. He may have worked this out on the basis of floor area or rateable value or otherwise, but the tenant will have agreed to the percentage when signing the lease and so (theoretically) there should be no grounds for dispute. However, the inflexibility of this may itself lead to problems, eg if the landlord should later want to add to the property. In *Pole Properties Ltd v Feinberg*[6], the defendant, a tenant in a block of flats, was due according to his lease to pay two-sevenths

3 [1976] 3 All ER 581, CA.
4 [1976] 3 All ER 581, CA at 587.
5 1988 SLT (Sh Ct) 43.
6 (1982) 43 P & CR 121, 259 EG 417, CA.

of any increase in the cost of central heating fuel. The landlords later extended the property by building a new block of flats on an adjoining site and making the central heating system common to both blocks. A new proportion had therefore to be worked out for the tenant's share, which he contested because it took no account of the fact that the new flats were more intensively heated, with radiators in more of their rooms. The court held that the situation had so radically altered that the terms of the lease no longer applied. The tenant would have to pay what was fair and reasonable in the circumstances, ie according to the heating facilities provided for him. Incidentally, this pinpoints a criticism that could be made of all the apportionment methods mentioned above: that they do not necessarily reflect the amount of the services which the respective tenants actually use or enjoy.

The lease will also require to specify the method of collection. This can either be done by the landlord charging a higher rent, to include the provision of services, or by providing that the cost of services may be recovered as a separate charge. The former method has the attraction of simplicity and is used widely in England, as it makes it easier to enforce the English remedy of forfeiture for non-payment of rent. This does not apply in Scotland, but including service charges as part of rent would at least make the landlord's hypothec available for their recovery[7]. However, for accounting and tax purposes, it is probably better from the landlord's point of view to have service charges shown as a separate item.

Finally, it is common for landlords to specify in the clause relating to service charges that the amount of the charge will be as certified by his surveyor or accountant. It is sometimes also provided that his surveyor will settle any disputes regarding service charges. Both of these practices, as well as being possibly unfair to the tenant, can be dangerous for the landlord. In *Finchbourne Ltd v Rodrigues*[8], the surveyors' certificates were held to be invalid because the surveyors were essentially the same persons as the lessors. This is not quite the same as the landlord having the certificates issued by a firm of surveyors who have been engaged as his agents. As we saw above, in *WW Promotions (Scotland) Ltd v De Marco*[9], the Scottish courts at any rate are prepared to hold such certificates to be valid; the Sheriff Principal in that case suggested that it might have been better for the surveyor to have been more independent, but did not express his opinion more strongly than

7 See ch 4 pt 2 above.
8 [1976] 3 All ER 581, CA.
9 1988 SLT (Sh Ct) 43.

that. However, it is probably safer for the landlord, as well as fairer on the tenant, to have certificates issued by someone other than the firm of surveyors who manage the property.

These cases concerned leases where the surveyor's function was to certify the **amount** of the charge. If the lease goes even further and provides for the landlord's surveyor to settle disputes, this can rebound upon the landlord. In *Re Davstone Estates Ltd's Leases*[10], such a provision was held to be void because it involved the surveyor in interpretation of the lease terms; that was a question of law, which was properly the jurisdiction of the courts.

3. THE LANDLORD'S OBLIGATION

The tenant's agent should ensure that the lease, as well as obliging the tenant to pay for services, actually contains an undertaking by the landlord to provide the services in the first place. One would have thought that this would be implied – it does not make much sense to charge the tenant for services he may not have received – but this is not necessarily the case. In the *Duke of Westminster v Guild*[11], the lease obliged the tenant to contribute to the maintenance of a drain, but there was no corresponding obligation on the part of the landlord actually to do the maintenance, and the court refused to imply a condition to this effect into the lease. It will depend, of course, on the wording of the lease in each individual case, but it is better if the tenant's agent makes sure that the landlord's obligation is clearly stated.

It is also worth noting that the Unfair Contract Terms Act 1977 applies to the provision of services by landlords. The Act does not apply to leases in general, but **does** specifically apply to services connected with the use of land[12]. This means that if the landlord purports in the lease to exempt himself from the breach of any obligation, arising from the express or implied terms of the contract, to take reasonable care or exercise reasonable skill in his provision of services, such a disclaimer may be ineffective. If his breach relates to death or personal injury, the exemption clause will be totally void; in other cases, the court will only enforce it if it considers the exemption to have been fair and reasonable when the contract was entered into[13].

10 [1969] 2 Ch 378, [1969] 2 All ER 849.
11 [1985] QB 688, [1984] 3 All ER 144, CA.
12 Unfair Contract Terms Act 1977, s 15.
13 Ibid s 16.

A tenant's agent, however, should not rely on the effect of the Act, which may be uncertain in view of the court's discretion to determine when a clause is fair and reasonable. Instead, he should resist any attempt of the landlord to include such disclaimers in his service charge clause.

4. SINKING FUNDS

Some leases provide for the establishment of a sinking fund, ie a common fund to which all tenants contribute and from which service charges are paid. This can be advantageous to tenants in that it will spread the load of charges evenly over a number of years. It is also fairer where there is a turnover of tenants. It means that one particular tenant will not have to bear the whole of a particularly heavy expense because he happens to be the one in occupation at the time it occurs; for example, in the case of repairs, it is reasonable that his predecessors and successors in the property should also contribute. A sinking fund can also provide the landlord with a build-up of capital to pay for major replacement work in the premises: it is obviously easier to pass such costs on to the tenant if it is done in a piecemeal fashion.

However, from a landlord's point of view, sinking funds also have disadvantages. The landlord may be liable for income tax or corporation tax on the sinking fund payments. This can be partially avoided by setting up a trust fund, but even then any income on the trust may be taxable. As a result of these tax complications, sinking funds have not been widely used in relation to commercial properties[14].

14 For a more detailed discussion of sinking funds and their tax implications, see *Ross and McKichan* paras 11.29-11.37.

12 Agricultural Holdings

1. INTRODUCTION

Since the late nineteenth century, leases of agricultural holdings have been subject to statutory control by a series of enactments generally known as the Agricultural Holdings Acts. The broad object of the Acts is to encourage tenants to farm well and to make any necessary improvements to their holdings, while at the same time ensuring that the landlords receive a proper economic rent. At common law, if a tenant carried out any improvements to his holding, eg adding new buildings or draining fields, these would accrue to the landlord at the end of the lease[1]. The lease contract might provide for him to be compensated for improvements, but there was no automatic right to this. As a result of this, in the last years of his lease, the tenant had no real incentive to farm well: not only might he be reluctant to add necessary improvements to the holding, but he would be tempted to overwork the land, leaving it infertile for his successor. It was therefore in the interests of both landlords and tenants for the matter to be regulated in some way.

This is mainly achieved by giving tenants, in many cases, the statutory right to stay in occupation beyond the expiry date contracted for in the lease, even where the landlord wants to regain possession of the farm; in other words, the tenant is granted extended security of tenure. In certain other cases, the landlord **will** be able to regain possession when the lease is due to end, but the tenant will be entitled to compensation for any improvements he has made to the holding. Because he is being forced to move, he will often (though not always) also have the right to disturbance compensation, as well as various other compensation claims.

The rights to security of tenure and to compensation form the foundation of the tenant's statutory protection under the Acts, and should therefore be regarded as their most important provisions. However, the Acts affect the landlord/tenant relationship in several

---

1 See ch 7, pt 1 above.

other respects. As well as regulating the terms of farm leases in a number of important ways, they provide comprehensive rules for the settlement of disputes by arbitration. Finally, the Acts recognise that much of the benefit that a tenant has worked for may be lost if the lease is terminated by his premature death; and so there is provision, in certain circumstances, for the tenancy of a holding to be inherited after his death by a member of the tenant's family. All of these matters are given consideration below.

Crofts and other small landholdings, although not expressly excluded from the Acts, are primarily regulated by their own separate legislation. These provisions are rather complex, but a brief outline of them is given at the end of the chapter.

The law of agricultural holdings is broadly the same in both England and Scotland. Scotland has its own series of Acts, enacted in parallel to the English ones, although, just to confuse matters, some of the amending Acts are common to both countries. Since the first Act of 1883, the legislation has from time to time been brought together in one consolidating Act, the most recent one being the Agricultural Holdings (Scotland) Act 1949. Since then, unfortunately, there have been a large number of amendments, without a further consolidating Act to tidy things up. The main changes were effected in the Agriculture Act 1958, the Agriculture (Miscellaneous Provisions) Act 1968, the Agriculture (Miscellaneous Provisions) Act 1976 and the Agricultural Holdings (Amendment) (Scotland) Act 1983.

There would not be much point in providing the tenant with such extensive statutory protection if it was possible for a farm lease to include a clause contracting out of the provisions of the Acts. Contracting out is not universally prohibited, but is expressly forbidden in respect of many of the Acts' more important functions; in some other cases, although there has been no express prohibition, the courts have held that the mandatory wording of the provision has precluded contracting out. It was suggested by the House of Lords in *Johnson v Moreton*[2], that, in the latter cases, the underlying distinction is between those provisions that affect only the private contractual interests of the parties (where contracting out is allowed), and those that involve the public interest, in the welfare of the tenant and in the proper farming of the land (where contracting out is forbidden). Accordingly, contracting out is prohibited, for example, in respect of the provisions for a written notice to quit[3],

2 [1980] AC 37, [1978] 3 All ER 37, HL.
3 Agricultural Holdings (Scotland) Act 1949, s 24(1).

entitlement to compensation[4], arbitration[5] and, most importantly of all, security of tenure[6].

As well as the wide scope which the Acts provide for reference of disputes to arbitration, considerable jurisdiction is given to the Scottish Land Court. This is a court of special jurisdiction, comprising a legally qualified chairman and four practical agriculturalists. It also has wide jurisdiction in relation to crofts and small landholdings, which were the main reason for its creation in 1911. The Scottish Land Court should **not** be confused with the Lands Tribunal for Scotland, which is an administrative tribunal with quite different functions, eg variation of land obligations[7] and settlement of disputes over compulsory purchase claims.

Definition of agricultural holding

The statutory definition may be broadly summed up as a lease of land used for agriculture as part of a trade or business[8]. Leases where the tenant is an employee of the landlord are excluded. 'Agriculture' is given a very comprehensive definition, but generally includes all arable, pastoral and livestock raising activity[9]. 'Lease' is defined as 'a letting of land for a term of years, or for lives and years, or from year to year[10]'. Market gardens are included, but are subject to certain special provisions regarding compensation and fixtures[11].

The Acts do not allow agricultural leases for a term of less than a year. If an agricultural lease is entered into purporting to be for less than a year, and it is one to which the Acts would otherwise apply, it will take effect as a lease from year to year, bringing it within the ambit of the Acts. There are one or two limited exceptions to this, namely grazing or mowing lets for a specified part of the year, or where the Secretary of State has granted permission for a let of less than a year. In these cases the Acts will not apply, either to these excepted tenants or to any of their subtenants[12]. Also, if the lease is an informal one for an unspecified term, there is a possibility that

4 Agricultural Holdings (Scotland) Act 1949, s 64.
5 Ibid s 75(1).
6 *Johnson v Moreton* [1980] AC 37, [1978] 3 All ER 37, HL.
7 See ch 6 pt 3 above.
8 Agricultural Holdings (Scotland) Act 1949, s 1.
9 Ibid s 93(1).
10 Ibid s 93(1).
11 Ibid ss 65-67 (as amended by the Agriculture Act 1958, Sch 1 pt II and Sch 2 pt II).
12 Agricultural Holdings (Scotland) Act 1949, s 2.

the Acts may be excluded because the lease does not meet the statutory definition of a lease in this context[13].

The Secretary of State is only likely to give permission for leases of less than a year, thereby excluding the Acts, if the public interest is in some way involved, or if granting a longer lease is in some way unreasonable or impracticable. For example, in a new town, it is normal for the development corporation to begin acquiring land within its designated area well in advance of the land being actually developed. Since much of this is likely to be farmland, it makes sense to lease it back to the farmers until such time as it is required; however, it would rather negate the point of this if the farmers could eventually claim security of tenure or lodge large compensation claims. In such a case, the Secretary of State will grant permission for the development corporation to grant farm leases for less than a year. There is no reason why such a lease cannot be renewed if the land is still not required by the termination date, provided the original term is for less than a year (eg 364 days) and a notice to quit is sent; if it is allowed to run on by tacit relocation, the Acts will probably apply.

2. GENERAL PROVISIONS REGARDING LEASE TERMS

Written leases[14]

Where there is no written lease embodying the terms of a tenancy, either party may require the other to enter into a written agreement for this purpose. This should include the basic terms included in Schedule 5 of the 1949 Act, as well as the provisions regarding maintenance of fixed equipment (see below). If, therefore, there is a written lease, but it does not incorporate these terms, either party may likewise require the other to enter into an amended lease that does. Six months written notice should be given by the party requiring the lease, or the amendment, failing which the terms of the lease will be referred to arbitration. In the case of *Grieve & Sons v Barr*[15], it was held that improbative writings validated by homologation or *rei interventus* amounted to a written lease for the purpose of the Acts.

---

13 *Stirrat v Whyte* 1967 SC 265, 1968 SLT 157; but see also *Morrison-Low v Paterson* 1985 SLT (HL) 255 and *Gairneybridge Farm Ltd and King, Applicants* 1974 SLT (Land Ct) 8.
14 Agricultural Holdings (Scotland) Act 1949, s 4.
15 1954 SC 414, 1954 SLT 261.

The basic lease terms laid down by Schedule 5 are as follows:
(1) The names of the parties.
(2) Particulars of the holding, with sufficient description to identify its extent, by reference to a map or plan of the fields and other parcels of land.
(3) The duration of the let, or durations if different, for different parts of the holding.
(4) The rent and the dates on which it is payable.
(5) An undertaking by the landlord to reinstate or replace any building on the holding damaged by fire, if this is required by the rules of good estate management. The landlord is also required to insure all such buildings for their full value. The insurance requirement does not apply to government departments or other landlords who, with the approval of the Secretary of State, have made provision for defraying the cost of such reinstatement; the reason for this is that landlords, such as the government, who own a large amount of property, may find that bearing the cost of any fire damage themselves is cheaper than paying the necessary insurance premiums.
(6) An undertaking by the tenant, so far as required by the rules of good husbandry, to return the full equivalent manurial value of any harvested crops destroyed by fire, which were grown on the holding for consumption there. The tenant is also required to insure all such harvested crops, as well as dead stock, though there is a similar exemption as in (5) where the tenant is a government department or the Secretary of State's permission has been given.

The first four of these conditions, of course, are basically the essential provisions that any lease must have at common law[16]. They would therefore have been legally necessary, even if the Act had not specifically included them.

Maintenance of fixed equipment[17]

The Acts provide for certain maintenance provisions to be included in every lease of an agricultural holding. The landlord is bound, before the commencement of the lease, to put the fixed equipment in a thorough state of repair and to provide the necessary buildings and other equipment. 'Fixed equipment' is defined in s 93(1) of the 1949 Act and, broadly speaking, means all permanent buildings or

---

16 See ch 2, pt 2 above.
17 Agricultural Holdings (Scotland) Act 1949, ss 5 and 6.

structures necessary for the holding, including farm buildings, fences, hedges and dykes, gates, ditches, drains, service roads and electrical equipment, among others. Both landlord and tenant have maintenance obligations in relation to the fixed equipment. The landlord is bound to make such replacement or renewal of the fixed equipment as is made necessary by natural decay or fair wear and tear. Otherwise, the maintenance obligation falls upon the tenant, ie to keep it in a good state of repair, fair wear and tear excepted.

Either party may agree to be responsible for the other's obligations regarding the fixed equipment, though any provision in a lease requiring the tenant to pay the whole or part of a fire insurance premium in respect of the fixed equipment will be null and void.

Rent reviews[18]

As with any other kind of lease, if its contractual duration is of any length, the landlord will have included provision for rent reviews at regular intervals. However, as we have already noted, it is one of the main purposes of the Acts that the tenant may be granted security of tenure beyond the termination date stated in his lease. In such cases, the provision of rent reviews will thereafter be regulated by the Acts.

Where a lease is due to expire and the Land Court has decided that it should continue under the security of tenure provisions[19], either the landlord or the tenant may serve a written demand on the other to have the question of rent referred to arbitration. The rent will be fixed by the arbiter on an open market value basis and may become effective as at the date of expiry of the original lease or at any time thereafter. Certain valuation criteria are laid down; for example the value of tenant's improvements should be disregarded, as well as the fact that the tenant is in occupation of the holding. Any deterioration caused to the holding by the tenant should also be discounted. After a new rent has been thus fixed, a further application cannot be made by either party until a period of three years has elapsed. If the original lease was for less than three years, no variation in rent can be made until three years have elapsed since the commencement of the tenancy.

This means in effect that a lease continuing under the security of tenure provisions is subject to three yearly rent reviews. The period for Scotland was formerly five years, but it was brought into line

---

18 Ibid s 7 (as amended by the Agriculture Act 1958, s 2 and Sch 2 pt 1 and the Agricultural Holdings (Amendment) (Scotland) Act 1983, s 2).
19 See pt 3 below.

with the English position by the Agricultural Holdings (Amendment) (Scotland) Act 1983. That Act also introduced the right in some circumstances to appeal to the Land Court against an arbiter's decision[20]. For a general discussion of relevant valuation considerations, including those introduced by the 1983 Act, see the undernoted references[1].

Apart from the above provisions, the rent may also be increased in certain circumstances when improvements to the holding have been made by the landlord[2].

Tenant's right to remove fixtures[3]

We saw above that the necessary buildings and other basic equipment necessary to run the farm have to be provided by the landlord as fixed equipment. However, the tenant, if he wishes, may add fixtures to the holding at his own expense. Since these are provided by him, he is entitled to remove them, either during the tenancy or within six months after the lease has ended. A fixture is defined as 'any engine, machinery, fencing or other fixture'. The same right applies to buildings erected by the tenant, other than ones for which he is entitled to compensation for improvements.

The tenant is entitled to remove a fixture or building only if he is up to date with his rent and has performed all other obligations of the lease. Also, before exercising his right, he must give the landlord one month's written notice of his intention, which will give the landlord the option of buying the fixture at its value to an incoming tenant of the holding. If the fixture is in fact removed, the tenant must make good all damage caused by its removal.

Record of holding[4]

Since disputes may arise, either during a tenancy or at its termination – regarding, for example, who provided certain fixtures, or whether neglect to a holding was inherited by the tenant or largely caused by him – it is useful to have some independent evidence by which to establish the facts. The 1949 Act therefore

---

20 Agricultural Holdings (Amendment) (Scotland) Act 1983, s 5; see also pt 5 below.
 1 *Aberdeen Endowments Trust v Will* 1985 SLT (Land Ct) 23; *Dunbar and Anderson, Joint Applicants* 1985 SLCR 1.
 2 Agricultural Holdings (Scotland) Act 1949, s 8.
 3 Ibid s 14.
 4 Ibid ss 5 and 17.

provides for written records of certain aspects of a holding to be made, some of them compulsory, some optional. Such a record is to be made by a person appointed by the Secretary of State, at the joint expense of the parties. The following are the types of record that may be made:

(a) A record of the condition of the fixed equipment. This **must** be made at the beginning of the tenancy and is deemed to form part of the lease.

(b) A record of the condition of cultivation of the holding and of the condition of the fixed equipment. This may be made at any time during the currency of the lease, but is not compulsory unless **either** the landlord **or** the tenant demands it.

(c) Any improvements made by the tenant, or fixtures or buildings which he is entitled to remove (see the preceding section). This only needs to be made if the **tenant** demands it.

In relation to (b) and (c), the parties may agree to make a record of only part of the holding, or of the fixed equipment only.

Removal for non-payment of rent[5]

It is important to remember that the security of tenure issues discussed below relate only to the tenant's position at the **end** of his lease. Like the tenant in any lease, whether or not it is one subject to statutory control, an agricultural tenant has a contractual right to remain in the property until the lease is due to expire, and the statutory provisions determine only whether he has the right to stay on **beyond** that date.

However, as with other types of lease, an agricultural lease can be terminated prematurely on one of the grounds (eg irritancy) specified in chapter 7. To this the Acts have added another ground of termination, which can apply either during the contractual duration or after the security of tenure provisions have been invoked. Where the tenant is six months or more in arrears with his rent, the landlord can raise an action in the sheriff court for his removal at the next term of Whitsunday or Martinmas. These terms (normally 15th May and 11th November) are specially defined in the 1949 Act as being 28th May and 28th November[6]. The sheriff will grant decree against the tenant unless the tenant can either pay the rent due or find sufficient security, to the sheriff's satisfaction,

5 Ibid s 19.
6 Ibid s 93(1); *Austin v Gibson* 1979 SLT (Land Ct) 12.

for the rent due and an additional one year's rent. A lease terminated in this way will be treated as if it had expired naturally at that term. The tenant will therefore be entitled to the usual going away rights such as compensation for improvements. He will not, however, be entitled to compensation for disturbance.

In effect, this provision amounts to a legal irritancy, imposed by statute, which can be purged by the tenant in the manner described above (ie by paying the rent, etc).

Miscellaneous provisions regarding lease terms

Apart from those mentioned above, the 1949 Act makes a number of other provisions regulating the relationship of landlord and tenant. These include the right of either party to refer to arbitration the question of whether or not the amount of permanent pasture on the holding should be reduced[7], the right of the tenant to adopt his own method of cropping and to dispose of the produce of the holding as he pleases[8], and the right of the landlord at any reasonable time to enter the holding to view its condition or carry out his responsibilities[9].

3. SECURITY OF TENURE

As mentioned above, one of the main purposes of the Acts is to provide greater security of tenure for agricultural tenants. Like the tenant in any other kind of lease, the tenant of an agricultural holding has the contractual right to stay on in the property until the expiry date of his lease. Like other tenants, he can only be removed before then in extraordinary circumstances, for example if he has committed a breach justifying irritancy, or the property has been destroyed. When the lease is due to end, the tenant may be able to stay on if the landlord agrees to a new lease, or if the old one is allowed to be renewed automatically by tacit relocation. However, in leases where the common law applies, a landlord who wants his tenant out at the expiry date has an absolute right to evict him, provided he sends a notice to quit in time[10].

---

7 Agricultural Holdings (Scotland) Act 1949, s 9 (as substituted by the Agriculture Act 1958, Sch 1, pt II).
8 Agricultural Holdings (Scotland) Act 1949, s 12 (as amended by the Agriculture Act 1958, Sch 1, pt II).
9 Agricultural Holdings (Scotland) Act 1949, s 18.
10 See ch 7, pt 1 above.

On the other hand, where the Agricultural Holdings Acts apply, a landlord who wants to remove a tenant at the end of his lease may be legally prevented from doing so. In certain cases the tenant will have the right to stay on in the property indefinitely, long after the contractual term of his lease has expired. This extended security of tenure is not automatic. In some exceptional cases the landlord will have an absolute right to remove the tenant, provided that he follows the correct statutory procedure. In all other cases the tenant will have the right to refer the matter to the Land Court. Once that happens, it will be in the hands of that court to decide whether or not the tenant should be granted security of tenure. There are certain statutory criteria which they should have regard to when reaching their decision, but they are not bound by them and have a wide discretion in each individual case.

The 1949 Act does not contain a specific prohibition against contracting out of the security of tenure provisions, but in *Johnson v Moreton*[11] the House of Lords held that the mandatory wording of the provisions precluded this. In a moving pastoral eulogy, Lord Hailsham spoke at some length of the tenant's 'years (sometimes generations) of patient and self-abnegating toil and investment to put heart into soil' and otherwise develop the holding. 'These are not simply matters of private contracts . . .' he concluded. 'It is a public interest introduced for the sake of the soil and husbandry of England of which both landlord and tenant are in a moral, though not of course a legal, sense the trustees for posterity. Silence is not an argument, particularly when the words are prima facie mandatory, for excusing a term in a contract introduced for the purpose of annulling the protection given to the tenant by s 24[12].'

Since the Scottish provision is virtually identical to the one considered in that case, it seems likely that the soil of Scotland is similarly protected.

Notice to quit

As in other types of lease, the tenant cannot be removed at all unless **either** party serves a notice to quit for the requisite period before the end of the lease. A landlord's notice should be in the form prescribed by the Sheriff Courts (Scotland) Act 1907[13]. In the case

11 [1980] AC 37, [1978] 3 All ER 37, HL.
12 *Johnson v Moreton* [1980] AC 37 at 59 and 60, [1978] 3 All ER 37, HL.
13 Agricultural Holdings (Scotland) Act 1949, s 24(4); *Rae & Cooper v Davidson* 1954 SC 361, 1955 SLT 25. See also *Gemmell v Andrew* 1975 SLT (Land Ct) 5 and *Taylor v Brick* 1982 SLT 25.

of tenancies subject to the Agricultural Holdings Acts, the statutory period of notice is not more than two years or less than one year before the date of expiry[14]. This provision cannot be contracted out of, ie any clause in the lease substituting a longer or shorter period of notice would not be enforceable[15]. If notice is not served, or is not served in time, the lease will continue from year to year by tacit relocation until proper notice is served; this is, of course, the common law rule for all leases, but in the case of agricultural lets it is given statutory reinforcement[16].

Exceptions to security of tenure[17]

If any of the grounds of removal listed below applies, the landlord has an absolute right to remove the tenant without the tenant being able to refer the matter to the Land Court. **The notice to quit must expressly state which of the six grounds of removal applies.** Otherwise the notice, although it may be valid for other purposes, will not be effective in excluding the jurisdiction of the Land Court and the matter may be referred to them by the tenant serving a counter-notice on the landlord (see below). Where recourse to the Land Court **has** been excluded, the tenant nevertheless has the right, within one month, to refer the matter to arbitration. However, if the landlord's stated ground does exist, this will do the tenant no good: the function of arbitration in this context is merely to determine whether the landlord was within his rights in claiming that one of the grounds of removal applies.

The six grounds of removal are as follows:

(1) The landlord has let permanent pasture to the tenant **for a definite period** to use as arable land **on condition** that the tenant sows grass again at the end of the let.

(2) The land is required for a use other than agriculture for which planning permission has been granted or is not required.

(3) Within the last nine months an application has been made to the Land Court and the Court has granted a certificate that the tenant was not fulfilling his responsibilities to farm in accordance with the rules of good husbandry[18].

---

14 Agricultural Holdings (Scotland) Act 1949, s 24(1).
15 *Duguid v Muirhead* 1926 SC 1078.
16 Agricultural Holdings (Scotland) Act 1949, s 3.
17 Ibid s 25 (2) (as amended by the Agriculture Act 1958, s 3 and Schs 1 and 2 and the Agriculture (Miscellaneous Provisions) Act 1976 ss 13 and 14).
18 *Luss Estates Co v Firkin Farm Co* 1985 SLT (Land Ct) 17, 1984 SCLR 1.

(4) The tenant is in arrears with his rent or is in breach of another term of the lease which is remediable (other than a breach in relation to the provision or maintenance of fixed equipment)[19]. The landlord must have given the tenant two months' notice to pay the rent arrears or a reasonable period of notice to remedy the breach[20].

(5) The landlord's interest has been materially prejudiced by the tenant's breach of a term of the lease which could not be remedied in reasonable time and at economic cost.

(6) The tenant is bankrupt.

If the ground of removal is breach of a lease condition (ie (4) or (5) above), that condition must not be inconsistent with the tenant's fulfilment of his responsibilities to farm in accordance with the rules of good husbandry. In other words, if the lease imposes an obligation which it would be bad farming practice for the tenant to obey, he cannot be removed for failure to observe it. The rules of good husbandry are defined as 'maintaining a reasonable standard of efficient production, as respects both the kind of produce and the quality and quantity thereof, while keeping the unit in a condition to enable such a standard to be maintained in the future'[1]. Specific mention is made of maintenance of grassland, handling of arable land, proper keeping of livestock, pest control, maintenance of equipment etc.

In all of the above cases except (2) (ie where the land is required for a use other than agriculture), the tenant loses his right to compensation for disturbance, although he retains other rights on removal, such as his right to compensation for improvements.

Examination of the above grounds of removal will show that in each case there is some justification for depriving the tenant of his right to appeal to the Land Court. In cases (3)-(6) listed above the tenant is at fault in some way, being a bad farmer, in breach of contract or bankrupt. Case (1) listed above is a special case where the landlord wishes to renew the soil by the transfer of grazing land to arable for a limited period, and presumably the tenant knew the position when he took the lease on.

In the remaining case, ie case (2) listed above, where the land is required for a non-agricultural use, the tenant is probably not at fault: it is just that the merits of the alternative use are considered to outweigh the needs of the tenant. However, here the tenant is in a better position. Of all the exceptions to security of tenure, this is the

19 Agriculture (Miscellaneous Provisions) Act 1976, s 13.
20 *Macnabb v A & J Anderson* 1955 SC 38, 1955 SLT 73.
 1 Agriculture (Scotland) Act 1948, Sch 6.

only one where he retains his right to compensation for disturbance. Also, where a planning application is being made in respect of land subject to an agricultural tenancy or tenancies, there is a statutory requirement for the applicant to serve notice of his application on all agricultural tenants on the land[2]. And so, even though it is too late for the tenant to challenge the landlord after planning permission has been obtained, he will have an opportunity at an earlier stage to lodge objections and in some cases there may even be a public enquiry regarding the proposals.

Security of tenure

In all cases other than (1)-(6) listed above the tenant may, within one month of receiving a notice to quit, serve a counter-notice on the landlord referring the matter to the Land Court[3]. The court will consent to the tenant's removal only where it is established that one of the following circumstances applies[4]:

(1) The carrying out of the purpose for which the landlord seeks to terminate the tenancy is desirable in the interests of good husbandry.

(2) The carrying out is desirable in the interests of sound estate management[5].

(3) The carrying out is desirable for the purposes of agricultural research, experiment, education etc.

(4) Greater hardship would be caused by withholding than by giving consent to the operation of the notice[6] **or**

(5) The landlord's purpose is to employ the land for a use other than agriculture for which planning permission is required but has not been granted.

The onus of proof is on the landlord to establish that one or more of the above grounds exists[7]. And even where the landlord succeeds

---

2 Town and Country Planning (Scotland) Act 1972, s 24.
3 Agricultural Holdings (Scotland) Act 1949, s 25 (1).
4 Ibid s 26 (as amended by the Agriculture Act 1958, s 3 and Schs 1 and 2 and by the Land Compensation (Scotland) Act 1973, s 44).
5 *Altyre Estate Trs v McLay* 1975 SLT (Land Ct) 12.
6 *Somerville v Watson* 1980 SLT (Land Ct) 14; see also *Hutchison v Buchanan* 1980 SLT (Land Ct) 17, *Prior v J & A Henderson Ltd* 1984 SLT (Land Ct), 51, 1983 SLCR 34 (a case where an attempt to remove the tenant failed under (a), (b) and (d) above), and *Lindsay-Macdougall v Peterson* 1987 SLCR 59.
7 *McLaren v Lawrie* 1964 SLT (Land Ct) 10.

in discharging that onus, the Land Court still have the discretion to refuse the landlord's application if it appears to them that a fair and reasonable landlord would not insist on possession[8].

It would be an unwise landlord who found himself in the Land Court arguing for repossession on number (5) of the above grounds. Where his alternative use requires planning permission, he should obtain that permission first, before sending his notice to quit. In that way he will qualify under the second exception to security of tenure and he will have an absolute right to remove the tenant, with the latter having no right to take him to the Land Court. If he serves his notice to quit **before** obtaining planning permission, the tenant may refer the matter to the Land Court and, because of the court's ultimate discretion, the outcome will be uncertain.

Notice to quit part of the holding

In some cases, the landlord may only want back part of the holding, and be happy for the tenant to remain on in the remainder. He may therefore serve on the tenant a notice to quit part of the holding at the lease's termination date. However, this may not suit the tenant, who may prefer to move elsewhere, or to retire, rather than farm a reduced holding. Furthermore, the smaller area may not be economically viable. Since the contractual period of the tenant's lease will be about to end, he will of course be perfectly entitled legally to call it a day: the effect of the Acts only gives a **tenant** the right to extend his lease, without a landlord having a reciprocal right to hold a tenant beyond the end of his lease term. And so, irrespective of the Acts, the tenant's basic right, if he so wishes, is to end the lease at its natural termination date by serving the landlord with at least a year's notice. If he receives sufficient notice of the landlord's intention to take back part of the holding, there will be no problem.

However, what if the landlord were to send his notice a bare year before the end of the lease? It would be unfair if the tenant were held by tacit relocation for a further year to only part of the holding, which he may not want on its own. Furthermore, we will see below that where a tenant is denied his security of tenure he generally has a right to compensation for disturbance of up to two years' rent. If a reduced holding is no use to him, would it be fair for him to get disturbance only for the part that the landlord wanted back? This is

---

8 *Altyre Estate Trs v McLay* 1975 SLT (Land Ct) 12.

where the Acts step in to give the tenant further rights in such circumstances.

Where the landlord serves a notice to quit for part of the holding the tenant, within twenty-eight days, may serve a counter-notice making the landlord's notice take effect for the full holding[9]. This allows the tenant to claim the compensation payable on his removal from the whole farm, should he not consider it desirable to continue in occupation of the reduced holding. However, if the part claimed back by the landlord is less than one-fourth of the holding either in area or rental value and the diminished holding is reasonably capable of being farmed as a separate unit, compensation for disturbance will be restricted to the part included in the landlord's notice to quit[10]. This means that the tenant, if he wants, can leave the whole holding; however, only if a significant part is being reclaimed by the landlord will he get a disturbance payment for all of the holding rather than just the part the landlord wants back.

Of course, to take the money and run is not the tenant's only option. Instead of giving in to the landlord by leaving the holding, he will usually have the alternative of referring the matter to the Land Court. It is therefore possible that they will grant him security of tenure for the whole holding, despite the landlord's notice.

4. TENANT'S COMPENSATION RIGHTS

Under the Agricultural Holdings Acts there are several compensation rights which a tenant may be entitled to claim from his landlord at the termination of his let. The oldest and most fundamental statutory right of the agricultural tenant, dating back from the very first Act in 1883, is to receive compensation for any improvements that he has made to the holding. Even the right to security of tenure came much later. In the case of compensation for improvements, it does not matter that it may have been the tenant's fault that he was removed from the holding. Even if he has been removed prematurely for non-payment of rent he will be entitled to his compensation. The reason for this is quite obvious. If he has added to the value of the holding, he is due reimbursement for that, whatever else he may have been guilty of.

However, that is not the end of the story. If the tenant has to be moved through no fault of his own, it is right that he should also

---

9 Agricultural Holdings (Scotland) Act 1949, s 33.
10 Ibid s 35(4).

receive some compensation for the inconvenience and expense of this. Thus he will sometimes also be entitled to compensation for disturbance. In addition, the Agriculture (Miscellaneous Provisions) Act 1968 added a further substantial payment for re-organisation of the tenant's affairs, to which he will be entitled in certain limited circumstances. It is a prerequisite for payment of this that the tenant is entitled to compensation for disturbance; however, it is not payable in all situations where disturbance is due.

These three heads of compensation are the basis of the possible claims a tenant can make at the end of his lease if he is denied extended security of tenure. In some cases he may get all three; in other cases he may be denied some or all of them, if he has made no improvements, for example, or has been in breach of his lease. There are, however, certain other compensation claims which a tenant may have under the Acts, two of which it is convenient to mention at this point. These are **not** rights which arise at the lease's termination. The first occurs if the lease contains a landlord's break at an intermediate point, and the landlord exercises that right, resulting in the tenant being removed prematurely. In that case, in addition to his other waygoing rights, he may be entitled to compensation for early resumption. Finally, at any time during the currency of his lease, or after it has been extended, the tenant's crops may suffer damage caused by game, and for this he also can claim compensation.

None of these rights can be contracted out of: in other words, any clause in an agricultural lease depriving the tenant of his rights of compensation, or any of them, will not be given effect to[11].

(1) Compensation for improvements

An agricultural tenant is entitled at the termination of his lease to obtain from the landlord a sum which fairly represents the value of certain improvements he may have made to the property[12]. In some cases the tenant will require to serve adequate notice on the landlord of his intention to carry out the improvements and in other cases he will require the landlord's written consent before carrying them out. If the tenant fails to comply with these requirements in the cases where they are necessary, he will lose his right to compensation[13]. Note that this right of compensation (unlike the ones which

11 Ibid s 64.
12 Ibid s 48.
13 Ibid ss 50-52 (as amended by the Agriculture Act 1958, Schs 1 and 2).

follow) can arise even if it is the tenant who gives the notice to quit: as observed above, he has added to the value of the holding, whatever the circumstances of his departure.

The amount of compensation payable will be calculated on the basis of the value of the improvements to an incoming tenant as agreed between the parties. Failing agreement, the compensation will be fixed by arbitration[14].

There are three categories of improvement that may qualify for compensation. The following is a brief selection of some of the types of improvement under each category; for the full list, the reader is referred to the Act[15]:

(a) *Permanent improvements.* To be entitled to compensation, the tenant must have obtained the landlord's written consent before carrying out the improvements. The category of permanent improvements includes laying down permanent pasture, making water meadows or works of irrigation and the planting of orchards or fruit bushes.

(b) *Drainage and associated improvements.* The tenant will not be due compensation unless he has given the landlord prior written notice of his intention to carry them out, not less than **three months** before he proceeds with the improvements.

Included in this category are land drainage, making or improvement of farm access or service roads, making or removal of permanent fences (including hedges, stone dykes and gates), erection, alteration or enlargement of buildings and repairs to fixed equipment. It should be noted in particular that the erection of buildings comes under this category, as it might have seemed more logical to regard it as a permanent improvement. If the landlord objects to the improvement, there is provision for the matter being determined by the Land Court[16].

(c) *Temporary improvements.* Here neither the consent of, or notice to, the landlord is required. Temporary improvements include protecting fruit trees against animals, eradication of bracken, whins or broom, application to the land of purchased manure and laying down of temporary pasture.

---

14 Agricultural Holdings (Scotland) Act 1949, s 49.
15 Ibid Sch 1.
16 Ibid s 52 (as amended by the Agriculture Act 1958, Schs 1 and 2); *Renwick v Rodger* 1988 SLT (Land Ct) 23.

(2) Compensation for disturbance[17]

Subject to certain exceptions noted below, compensation for disturbance is paid where the tenant has left the holding in the following circumstances:

(1) The landlord has given the tenant notice to quit the holding. If it is the other way around and the tenant has given the landlord notice, the tenant will not be entitled to compensation for disturbance. He can hardly claim for the inconvenience of having to move if he is doing so on his own initiative.

(2) The landlord has given the tenant notice to quit **part** of the holding and the tenant has served a counter-notice requiring the notice to quit to take effect for the full holding. We saw above that, provided the part claimed is sufficiently substantial, the tenant can claim disturbance for the whole holding. This does not mean that he will be denied disturbance compensation if the landlord only wants less than a quarter of the holding, or if he decides to accept the landlord's notice and stay on in the reduced holding. In such cases, he will be entitled to reduced compensation, proportionate to the area which the landlord has reclaimed[18].

The minimum amount of compensation payable is one year's rent at the rate payable immediately before the termination of the tenancy (subject to certain minor deductions). If the tenant can prove additional loss directly attributable to his removal, he can claim additional compensation up to a maximum total compensation of two years' rent.

Compensation for disturbance is excluded in the following circumstances:

(1) In all cases (with one exception) where the landlord has an absolute right to remove the tenant without being taken to the Land Court[19]. As we saw earlier, the exception is the second of the six cases, ie where the land is required for a use other than agriculture for which planning permission has been granted or is not required.

(2) In certain cases where the tenant is the successor of a deceased tenant[20].

---

17 Agricultural Holdings (Scotland) Act 1949, s 35 (as amended by the Agriculture Act 1958, Sch 3 and the Agriculture (Miscellaneous Provisions) Act 1968, ss 9, 11, 12, 14, 16 and Sch 5).
18 Agricultural Holdings (Scotland) Act 1949, s 60.
19 See pt 3 above.
20 See pt 6 below.

(3) Sum for reorganisation of tenant's affairs[1]

Where (and only where) compensation for disturbance is payable, the landlord may also have to pay, in certain circumstances, a sum to assist in the reorganisation of the tenant's affairs. The amount of this sum is four times the annual rent of the holding at the rate payable immediately prior to the termination of the tenancy. Where compensation for disturbance is only payable in respect of **part** of the holding, the sum is four times the appropriate portion of the annual rent. In *Copeland v McQuaker*[2], it was held that the sum for reorganisation was payable even although additional loss could not be proved; it was not compensation as such, but a fixed sum which, if it was applicable, was paid regardless of loss.

The provisions which govern when the sum for reorganisation is payable are extremely complex and the 1968 Act is not one that is likely to win any prizes for lucidity. However, broadly speaking, it appears that the sum need only be paid where the landlord wants the land for some use other than agriculture. In all other cases payment can be avoided, provided that the landlord states in his notice to quit the reason why he requires to resume possession. The reasons he may give roughly corrrespond to the Land Court's four other criteria for removal (ie interests of good husbandry, interests of sound estate management, required for agricultural research etc, hardship to the landlord)[3]. There is therefore an onus on the landlord to ensure that he words his notice to quit correctly if he wants to avoid making an unnecessary payment. Even so, if the matter has gone to the Land Court, he may still be required to pay the sum if the Court is satisfied that the land **is** required for a use other than agriculture, even though the landlord stated another ground as the basis of his right to terminate[4].

In the situation where the lease can be terminated without the tenant being able to refer the matter to the Land Court, the sum for reorganisation will likewise only be payable when the land is required for a use other than agriculture. The reason for this is simply that the sum for reorganisation is only paid along with disturbance, and no disturbance compensation is payable in the other five cases where the Land Court's jurisdiction can be excluded[5].

1 Agriculture (Miscellaneous Provisions) Act 1968, ss 9 and 11.
2 1973 SLT 186.
3 See pt 3 above; see also *Barns-Graham v Lamont* 1971 SC 170, 1971 SLT 341 and *Copeland v McQuaker* 1973 SLT 186.
4 Agriculture (Miscellaneous Provisions) Act 1968, s 11(2)(b).
5 See pt 3 above.

(4) Compensation for early resumption[6]

Where the landlord, in exercise of a provision in the lease, resumes (ie takes back from the tenant) part of the holding for non-agricultural purposes, the tenant is entitled to compensation for early resumption. This is worked out on the basis of the 'amount which is equal to the value of the additional benefit (if any) which would have accrued to the tenant if the land had, instead of being so resumed, been resumed at the expiration of twelve months from the end of the year of tenancy current at a date two months before the date of resumption'. This is yet another instance where the draftsman of the 1968 Act is rather coy about revealing his meaning. What it means is that the tenant is due roughly a year's loss of profit from the resumed land. The exact amount depends on when the date of resumption falls in relation to the anniversary of the lease's date of entry. If, therefore, the resumption date is on the anniversary of the lease, exactly a year's loss of profits will be payable; otherwise, it may be slightly less or slightly more than that.

It is important to note that this payment can only be made when the lease has been terminated prematurely: it is **not** payable in cases where the tenant has been denied security of tenure, but has nevertheless occupied the holding for the full contractual period of his lease.

(5) Compensation for damage by game[7]

An agricultural tenant has the right to claim compensation from his landlord for damage caused to his crops by game, provided that the damage exceeds twelve pence per hectare of the area over which it extends. It does not matter if the landlord is not at fault, eg where deer come from the land of a neighbouring proprietor[8]. 'Game' is defined as 'deer, pheasants, partridges, grouse and black game'. Compensation is not payable if the tenant has written permission from the landlord to kill the game himself[9]. Note that this right of compensation can arise **at any time** and is not related to removal of the tenant from the holding, or any part of it.

---

6 Agriculture (Miscellaneous Provisions) Act 1968, s 15.
7 Agricultural Holdings (Scotland) Act 1949, s 15 (as amended by the Agriculture (Adaptation of Enactments) (Scotland) Regulations 1977, SI 1977/2007).
8 *Thomson v Earl of Galloway* 1919 SC 611.
9 *Ross v Watson* 1943 SC 406.

5. ARBITRATION UNDER THE AGRICULTURAL HOLDINGS ACTS

Section 74 of the 1949 Act reads as follows:

'Save as otherwise expressly provided in this Act, any question or difference of any kind whatsoever between the landlord and the tenant of an agricultural holding arising out of the tenancy or in connection with the holding (not being a question or difference as to liability for rent) shall, whether such question or difference arises during the currency or on the termination of the tenancy, be determined by arbitration.'

This means that virtually every dispute between the parties, with very few exceptions, must be referred to arbitration. Recourse must even be had to arbitration where the dispute relates to the landlord's attempt to remove the tenant, by irritancy or otherwise[10]. As can be seen from s 74, arbitration is excluded where the dispute relates to liability for rent. Arbitration is also excluded where the dispute relates to valuations of sheep stocks, dung, fallow, straw, crops, fences and other property of an outgoing tenant, which is being taken over by the landlord or an incoming tenant[11]. The courts also have jurisdiction, rather than an arbiter, when the issue is whether there is a landlord/tenant relationship at all[12].

Procedure

Arbitrations are to be heard by a single arbiter[13] selected from a panel appointed by the Lord President of the Court of Session[14]. The choice of arbiter is made by the parties or, if they cannot agree on the choice, by the Secretary of State[15]. Where the arbiter is selected by agreement, this must be done in a formal deed signed by both parties and an exchange of letters is not sufficient[16]. The procedure for arbitrations is set out in Schedule 6 of the 1949

---

10 *Houison-Craufurd's Trs v Davies* 1951 SC 1, 1951 SLT 25; *Brodie v Ker* 1952 SC 216, 1952 SLT 226.
11 Agricultural Holdings (Scotland) Act 1949, s 75(4).
12 *Cormack v McIldowie's Exrs* 1974 SLT 178.
13 Agricultural Holdings (Scotland) Act 1949, s 75(1).
14 Ibid s 76(1).
15 Ibid Sch 6, para 1.
16 *Chalmers Property Investment Co Ltd v MacColl* 1951 SC 24, 1951 SLT 50.

Act[17]. Provisions are made regarding submission of particulars of a claim[18], the production of evidence[19] and the making of the award, which must normally be done within three months of the arbiter's appointment[20].

Appeals

Apart from disputes relating to rent reviews which now have their own special rules (treated separately below), the rights of appeal from an arbiter's award are fairly limited. The arbiter's decision is binding on points of fact but, at any stage of the proceedings, a stated case may be made to the sheriff on points of law arising during the course of the arbitration. This can either be made as a result of direction by the arbiter, or by the sheriff himself on the application of either the landlord or the tenant[1]. It should be noted that the wording of this provision means that the appeal by stated case can only be made during the proceedings and not after the issue of the arbiter's award; once made, the award is final and binding on both parties[2]. However, in those cases which have gone to the sheriff, a further appeal may be made from the sheriff's decision to the Court of Session[3]. After a decision in law has been made by the sheriff court or Court of Session, the arbiter is bound to apply it, or he will be guilty of misconduct[4].

In the case of disputes relating to rent reviews, an exception to the above rules was introduced by the Agricultural Holdings (Amendment) (Scotland) Act 1983[5]. It was felt that, because of the large sums at stake in rent review disputes, the decision should not rest on a single arbiter alone. In such cases, therefore, there is introduced a new right of appeal from the arbiter's award on any question of fact or law[6]. This right of appeal is to the Land Court, and must be made

---

17 Agricultural Holdings (Scotland) Act 1949, Sch 6 (as amended by the Agriculture (Miscellaneous Provisions) Act 1968, s 11(5), the Agriculture (Miscellaneous Provisions) Act 1963, s 20 and the Agricultural Holdings (Amendment) (Scotland) Act 1983, s 5).
18 Agricultural Holdings (Scotland) Act 1949, Sch 6, para 5.
19 Ibid Sch 6, paras 6 and 7.
20 Ibid Sch 6, para 8 (as amended by the Agricultural Holdings (Amendment) (Scotland) Act 1983, s 5).
1 Agricultural Holdings (Scotland) Act 1949, Sch 6, para 19.
2 Ibid Sch 6, para 14.
3 Ibid Sch 6, para 20.
4 *Mitchell-Gill v Buchan* 1921 SC 390.
5 Agricultural Holdings (Amendment) (Scotland) Act 1983, s 5.
6 *Earl of Seafield v Stewart* 1985 SLT (Land Ct) 35.

within two months of the award. There is still provision for a stated case on points of law to be made before the issue of the award, but in rent review cases it must now be made to the Land Court. In both of these instances, the Land Court's decision is final. This seems rather anomalous, in view of the fact that appeals can be made from the sheriff to the Court of Session in other types of dispute.

It should also be noted that these provisions in respect of rent review disputes only apply when the arbiter has been appointed by the Secretary of State, not when he has been appointed by the parties themselves. In the latter case, appeals in rent review arbitrations are still subject to exactly the same rules as any other type of arbitration under the Agricultural Holdings Acts (ie stated case to the sheriff on points of law before the issue of the award). In rent review disputes, therefore, even where the parties can agree on a choice of arbiter, it might be in their interest to have him appointed by the Secretary of State, so that they can enjoy the wider rights of appeal introduced by the 1983 Act.

6. SUCCESSION TO AGRICULTURAL TENANCIES

Introduction

We saw in chapter 7 that a lease may be inherited either under testate succession (where the tenancy has been bequeathed in the tenant's will) or under intestate succession (where the tenant has either not left a will, or has left one but has failed to dispose of the lease in it)[7]. We also saw that, in some cases, the landlord could object to the succession and prevent the transmission to the new tenant. The same is broadly true of succession to agricultural holdings; however, the matter is here entirely regulated by statute and is, unfortunately, a little more complex. The provisions of the 1949 Act have been amended several times, by the Succession (Scotland) Act 1964, the Agriculture Act 1958, the Agriculture (Miscellaneous Provisions) Act 1968 and the Agricultural Holdings (Amendment) (Scotland) Act 1983. Fortunately, the 1983 Act has made things a little easier by incorporating the changes of the 1958 and 1968 Acts, and restating them, along with its own changes, as amendments to the 1949 Act.

7 See ch 7, pt 1 above.

Bequest of lease (testate succession)[8]

The tenant of an agricultural holding is entitled to bequeath his lease under his will. Since a bequest is virtually a form of assignation, this therefore forms an exception to the common law rule that agricultural leases, other than those of unusual duration, cannot be assigned without the landlord's consent[9]. However, this particular provision of the 1949 Act is one where there is no express prohibition against contracting out. And so in *Kennedy v Johnstone*[10] it was held that s 20 **could** be contracted out of, and that a provision in a lease expressly excluding the tenant's legatee was valid.

Moreover, the Act does not give a tenant the right to bequeath his lease to anyone at all, but only to a person selected from a limited class of individuals. It must be bequeathed to someone who, had the tenant not left a will, might have been entitled to succeed him under the law of intestate succession; alternatively, it may be bequeathed to either his son-in-law or his daughter-in-law. Apart from these last two relatives by marriage, this mainly means that it must be left to a blood relative, probably a child, but possibly also a brother or sister or even a parent or more remote member of the family. It may also be left to the tenant's wife or husband[11]. The bequest does not have to be to the first person in line of succession, as long as it is to someone among the class of possible intestate successors. For example, even though he has children, he could leave the lease to his brother, or bypass his blood relatives entirely and leave it to his son-in-law.

It is of course possible that the legatee may not be a willing recipient; after all, a lease, like any other contract, involves responsibilities as well as benefits. If the legatee wants the tenancy, therefore, he must notify the landlord of this within twenty-one days of the tenant's death, unless he is prevented from doing so by some unavoidable cause. In *Coats v Logan*[12], the legatee failed to notify the landlord in time and was prevented from acquiring the tenancy; moreover, since he had actually accepted the bequest and this fact had been recorded in the confirmation, the tenant's executors were unable to dispose of the tenancy as intestate estate.

---

8 Agricultural Holdings (Scotland) Act 1949, s 20 (as amended by the Succession (Scotland) Act 1964, Sch 2).
9 See ch 5, pt 1 above.
10 1956 SC 39, 1956 SLT 73.
11 Succession (Scotland) Act 1964, s 2.
12 1985 SLT 221.

The result was that the landlords were able to regain possession of the holding. However, in *Morrison-Low v Paterson*[13], the tenant's two sons carried on in occupation of the holding for six years after their father's death, continuing to pay rent and otherwise interacting with the landlord. It was held that a tenancy had been constituted by the actings of the parties.

The landlord may object to the bequest by sending, within one month of the legatee's notice, a counter-notice referring the matter to the Land Court. The Land Court will thereafter either confirm the bequest or, if it thinks that the landlord has a reasonable objection, it may declare the bequest to be null and void.

Intestate succession

The lease of an agricultural holding may also be inherited under the rules of intestate succession. As stated above, this will apply if the tenant has either not left a will, or has left one but has failed to dispose of the lease under it. However, the lease may also pass under the rules of intestacy where there has been a bequest, but the legatee has declined to accept it or the landlord's objection to him has been upheld by the Land Court[14]. As with other types of lease, the lease will initially pass to the executor, who has power to transfer it to any of the people entitled to succeed the tenant under the rules of intestate succession[15]. This does not mean that the executor has as much scope as a tenant making a bequest under his will, where the lease could be bequeathed to any possible intestate successor, not necessarily the first in line of succession. The executor has to choose one of the class of people who are first in line of succession, eg one of the tenant's children. The reason why he is given the right to choose only one out of that class is to avoid creating a joint tenancy among two or more heirs.

The executor's right to transfer the tenancy applies even where the lease contains an express or implied prohibition against assignation[16].

The landlord has a right to object to the new tenant, very much along the same lines as in the case of a bequest. Within twenty-one days of acquiring the lease, the new tenant must notify the landlord

---

13 1985 SLT (HL) 255.
14 Agricultural Holdings (Scotland) Act 1949, s 20(7) (as substituted by the Succession (Scotland) Act 1964, Sch 2).
15 Succession (Scotland) Act 1964, s 16.
16 Succession (Scotland) Act 1964, s 16(1) and (2).

of the fact, and the landlord may within one month send a counter-notice referring the matter to the Land Court. The Land Court has a power, similar to that which it has with bequests, to either confirm the succession or terminate the tenancy[17].

Security of tenure

What we have been discussing so far are situations where the tenant dies before the contractual term of his lease has ended. What the successor inherits, therefore, whether by bequest or through intestacy, is the unexpired portion of the lease. However, if the original tenant had survived, he might well have had a right under the Acts to claim extended security of tenure beyond the lease's contractual expiry[18]. The question that now arises is whether a tenant by inheritance has a similar right when the expiry date arrives.

Because of the number of changes in the law since the 1949 Act, the position is somewhat complex, and it may be more easily understood if we first take a brief look at the history of these changes. Originally a successor tenant had the same right to claim security of tenure as the original tenant. This was changed by the Agriculture Act 1958, which deprived the original tenant's successor of any right to security of tenure when the lease expired. The situation was partially reversed by the Agriculture (Miscellaneous Provisions) Act 1968, which distinguished two categories of successor, a near relative successor (the tenant's child or spouse), and all others. The right to claim security of tenure was reinstated for near relative successors, but was still denied to the others. However, being granted security of tenure was made harder for the near relative successor than it would have been for the original tenant; in addition to the normal Land Court criteria for terminating a lease, the 1968 Act provided additional grounds of termination which applied only in the case of near relative successors. Finally, the Agricultural Holdings (Amendment) (Scotland) Act 1983 made it even more difficult for a near relative successor to be granted security of tenure by placing further legal hurdles in his way; however, in order not to spoil the reasonable expectations of existing tenants and their families, these additional rules were only made applicable to new leases, granted after 1 January 1984.

17 Agricultural Holdings (Scotland) Act 1949, s 21 (as substituted by the Succession (Scotland) Act 1964, Sch 2).
18 See pt 3 above.

This leaves us at present with three categories of successor tenant, each in a separate legal position regarding his right to claim security of tenure when the lease expires: (1) a successor who is not a near relative; (2) a near relative successor to a lease granted **before** 1 January 1984, and (3) a near relative successor to a lease granted **after** 1 January 1984. In each of these cases, the tenant may either have succeeded through a bequest or under intestacy. In all of them, a landlord, who may have objected unsuccessfully to the succession when the original tenant died, will now get a second bite at the cherry at the end of the lease. His chances of success will vary depending upon which of the above categories the original tenant's successor falls into.

Successors other than a near relative[19]

The most straightforward situation is where the successor is other than a near relative. The tenant (subject to a minor qualification noted below) has no right to security of tenure beyond the lease's termination date and no right to refer the matter to the Land Court. The fact that he is the original tenant's successor and not a near relative is added as an additional ground under s 25 of the 1949 Act, giving the landlord an absolute right to terminate the lease at the expiry date stated in the notice to quit[20]. This will be the original termination date of the lease if the lease had more than two years to run when the successor acquired the tenancy. However, if there was less than two years of the lease left at that date, the tenant may be able to stay on a little longer. In such a case, the notice to quit may terminate the tenancy at a subsequent anniversary of the original expiry date, as long as the new date is not less than one or more than three years after the successor's acquisition of the tenancy. This means that the successor tenant cannot be removed before the original expiry date, but may have it extended for a period of up to two years. In practice, however, if the landlord really wants the tenant out, he will be able to terminate the lease, at the latest, by the first anniversary of the termination date: even if the new tenant succeeded to the tenancy in the last year of the lease, there will be time to give him the statutory minimum of one year's notice and get him out only a year late.

It should be noted that the operative date from which these time

19 Agricultural Holdings (Scotland) Act 1949, s 25(2)(h) and (2A) (added by the Agricultural Holdings (Amendment) (Scotland) Act 1983, s 3).
20 See pt 3 above.

limits run is the successor's **date of acquisition** of the tenancy, **not** the date of the tenant's death.

This last provision will apply in situations where, prior to the tenant's death, the original lease had expired and was continuing on a yearly basis by tacit relocation. Its effect is to ensure that the successor tenant is assured of his minimum year's notice to quit.

Near relative successors – old leases[1]

The term 'old leases' relates to holdings let prior to 1 January 1984. 'Near relative' means a surviving spouse or child, including an adopted child[2]. Here the landlord does not have an absolute right to end the tenancy at the expiry date of the lease. If he attempts to terminate by sending a notice to quit, the successor tenant has the same right as the original tenant would have had to send a counter-notice within one month, referring the matter to the Land Court. However, in addition to the usual grounds, the Land Court has additional criteria which it may invoke to terminate the lease[3]:

(1) The tenant has neither sufficient training in agriculture nor sufficient experience in the farming of land to enable him to farm the holding with reasonable efficiency[4].

(2) The holding is not a two man unit (ie not big enough to provide work for two or more men) and the landlord, within two years, wants to amalgamate it with another holding, which he specifies[5].

(3) The tenant is himself the occupier of a separate two man unit, which he has occupied since before the death of the tenant whom he succeeded[6]. 'Occupier' has been interpreted as referring to the occupation of an individual, and the Land Court have refused to terminate a lease under criterion (3) where the tenant was a partner of a firm that occupied other holdings[7]. This remains the case for

1 Agricultural Holdings (Scotland) Act 1949, s 26A and Sch 9, pt I (added by the Agricultural Holdings (Amendment) (Scotland) Act 1983, s 4 and Sch 1).
2 Agricultural Holdings (Scotland) Act 1949, Sch 9, Part III, para 1 (added by the Agricultural Holdings (Amendment) (Scotland) Act 1983, Sch 1).
3 Agricultural Holdings (Scotland) Act 1949, Sch 9 (added by the Agricultural Holdings (Amendment) (Scotland) Act 1983, Sch 1).
4 *Macdonald v Macrae* 1987 SLCR 72.
5 *Mackenzie v Lyon* 1984 SLT (Land Ct) 30, 1983 SLCR 22; *Trustees of the Main Calthorpe Settlement v Calder* 1988 SLT (Land Ct) 30.
6 Agricultural Holdings (Scotland) Act 1949, Sch 9, cases 1-3 (as added by the Agricultural Holdings (Amendment) (Scotland) Act 1983, Sch 1; see also *Mackenzie v Lyon* 1984 SLT (Land Ct) 30, 1983 SLCR 22.
7 *Haddo House Estate Trs v Davidson* 1982 SLT (Land Ct) 14.

leases entered prior to 1 January 1984, but has now been changed in the case of new leases (see section below).

Where the successor acquired the lease within two years of its date of expiry, the termination date in the notice to quit is worked out along the same lines as with successors who are not near relatives (see above). This means that if security of tenure is refused, there may still be a right to a slight extension beyond the original termination date.

Near relative successor – new leases[8]

The term 'new leases' relates to holdings let **after** 1 January 1984. Broadly speaking, the successor is in a similar position to that of a successor under an older lease, with the same right to refer the matter to the Land Court on receiving the landlord's notice to quit. However, the termination grounds have been considerably tightened up, making it even harder for a successor to be granted security of tenure. All the termination grounds applying to older leases apply here also. In addition, the following significant changes have been made:

(1) A new termination ground has been added, ie that the tenant does not have sufficient financial resources to enable him to farm the holding with reasonable efficiency.

(2) In the case of ground (1) above and also where the ground is the tenant's lack of training or experience, the Land Court's discretion is curtailed. Until now there has always been a proviso that the court should withhold their consent to a termination if it appeared to them that a fair and reasonable landlord would not insist on possession. With regard to the two grounds mentioned above, this proviso has been removed.

(3) In the case of three of the grounds, the burden of proof has now been shifted to the tenant. We saw above that the onus is normally on the landlord to establish that one or more of the termination grounds exists[9]. Now, in all the 1983 Act cases except where the landlord desires to amalgamate holdings (ie tenant's lack of financial resources, insufficient training or experience, tenant also the tenant of a separate two man unit), it is now the tenant who has to satisfy the court that the termination ground does not apply.

---

8 Agricultural Holdings (Scotland) Act 1949, s 26A and Sch 9, pt II (added by the Agricultural Holdings (Amendment) (Scotland) Act 1983, s 4 and Sch 1).
9 *McLaren v Lawrie* 1964 SLT (Land Ct) 10.

(4) Where the ground is the tenant's insufficient training and experience, the ground will not apply where the tenant has, since the death of the original tenant, been involved in a course of agricultural training which he is expected to complete satisfactorily within four years. He must also have made satisfactory interim arrangements for the farming of the holding. This, alone out of all the changes, operates in the tenant's favour.

(5) Where the ground is that the tenant already occupies a separate two man unit, occupation is defined to include cases where the other unit is occupied by a company controlled by the tenant or by a firm of which he is a partner[10]. This negates the case of *Haddo House Estate Trs v Davidson*[11] in respect of new leases (see preceding section).

Where the successor acquired the tenancy within two years of the tenancy's termination date, the same rules apply as before with regard to the termination date in the notice to quit.

7. CROFTS AND SMALL LANDHOLDINGS

Introduction

If an agricultural unit is small enough, or the rent is very low, it will in some cases be subject to the legislation for crofts and small landholdings. The law relating to these is rather complex, and to examine it in depth would take much more space than is available here[12]. However, an attempt will be made to outline the basic principles involved.

One of the reasons for the complexity is that there are at least four different types of small landholders, each subject to different rules, in some cases to separate legislation. These are (a) small landholders, (b) statutory small tenants, (c) crofters and (d) cottars. To understand how this disparity came about, we must first take a very brief look at the history of the relevant legislation.

The first Act, the Crofters Holdings (Scotland) Act 1886, had as its purpose the alleviation of hardship suffered by crofters in the

---

10 Agricultural Holdings (Scotland) Act 1949, Sch 9, pt III (added by the Agricultural Holdings (Amendment) Scotland Act 1983, Sch 1).
11 *Haddo House Estate Trs v Davidson* 1982 SLT (Land Ct) 14.
12 For a more detailed account of the legislation in this area, see Gloag and Henderson *Introduction to the Law of Scotland* (9th edn, 1987) paras 33.6-33.44 and Paton and Cameron *Landlord and Tenant* (1987), ch 19.

highlands and islands of Scotland. It applied only to the crofting counties in the highlands, ie Argyll, Caithness, Inverness, Orkney, Ross and Cromarty, Sutherland and Zetland. It conferred on a crofter a statutory right to a fair rent, security of tenure, compensation for improvements at the end of his lease and the right to bequeath the tenancy to a member of his family. Although parallel rights are now enjoyed by agricultural tenants generally, the 1886 Act went far beyond the scope of the agricultural holdings legislation at that time. There was also set up a body known as the Crofters Commission to implement the Act.

The next stage occurred in 1911, when the Small Landholders (Scotland) Act 1911 extended this statutory protection beyond the crofting counties to the whole of Scotland. A distinction was made between a small landholder and a statutory small tenant, the former enjoying more legal privileges because he (or his predecessors) had provided most of the buildings and permanent improvements on the holding. Also, the Crofters Commission was replaced by the newly set up Scottish Land Court.

Finally, the special needs of the crofting counties were recognised again when they were given separate legal status by the Crofters (Scotland) Act 1955. Among other things, this abolished, in the crofting counties, the distinction between small landholders and statutory small tenants. However, the distinction persists in the rest of Scotland, in respect of which the earlier legislation, as amended, remains in force.

The main Acts now in force are (for the whole of Scotland apart from the crofting counties) the Crofters Holdings (Scotland) Act 1886, as amended by the Small Landholders (Scotland) Act 1911, the Land Settlement (Scotland) Act 1919 and the Small Landholders and Agricultural Holdings (Scotland) Act 1931. The crofting counties are regulated by the Crofters (Scotland) Act 1955, as amended by the Crofters (Scotland) Act 1961 and the Crofting Reform (Scotland) Act 1976. It will be noticed that, paradoxically, while the 1886 Act originally applied only to crofts, it has been replaced with regard to them by the later crofting legislation, but remains as the basis of the law relating to other small landholdings.

Before looking more closely at this interesting selection of different tenures, it may help us to get things into perspective and alleviate confusion if we first gain some idea of how often the various tenures are encountered in practice. If we take the number of reported Land Court cases as a guide, we get the impression that crofting tenure is the only one that remains anything like a vital force. While there is a steady annual stream of crofting decisions, there have been only a handful of reported cases on small landholders and statutory small tenants since the crofting legislation went its separate way in 1955. It would appear, therefore, that while the phenomenon of small holdings remains widespread in the crofting counties of the highlands, it is much more of an anachronism elsewhere in Scotland. Even so, the legislation on small landholdings remains in force and the occasional case still turns up.[13]

Small landholders

Definition. For a tenant to be a small landholder, his holding must have had a rent of not more than £50 a year in April 1912 **or** must be not more than twenty hectares in extent.[14] Also, the tenancy must have already been in existence in 1911[15]. This could be the case if the present holder inherited the holding from the original tenant or a member of his family; alternatively the tenant (or his predecessor) may have been registered subsequently as a new holder[16]. It is necessary for the landholder to cultivate the holding by himself or with his family, with or without hired labour[17]. Finally, the tenant or his predecessor in the same family must have provided or paid for the whole or greater part of the buildings and permanent improvements on the holding; otherwise, he will be a statutory small tenant[18].

Small landholder's rights. The small landholder enjoys the right to a fair rent[19], security of tenure[20], compensation for improvements[1], and the right to bequeath his tenancy[2]. These are of course similar to the rights of agricultural tenants generally, though they differ on

---

13 For example, *Clark v Moffat's Exrs* 1982 SLCR 137; *Arran Properties Ltd v Currie* 1983 SLCR 92.
14 Small Landholders (Scotland) Act 1911, s 26 (as amended by the Agriculture (Adaptation of Enactments) (Scotland) Regulations 1977).
15 Small Landholders (Scotland) Act 1911, s 2(1) (as amended by the Agriculture (Adaptation of Enactments) (Scotland) Regulations 1977).
16 Small Landholders (Scotland) Act 1911, s 7 (as amended by the Land Settlement (Scotland) Act 1919, s 9).
17 Small Landholders (Scotland) Act 1911, s 10(1).
18 Ibid s 2(1)(iii).
19 Crofters Holdings (Scotland) Act 1886, s 6.
20 Ibid s 1 (as amended by the Small Landholders (Scotland) Act 1911, s 10).
 1 Crofters Holdings (Scotland) Act 1886, s 8 (as amended by the Small Landholders and Agricultural Holdings (Scotland) Act 1931, s 12).
 2 Ibid s 16 (as amended by the Small Landholders (Scotland) Act 1911, s 20 and the Succession (Scotland) Act 1964, Sch 2).

points of detail. For example, the landholder can lose his security of tenure for opening a public house without the landlord's consent. The landlord, with the Land Court's consent, has the right to resume the holding for some reasonable purpose[3]. The landholder has no general power to assign or sublet without the landlord's consent, though a limited right to assign may be granted by the Land Court[4].

Statutory small tenants

As indicated above, the statutory small tenant is someone who would have qualified as a small landholder, except that neither he nor a predecessor in the same family provided the greater part of the buildings and permanent improvements on the holding[5]. He is denied most of the rights enjoyed by the small landholder, though he may apply to the Land Court for a renewal of his lease at the end of his tenancy, and either he or the landlord can apply to the Land Court to fix an 'equitable' rent; the formula for this suggests that it should be worked out on more of a market basis than the fair rent enjoyed by the small landholder[6]. The Small Landholders and Agricultural Holdings (Scotland) Act 1931 gave the statutory small tenant the option of converting his status to that of landholder, for the sake of becoming entitled to compensation for improvements[7].

Crofters

Definition. The Crofters (Scotland) Act 1955 reintroduced crofts as a separate form of tenure in respect of the crofting counties only. All holdings occupied by small landholders or statutory small tenants immediately prior to the Act now became crofts[8]. Provision was made for the creation of new crofts by order of the Land Court followed by registration under the 1955 Act; this system was abolished by the Crofters (Scotland) Act 1961, since when new

---

3 Crofters Holdings (Scotland) Act 1886, s 2 (as amended by the Small Landholders (Scotland) Act 1911, s 19).
4 Small Landholders (Scotland) Act 1911, s 21 (as amended by the Succession (Scotland) Act 1964, Sch 2, para 15).
5 Small Landholders (Scotland) Act 1911, s 2(1)(iii).
6 Ibid s 32.
7 Small Landholders and Agricultural Holdings (Scotland) Act 1931, s 14.
8 Crofters (Scotland) Act 1955, s 3 (as amended by the Crofters (Scotland) Act 1961, Sch 1, para 9).

crofts can be created by direction of the Secretary of State[9]. If the landowner and the crofter agree, the croft may later be enlarged by the addition of non-crofting land, provided the total area (exclusive of common pasture or grazing) is not more than thirty hectares and the rent more than £100[10].

The 1955 Act revived the Crofters Commission, but only for the administration of the crofting system. Judicial and other legal jurisdiction remained, and still remains, with the Land Court.

Crofters' rights. Like the small landholder, the crofter has the right to a fair rent[11], compensation for improvements[12], security of tenure[13], and the right to bequeath his lease[14]. The provisions are broadly similar to those applying to the small landholder but differ in detail. In particular, the crofter now has greatly improved compensation rights in respect of permanent improvements, and in the event of the croft being resumed by the landowner.

Acquisition right. The Crofting Reform (Scotland) Act 1976 gave a crofter the right to buy his croft from the landowner[15]. If terms cannot be agreed with the owner, the matter will be dealt with by the Land Court. His right to buy the house and any garden ground is absolute, but whether or not he can acquire the rest of the land is at the discretion of the Land Court[16].

Cottars

A cottar enjoys a special kind of a tenure which, like crofts, occurs only in the crofting counties. A cottar is someone who occupies a house, with or without garden ground, either rent free, or under a yearly tenancy at a rent of not more than £6 per year[17]. The difference between a cottar who pays no rent and a squatter is that

---

9 Crofters (Scotland) Act 1961, s 2 (as amended by the Crofting Reform (Scotland) Act 1976, Sch 2, para 17).
10 Crofters (Scotland) Act 1961, s 2(2) (as amended by the Crofting Reform (Scotland) Act 1976, Sch 2, para 17).
11 Crofters (Scotland) Act 1955, s 5.
12 Ibid s 14 (as amended by the Crofters (Scotland) Act 1961, s 6 and the Law Reform (Miscellaneous Provisions) (Scotland) Act 1968, Sch 2).
13 Crofters (Scotland) Act 1955, s 13.
14 Ibid s 10 (as amended by the Law Reform (Miscellaneous Provisions) (Scotland) Act 1968, Sch 2).
15 Crofting Reform (Scotland) Act 1976, s 1.
16 Ibid, s 2.
17 Crofters (Scotland)) Act 1955, s 28(4).

the former has the landowner's permission to occupy the property[18]. If he is removed from the property, a cottar is entitled to compensation for permanent improvements[19]. Under the Crofting Reform (Scotland) Act 1976, a cottar has the same right as a crofter to buy the house he occupies from the landowner[20].

18 *Duke of Argyll's Trs v MacNeill* 1983 SLT (Land Ct) 35, 1982 SLCR 67.
19 Crofters (Scotland) Act 1955, s 28(1).
20 Crofting Reform (Scotland) Act 1976, s 1(2) and (4).

13 Residential Leases: The Private Sector

1. INTRODUCTION: THE RENT ACTS

We now come to the area of lease law where statutory control of leases has for long been at its most prolific and confusing. Since the middle of the 1914-18 war, lets of dwellinghouses by private landlords have been largely subject to a series of statutes known originally as the Rent Restriction Acts and, more recently, as the Rent Acts. It is a field that has traditionally been fraught with difficulty and controversy. 'Even the most casual inspection of any recent volume of the King's Bench Reports will disclose the inhuman bondage in which the Rent Acts hold the legal profession'. These words of RE Megarry[1] have for long summed up the opinion of lawyers on the subject; this view was held not least by judges, who have described the Acts as 'this chaotic series of Acts' or 'that chaos of verbal darkness', to mention only two of the more flattering descriptions[2].

Before our by now punch-drunk reader scuttles off in panic, it should be said that the situation in recent years has much improved. In 1967 Paton and Cameron quoted no less than eighteen Rent Acts that were wholly or partly in force at that time[3]. Since then the legislation has twice been consolidated, in 1971 and, most recently, by the Rent (Scotland) Act 1984. However, this welcome simplification is already proving short-lived, and fundamental changes to the system have now been introduced by the Housing (Scotland) Act 1988.

It is not within the scope of this book to comment on the political implications of the law that is here expounded. Nevertheless, an exception must be made in the case of the Rent Acts. Without some

---

1 R E Megarry *The Rent Acts* (10th edn, 1967), quoting the preface to the 6th edn, 1951.
2 Lord Justice Mackinnon quoted in *Megarry*, introduction to 10th edn and in Paton & Cameron *Landlord and Tenant* (1967), p 497.
3 *Paton & Cameron*, pp 497-498.

explanation of the social reasons that brought about their introduction, and the political controversy surrounding them since, they
might seem no more than a sadistic exercise in keeping the ordinary
person, not to mention his legal adviser, confused about his legal
rights.

The purpose of the Rent Acts was to protect tenants of
dwellinghouses in the private sector from exploitation by landlords.
This was attempted mainly by means of rent control and by
providing the tenant with security of tenure; to these there has been
more recently added protection from harassment and unlawful
eviction. The first Act was introduced (as a temporary measure!) in
1915, because of an acute shortage of houses for working-class
people during the 1914-18 war. This shortage was caused partly by
the diversion of resources away from house building and into the
war effort, and partly by the widespread migration of workers from
rural areas into the towns to work in munitions factories. Since then,
however, housing shortages have never quite gone away, and
neither have the Rent Acts; unfortunately, neither did the illusion
that they were temporary measures, and so after the first consolidating Act in 1920, there was no further consolidation until 1968 (in
England) and 1971 (in Scotland). This accounts for much of the
traditional confusion in this area.

But much more of the blame derives from the fact that, virtually
from the start, the subject of rent control has been something of a
political football. Conservative governments have tended to favour
the position of the landlord and to relax restrictions; Labour
governments, on the other hand, have been more inclined to favour
tenants and to reimpose controls. This has, arguably, created a
situation in which neither landlord nor tenant has been done full
justice.

Few people would disagree that it is desirable to protect tenants
from exploitation of housing shortages by unscrupulous landlords. But even the stoutest defenders of the Rent Acts will
acknowledge that the Acts have not, in the long run, been an
unqualified success, and that their well-intentioned intervention
has had a counter-productive effect. The imposition on landlords of
low rents, which for many years were allowed no adjustment to take
account of inflation, meant that essential repairs and maintenance
were often not carried out, hastening the decline of properties into
slum condition. These rent levels, and the inability of landlords to
regain possession of their properties when they wanted them, meant
that owners who might otherwise have leased their properties were
disinclined to do so; and those who did lease them were liable, when
the properties eventually became vacant, to sell them off rather than

relet them. Finally, private investment in this area virtually came to a halt, so that few new houses were built for letting by the private sector.

This situation was recognised by the then Labour government in 1965 when they substantially overhauled the system by introducing a system of fair rents that were designed to meet the needs of both landlords and tenants. This has remained the basis of the system until the present day, but it did not go far enough for the present government, who have now begun the process of replacing it with a system of market rents.

To properly see the matter in perspective, however, we must remember that the decline in private sector house letting over the course of the century has been accompanied by an unprecedented increase, particularly since the last war, in the provision of public sector houses for let. When the first Rent Act was introduced in 1915, most people leased their dwellinghouse from a private landlord. Now the situation is quite different, with public sector tenancies being the dominant tenure, along with a rise in the incidence of owner-occupation. Nevertheless, the private sector element remains substantial, particularly in the realm of bedsits and other temporary furnished accommodation. The purpose of the latest legislation is to reverse the trend by attracting private investment back to the house letting market.

We can sum up our historical outline, therefore, by dividing the legislation into three main phases:

(1) Controlled tenancies

The system of controlled tenancies was the main system from the onset of rent control until the system of regulated tenancies was introduced in 1965. However, the two systems continued in parallel until controlled tenancies were abolished in 1980. The tenant paid a standard rent which was not subject to increase except in very limited circumstances, eg where the landlord had carried out improvements. The result was that, especially in the years after the second world war, the rents paid under controlled tenancies became very low in real terms, being very far below market value. In 1957 the then Conservative government abolished rent control for all new tenancies and de-controlled all existing tenancies, apart from those with fairly low rateable values (those below £40 in London and below £30 elsewhere)[4]. The latter remained controlled, but for

---

4 Rent Act 1957, s 11(1).

the standard rent there was substituted one linked to gross annual value. Many of those existing controlled tenancies, though gradually dwindling in number, continued in existence for some years, before being transformed into regulated tenancies in 1980[5].

Controlled tenancies are therefore now obsolete, and we need concern ourselves with them no further; this alone makes our task considerably easier, as it was in the heyday of controlled tenancies that the Rent Acts were at their most prolific and confusing. It should be said that the above brief account of controlled tenancies is an extremely general and simplified one: it is, thankfully, no longer necessary to consider their considerable complexities in further detail.

(2) Regulated tenancies

Regulated tenancies remain in force today. From 1980 until 1988 they enjoyed a brief period of being the **only** extant system. This is no longer the case and they are destined to be eventually superseded by a new system of assured tenancies; this assumes, of course, that the position will not be further changed after a future change of government, and if anything has been learned from the present brief historical excursion, it is surely the unsafe nature of such an assumption! However, whatever the future may hold, both regulated and assured tenancies are likely to exist side by side for some years to come, and so it is necessary to consider both systems in some detail.

Regulated tenancies were introduced in 1965 by the Labour government in power at that time[6]. The massive decontrol in 1957 had led to many cases of poor tenants being exploited by slum landlords; one such landlord, a certain Mr Rachman, was even given the dubious honour of having his name incorporated into the English language, and the word 'rachmanism' came to stand for such exploitation. The Labour government, therefore, decided to reimpose controls, but sought to avoid the mistakes of the past by changing the system in a fundamental way. Tenants of dwelling-houses once again enjoyed security of tenure and freedom from eviction. In place of the old 'standard rent' there was introduced a system of 'fair rents', to be fixed in individual cases by the local rent officer, a government official appointed for the purpose, and with

5 Tenants Rights Etc (Scotland) Act 1980, s 46.
6 Rent Act 1965.

rights of appeal to a rent assessment committee. The fair rent was intended to provide a balance between the needs of landlords and tenants, by giving landlords a reasonable return on their investment, but ignoring any market forces caused by housing shortages. It also allowed for rents to be periodically reviewed to take account of inflation.

Under the old system of controlled tenancies, and initially under regulated tenancies, there was one major exception to Rent Act control. Furnished tenancies did not enjoy full Rent Act protection; instead they were subject to a much more limited form of protection, with rents fixed by rent tribunals. This distinction was virtually abolished in 1974 when full protection was extended to most furnished tenancies; the former system of limited protection (known as Part VII protection) remained in force, however, for certain exceptional cases of furnished tenancies where full protection was still denied, as well as to tenants of resident landlords, who were now denied full protection, whether or not the tenancy was a furnished one[7].

(3) Assured tenancies

Since 2 January 1989 (when the appropriate part of the Housing (Scotland) Act 1988 came into force), there can, apart from a few limited exceptions to cover transitional cases, be no new regulated tenancies. Instead, new tenancies of dwellinghouses will be subject to a system of assured tenancies, although existing regulated tenancies will continue to be subject to the old system. Security of tenure remains, though the grounds of repossession have been modified somewhat in favour of landlords. However, the right of either the landlord or the tenant to apply to the rent officer to have a fair rent fixed has been abolished; instead, the parties will negotiate a market rent. The rent assessment committees will continue to have a function in hearing appeals; however, in relation to assured tenancies they will be fixing, not fair rents under the old formula, but market rents. In this way the present government is hoping to attract private investment back into the private rented sector. Would-be private landlords are also given encouragement by a system of **short assured tenancies**, where security of tenure may be limited to no more than six months; an earlier version of these has already since 1980.

---

7 See pt 2 below.

Application to Scotland

The original Rent Acts were United Kingdom statutes, dispensing their horrors indiscriminately both north and south of the Border. In more recent years, Scotland has had its own separate legislation, although the law has remained substantially the same in both countries, and the decisions of English courts in this field remain highly persuasive. The present Scottish law is mainly contained in the Rent (Scotland) Act 1984 and the Housing (Scotland) Act 1988.

2. REGULATED TENANCIES

As stated above, the system of regulated tenancies is intended eventually to become obsolete. However, existing regulated tenancies entered into before Part II of the Housing (Scotland) Act 1988 came into force (ie 2 January 1989) will continue to have protection under the Rent (Scotland) Act 1984, and to enjoy a system of fair rents. Also, new regulated tenancies can be created in certain special circumstances[8]: (a) where the tenancy is entered in pursuance of a contract made before 2 January 1989 (b) where, immediately before the tenancy was granted, the tenant was a protected or a statutory tenant of the same landlord (ie not only where an existing regulated tenancy is being renewed, but also where the same landlord grants a tenancy of a different property), and (c) where the tenant was entitled to alternative accommodation on the termination of a previous regulated tenancy (or of a secure tenancy from a public sector landlord – see chapter 14); this provision would apply, for example, where the availability of alternative accommodation had been the ground of repossession. It is therefore still necessary to give an account of the main provisions relating to regulated tenancies.

Terminology

A number of different terms are used to describe the types of tenancy that fall within the ambit of the Rent Acts, and we are just about to enter a section where they begin to proliferate. It will therefore help to avoid confusion if we pause for a moment to clear the ground a little. The term 'regulated tenancy' has already been introduced as the general term for tenancies under the system

---

8 Housing (Scotland) Act 1988, s 42(1).

introduced in 1965 and now governed by the Rent (Scotland) Act 1984[9]. This distinguishes it from the now obsolete 'controlled tenancy' and the new 'assured tenancy' introduced by the 1988 Act. Within the broad definition of 'regulated tenancy', however, there are several sub-categories. The term 'protected tenancy' is used generally for a tenancy that satisfies the criteria set out below for entitlement to security of tenure and rent regulation under the 1984 Act; it specifically applies to tenancies where the expiry date of the lease has not arrived, or where it has arrived and the lease is continuing under tacit relocation[10]. The term 'contractual tenancy' is sometimes used instead here, since it describes the period when the tenant's right to occupy the property derives from the lease contract, as with any other lease. However, as soon as the security of tenure provisions actually require to be invoked (ie when the landlord has served a notice to quit), the tenancy is described instead as a 'statutory tenancy'[11].

Protected tenancies

Rateable value limit. The 1984 Act applies only to houses under a certain rateable value limit. The relevant limit is such, however, that it includes most houses likely to come on the normal letting market. The result is that only properties at the very top end of the market (apart from those excluded for one of the other reasons stated below) will be free from statutory protection. In most cases the relevant rateable value limit is not the current rateable value of the property, but a historic one, ie its rateable value when the system of regulated tenancies was first introduced by the Rent Act 1965. If, therefore, the property in question was in existence in 1965, any subsequent tenancy of it will be protected if it had a rateable value of under £200 on 23 March 1965 (the date when the Rent Act 1965 came into force), irrespective of its rateable value now.

As we saw in the introductory section above, one effect of the Rent Acts has been that few new dwellinghouses have been built by the private sector for letting. This means that most of the houses on the private letting market are older properties which were in existence in 1965 and which appeared on the valuation roll at that date. In most cases, therefore, the property will have a historic rateable value, and reference to this will determine whether or not a

9 Rent (Scotland) Act 1984, s 8.
10 Ibid ss 1 and 2.
11 Ibid s 3.

tenancy comes within the limit for protection. But it is nevertheless possible that properties built since 1965 may be let and may be of a comparable value to those older properties that enjoy protection; however, since there have been several rating revaluations since 1965, such properties may have entered the valuation roll for the first time at a level above £200. For such properties, therefore, it has been necessary to provide higher rateable value limits.

To sum up, therefore, a house will be within the rateable value limit for a protected tenancy in the following circumstances[12]:

(a) If it was already on the valuation roll on 23 March 1965 at a rateable value of under £200. As explained above, most protected tenancies are of older properties and will come under this heading.

(b) If it first appeared on the valuation roll between 23 March 1965 and 1 April 1978 with a rateable value under £200.

(c) If it first appeared on the valuation roll between 1 April 1978 and 1 April 1985 with a rateable value under £600.

(d) If it first appeared on the valuation roll after 1 April 1985 with a rateable value under £1,600.

In each of (b), (c) and (d), the relevant value is that when the property first appeared on the roll. The Secretary of State has power under the 1984 Act to further raise the limit from time to time to allow for future rating revaluations[13]. It will be noted that this has already happened in the case of category (d) above, in order to take account of the 1985 revaluation.

Further criteria for protection. Subject to the exceptions noted below, every tenancy will be a protected tenancy under the 1984 Act where a dwellinghouse within the appropriate rateable value limit is let as a separate dwelling. This includes flats as well as self-contained dwellinghouses[14]. It also may include part of a house, possibly no more than a single room, if it is let as a separate dwelling[15]. As long as there is a part that is held exclusively by the tenant, it does not matter if some of the accommodation is shared with other tenants[16]. On the other hand, where the house which is the subject of let contains a number of units of habitation (which

---

12 Rent (Scotland) Act 1984, s 1(1)(a); Protected Tenancies and Part VII Contracts (Rateable Value Limits) (Scotland) Order 1985, SI 1985/314.
13 Rent (Scotland) Act 1984, s 1(2).
14 *Langford Property Co Ltd v Goldrich* [1949] 1 KB 511, [1949] 1 All ER 402, CA.
15 *Cole v Harris* [1945] KB 474, [1945] 2 All ER 146, CA.
16 Rent (Scotland) Act 1984, s 97(1).

may be sublet by the tenant), then there is no protection, because the leased property is not a separate dwelling but a number of dwellings[17]. Subtenancies fall within the Act's definition of a tenancy, and so are also protected[18].

Where a house is occupied by an employee of the owner, and it is necessary for the employee to live there in order to do his job, the arrangement may be classified as a service occupancy rather than a lease. In such a case there will be no protection. However, it is necessary for the occupancy to be integral to the contract of service; the mere fact that the landlord is the tenant's employer is not enough to prevent there being a protected tenancy[19].

The following categories of tenancy are **not** protected. Many of these exceptions (though there are important differences) also apply in the case of assured tenancies:

1. *Where no rent is payable or the rent is less than two-thirds of the appropriate rateable value limit*[20]. This refers to the historic rateable value that qualified the tenancy for protection[1]. In most cases this will be the rateable value in 1965. Special provision is made for tenancies that were controlled tenancies prior to the final abolition of that system in 1980. Since it was a characteristic feature of controlled tenancies that rents were often very low indeed, possibly less than two-thirds of the appropriate rateable value, this fact alone did not prevent them being converted into regulated tenancies in 1980[2].

2. *Where the house is bona fide let at a rent which includes payments for board or attendance*[3]. 'Board' means the provision of food and 'attendance' means personal services such as cleaning or laundry services. In the case of attendance, the amount of rent attributable to it must form a substantial part of the whole rent[4]. This provision was probably only intended to exclude from protection people like lodgers and residents of boarding houses or hotels. However, it has

---

17 *Horford Investments Ltd v Lambert* [1976] Ch 39, [1974] 1 All ER 131, CA; *St Catherine's College v Dorling* [1979] 3 All ER 250, [1980] 1 WLR 66, CA.
18 Rent (Scotland) Act 1984, s 115(1).
19 *Macgregor v Dunnett* 1949 SC 510, 1949 SLT 412.
20 Rent (Scotland) Act 1984, s 2(1)(a); see also *Thomson v Lann* 1967 SLT (Sh Ct) 76 and *Fennel v Cameron* 1968 SLT (Sh Ct) 30.
1 Rent (Scotland) Act 1984, s 7(3).
2 Ibid s 2(2).
3 Ibid s 2(1)(b).
4 Ibid s 2(4); see also *Marchant v Charters* [1977] 3 All ER 918, [1977] 1 WLR 1181, CA.

been exploited as a loophole by which landlords have attempted to exclude tenancies from protection by creating the notorious 'bed and breakfast lets'. This common method of evasion is considered in more detail below[5].

3. *Student lets, where the landlord is the student's educational institution*[6]. This is a sensible provision that allows universities and colleges to remove ex-students from their properties in order to make way for new students. It has, however, also been used as a method of evasion, by which other private landlords can avoid creating protected tenancies. This is done by letting the property to a university or college, which do not qualify for protection and which can thereafter sublet to their students. A student who leases directly from a private landlord has the same rights as any other tenant; only where his university or college is the immediate landlord is he denied protection.

4. *Holiday lets*[7]. It makes sense that someone who takes a lease of a house in (say) Rothesay for a fortnight's holiday should not be able to claim the right to stay there for ever and have a fair rent registered. However, the word 'holiday' is not defined by the 1984 Act, and the concept of a holiday let has been extended by the courts to cover some rather unlikely holiday situations. In *McHale v Daneham*[8], the tenants of premises in Maida Vale were foreign visitors working in London and the tenancy had endured for over six months before repossession was claimed. The court held that it was nevertheless a holiday let and the tenants were denied protection. Nevertheless, the court will not necessarily confirm a let to be a holiday let merely because the lease says so, if there is other evidence to show that this is a sham by the landlord to evade Rent Act protection[9].

5. *Where the house is let along with agricultural land exceeding two acres*[10]. Such tenancies, of course, are likely to enjoy the alternative protection of the Agricultural Holdings Acts, and so Rent Act protection is not necessary[11].

---

5 See pt 5 below.
6 Rent (Scotland) Act 1984, s 2(1)(c).
7 Ibid s 2(1)(d).
8 (1979) 249 EG 969.
9 *Buchmann v May* [1978] 2 All ER 993, (1976) 240 EG 49, CA; *Francke v Hakmi* (1984) CLY 1906.
10 Rent (Scotland) Act 1984, s 1(3) and s 2(1)(e).
11 See ch 12 above.

6. *Public sector tenancies.* These include lets from district and regional councils and new town and urban development corporations[12]. Most tenancies in this category, however, have alternative statutory protection under the Housing (Scotland) Act 1987. Protection under the 1984 Act is also excluded where the landlord is the Crown or a government department, with the exception of property under the management of the Crown Estate Commissioners[13].

7. *Where the landlord is resident*[14]. This provision was first introduced by the Rent Act 1974 and applies only to tenancies entered into after 14 August 1974. Protection is denied where the landlord and the tenant occupy different parts of the same house. There is no requirement that the let should be a furnished one. It does not apply, however, where the landlord and tenant occupy separate flats in a purpose built block of flats, and such a tenant may qualify for protection.

For the tenancy to escape protection, the landlord must have been resident when the tenancy was granted and have continued to be resident thereafter. When there is a change of landlord, as a result of death or otherwise, exemption from the requirement for continuous occupation is allowed for a limited period to allow time for the changeover; however, where the change is not due to the death of the original landlord (eg where he has sold the property), the tenant will be given full protection until such time as the new landlord takes up residence[15]. Where the tenancy is granted by joint landlords only one of whom is resident, this will be sufficient to avoid protection[16].

The Rent Act 1974 was unintentionally ambiguous in its wording of the exemption for purpose built flats; it was only intended to exclude cases where the landlord and tenant occupied separate flats in the same block, but it accidentally extended the exception to cases where the landlord and tenant both lived within the same flat. This was remedied in 1980 and the revised wording is incorporated in the 1984 Act[17]. However, the rights of tenants of resident landlords who were inadvertently given full protection as a result of this loophole are preserved. As a result, a tenant who shares a flat (as

---

12 Rent (Scotland) Act 1984, s 5.
13 Ibid s 4.
14 Ibid s 6.
15 Ibid s 6(3) and (4).
16 *Cooper v Tait* (1984) 271 EG 105, (1984) 48 P & CR 460, CA.
17 Rent (Scotland) Act 1984, s 6(1) (a).

opposed to a house) with his landlord may have a protected tenancy where the tenancy was entered into between 14 August 1974 and 1 December 1980; in the case of tenancies entered **after** the latter date, protection will be denied in the case of **all** resident landlords, in accordance with the original intention.

8. *Business premises*[18]. Where a property is used exclusively for commercial purposes, it will not qualify as a dwellinghouse within the meaning of the 1984 Act. However, where it is used partly for business and partly for residential purposes, it may still be protected, provided that the residential element is substantial[19]. Public houses and shops are totally excluded from protection, however, even where there is a residential element. This is presumably because the dwellinghouse element is an adjunct of a commercial let.

Security of tenure

The result of a tenancy being a protected tenancy is, of course, that the tenant enjoys the benefits conferred by the Rent (Scotland) Act 1984. This means, among other things, that he has the right to have a fair rent registered with the rent officer and that the terms of his lease contract will generally only be effective to the extent that they are consistent with the terms of the 1984 Act. However, his right to remain in occupancy of the dwellinghouse will not initially derive from the provisions of the Act; like any other tenant, it will depend upon the contractual duration of his lease, and any extension to that term by the process of tacit relocation. It is only when the landlord has attempted to terminate the tenancy by sending a notice to quit that the statutory provisions for security of tenure come into force. The period of notice will be as stated in the lease, except that it cannot be less than four weeks[20].

Statutory tenancies. Once a landlord has terminated a protected tenancy by sending a notice to quit, the tenant is not obliged to leave the property at the expiry date. Instead, provided that he is still in possession of the property and remains so after the expiry date, his

---

18 Rent (Scotland) Act 1984, s 10.
19 *Cargill v Phillips* 1951 SC 67, 1951 SLT 110; *Cowan & Sons v Acton* 1952 SC 73, 1952 SLT 122. In these cases, however, the business element was in fact primary and the tenancies were *not* protected.
20 Rent (Scotland) Act 1984, s 112.

tenancy will become a statutory tenancy, which will give him the right to stay on in the property indefinitely[1]. This will continue to be the case, even after the Housing (Scotland) Act 1988, provided that the original contractual tenancy was already in existence at 2 January 1989; the reason for this is that the contractual and the statutory periods are considered to be different parts of the one regulated tenancy[2]. As with with any other tenancy, the landlord will only be able to evict the tenant by obtaining a court order; in the case of a statutory tenancy, however, the court will not grant such an order unless it is satisfied that one of the statutory grounds of possession applies. Any attempt by a landlord to evict a tenant without a court order is not only invalid, but also a criminal offence, as is any attempt to harass the tenant with a view to making him abandon his tenancy; however, these provisions apply not only to regulated tenancies, but to residential tenancies generally, and will be considered in more detail in part four below.

As noted above, a tenant requires to remain in personal occupation of the dwellinghouse to retain his statutory protection. He may be protected even although he only resides there part of the time, but if his absence is prolonged the onus is on him to establish an intention to return, and the court will look with particular care at two-home cases[3]. A tenant who sublets the property in its entirety[4], or allows someone else (eg a mistress) to occupy in his place while living elsewhere himself[5], will lose his right to security of tenure. However, a tenant who sublets part of the property, while remaining in occupation of the rest, will not lose his protection provided that he intends at some future date to reoccupy the part sublet[6]. This requirement for personal possession also means that there is no security of tenure where the tenant is not an individual human being, eg where the tenant is a limited company.

Paradoxically, the possession requirement is not necessary for a tenancy to be a protected tenancy in the first place; thus a tenant who does not personally occupy the property[7], including a limited company[8], has the right to have a fair rent registered for the property, but may be evicted when the contractual period of the

1 Ibid s 3.
2 Ibid s 8.
3 *Brickfield Properties v Hughes* (1988) 20 HLR 108, CA.
4 *Menzies v Mackay* 1938 SC 74, 1938 SLT 135.
5 *Colin Smith Music Ltd v Ridge* [1975] 1 All ER 290, [1975] 1 WLR 463, CA.
6 *Regalian Securities Ltd v Ramsden* [1981] 2 All ER 65, [1981] 1 WLR 611, HL.
7 *Feather Supplies Ltd v Ingham* [1971] 2 QB 348, [1971] 3 All ER 556, CA.
8 *Ronson Nominees Ltd v Mitchell* 1982 SLT (Sh Ct) 18.

tenancy has come to an end[9]. This loophole has now been plugged in relation to assured tenancies[10].

Terms of statutory tenancies. The terms and conditions of a statutory tenancy are the same as those in the original contract of tenancy, so far as they are consistent with the provisions of the 1984 Act[11]. In particular, the tenant must allow the landlord access to execute repairs[12]. The period of notice of termination by either party will be the same as in the lease contract except that (a) if no period of notice is stated, a tenant who wishes to terminate will require to give the landlord at least three months' notice and (b) in all cases, a landlord wishing repossession must give a minimum of four weeks' notice[13].

Assignations and sublets. A statutory tenant is entitled to assign his tenancy, provided that he obtains the landlord's consent, and the assignee will become a statutory tenant in his place[14]. As noted above, a statutory tenant who sublets the property in its entirety will lose his protection as he is no longer in personal possession of it. Nor is subletting allowed if it is against the terms of the original tenancy. Otherwise, the tenancy may be sublet in whole or in part, and if the principal tenancy is terminated, the subtenant will be allowed to stay on as a statutory tenant[15]. However, if the sublet was furnished and the principal let was not, the sublet will continue as an unfurnished one[16]; in other words, if the principal let is terminated, any furniture belonging to the principal tenant may be removed by him and the landlord will not be obliged to replace it for the subtenant's benefit.

Termination of statutory tenancies. The grounds of repossession by the landlord are contained in Schedule 2 of the 1984 Act and are divided into two categories: those where the court has discretion whether or not to grant a repossession order, and those where the court has no option but to grant an order where the relevant ground applies. Many of these grounds are the same, or substantially similar, to the grounds for termination of an assured tenancy under

---

9 *Hiller v United Dairies (London) Ltd* [1934] 1 KB 57, [1933] All ER 667, CA.
10 Housing (Scotland) Act 1988, s 12(1); see also pt 3 below.
11 Rent (Scotland) Act 1984, s 15(1).
12 Ibid s 15(2).
13 Ibid s 15(3) and (4); s 112.
14 Ibid s 17.
15 Ibid s 19; see also discretionary ground 6 below.
16 Ibid s 20.

the Housing (Scotland) Act 1988, though there are significant differences which will be noted below. This means, however, that much of the case law in this area will also be relevant to assured tenancies, especially until there has been time for a body of case decisions to build up in relation to the latter tenure.

Discretionary grounds of repossession[17]. In these cases, the court will not grant a landlord an order for possession of the premises unless it considers that it is reasonable to do so and either (a) there is suitable alternative accommodation available or (b) there exists one or more of the grounds specified in Part I of Schedule 2 of the 1984 Act. It is this overriding requirement of reasonableness that gives the court their considerable discretion. It is quite open to them, for example, to decide that, although a ground exists under Part I of Schedule 2, it would not be reasonable to grant an order for possession, eg on a technicality, or (where the ground is rent arrears) if the arrears are not extensive. Moreover, the court has a duty to take the question of reasonableness into account even if the issue was not pleaded or raised by the tenant[18]. In the case of these discretionary grounds (but not the mandatory ones) the court has power to delay the proceedings in various ways, including adjournment of the case[19]. This power would normally be used in cases of rent arrears in order to give the tenant time to pay.

The grounds for deciding whether or not suitable alternative accommodation is available are set out in Schedule 2, Part IV. Factors to be taken into account include the proximity to the tenant's place of work, the rent level and the extent and character of the accommodation. Environmental factors such as noise or smell may make the property unsuitable[20]. However, the alternative accommodation only requires to be reasonably suitable to the needs of the tenant, and it is not necessary for it to keep him in the style to which he has become accustomed. Thus in *Hill v Rochard*[1], the tenants, an elderly married couple, had the tenancy of a period country house with many spacious rooms, a staff flat, outbuildings, a stable, and one and a half acres of land, including a paddock, where the tenants kept a pony. It was held that a house with a mere four bedrooms, occupying a paltry eighth of an acre and having no stable

17 Rent (Scotland) Act 1984, s 11 and Sch 2 pt I.
18 *Smith v Poulter* [1947] KB 339, [1947] 1 All ER 216.
19 Rent (Scotland) Act 1984, s 12.
20 *Redspring Ltd v Francis* [1973] 1 All ER 640, [1973] 1 WLR 134, CA.
 1 [1983] 2 All ER 21, [1983] 1 WLR 478, CA; see also *Siddiqui v Rashid* [1980] 3 All ER 184, [1980] 1 WLR 1018, CA.

or paddock, was nevertheless suitable alternative accommodation, and the landlords were granted possession. It seems odd that such princely quarters as the subject of the original tenancy should have had a low enough rateable value to be protected in the first place.

A certificate of the housing authority for the district in which the house is situated, certifying that the authority will provide suitable alternative accommodation for the tenant by a particular date, is conclusive evidence that suitable alternative accommodation will be available by that date[2].

The grounds specified in Part I of Schedule 2 are:

(1) Non-payment of rent or breach of another tenancy obligation[3].

(2) Conduct which is a nuisance to adjoining proprietors, or where there is a criminal conviction for using the house or allowing it to be used for immoral or illegal purposes[4]. It is not necessary that there should be a specific reference to using the premises in the criminal charge provided that sufficient evidence is produced to show that the house was in fact used for the crime[5]. In the case of nuisance, it may be either the tenant or some other person occupying the house who is responsible, and in the latter case it is probably not necessary that the tenant should have been aware of any conduct constituting a nuisance, eg where it was caused by the tenant's wife while he was in prison[6]. Also, the adjoining proprietors only need to be nearby (eg in the same building) and not necessarily physically contiguous[7].

(3) Deterioration of the condition of the house because of the neglect or default of the tenant or anyone living with him[8]. This includes neglect of a garden attached to the house[9]. With this ground (and with ground (4) below) the tenant may only be removed for the act or default of a lodger or subtenant where he has failed to take any reasonable steps to remove the person concerned.

(4) In the case of a furnished let, deterioration in the condition of the furniture because of ill treatment by the tenant or anyone living with him[10].

---

2 Rent (Scotland) Act 1984, Sch 2, pt IV, para 1.
3 Ibid Sch 2, pt I, case 1.
4 Ibid Sch 2, pt I, case 2.
5 *Abrahams v Wilson* [1971] 2 QB 88, [1971] 2 All ER 1114, CA.
6 *Scottish Special Housing Association v Lumsden* 1984 SLT (Sh Ct) 71.
7 *Cobstone Investments Ltd v Maxim* [1985] QB 140, [1984] 2 All ER 635, CA.
8 Rent (Scotland) Act 1984, Sch 2, pt I, case 3.
9 *Holloway v Povey* (1984) 271 EG 195, (1984) 15 HLR 104, CA.
10 Rent (Scotland) Act 1984, Sch 2, pt I, case 4.

(5) Where the tenant has given notice to quit, as a result of which the landlord has contracted to sell or re-let the house, or has taken some other step that would prejudice him if the tenant changed his mind[11].

(6) Assignation or subletting of the house without the consent of the landlord[12]. Even if a lease does not expressly prohibit assignations or sublets, the words 'without the consent of the landlord' in the Act allow the landlord to repossess if his consent was not in fact obtained[13]. However, in the case of a subletting, the subtenant may be able to claim protection, since the sublet will in fact be lawful[14]. This of course assumes that (the lease being silent) assignation or subletting is not prohibited at common law; in the case of furnished lets, where there is *delectus personae*, the common law **does** require the landlord's consent[15].

Where the landlord's consent **is** required, it may be obtained either expressly or by implication. Thus in *Hyde v Pimley*[16], where the landlord continued to accept rent from the principal tenant after becoming aware of the sublet, he was denied possession because his conduct amounted to a consent.

(7) Where the house is reasonably required by the landlord as a residence for his employee. Except where the house is required for an agricultural worker, the tenant must be a former employee of the landlord and have been granted the let in consequence of that employment[17]. The words 'reasonably required' (in this and the following ground) mean more than just that the landlord desires the property, but something less than absolute necessity will do[18]. It should be noted that with the first of the mandatory grounds below (Case (11)) the word 'reasonably' is not used, and the criterion is less strict. With this ground and ground (8) below, the landlord may be liable to the tenant in compensation if the order was obtained as a result of misrepresentation or concealment on the landlord's part[19].

---

11 Ibid Sch 2, pt I, case 5.
12 Ibid Sch 2, pt I, case 6.
13 *Regional Properties Co Ltd v Frankenschwerth* [1951] 1 KB 631, [1951] 1 All ER 178, CA.
14 Rent (Scotland) Act 1984, s 19; *Leith Properties Ltd v Byrne* [1983] QB 433, sub nom *Leith Properties Ltd v Springer* [1982] 3 All ER 731, CA.
15 See ch 5, pt 1 above.
16 [1952] 2 QB 506, [1952] 2 All ER 102, CA.
17 Rent (Scotland) Act 1984, Sch 2, pt I, case 7.
18 *Aitken v Shaw* 1933 SLT (Sh Ct) 21.
19 Rent (Scotland) Act 1984, s 21.

(8) Requirement of the house by the landlord for occupation as a residence for himself or an immediate member of his family (ie a child over eighteen or a parent of the landlord or of the landlord's wife or husband)[20]. This will not normally apply where the tenancy was already in existence when the landlord bought the property, ie where the landlord purchased the property subject to the sitting tenancy[1]. The word 'purchased' is used here in its normal sense, and does not include a situation where the landlord inherited the property subject to the sitting tenancy[2]. In relation to this ground, the court must have regard to whether greater hardship would be caused by granting the repossession order than by refusing it[3]. It should be noted that this discretionary ground will generally only apply in cases where the landlord has not previously occupied the property; in cases where he has, the court will not normally have discretion and will be bound to grant the landlord possession[4].

(9) Subletting at an excessive rent, ie in excess of the maximum fair rent that might be registered for the house[5].

(10) Overcrowding, where the tenant has failed to take reasonable steps to alleviate the situation[6].

Mandatory grounds of repossession[7]. These are situations where the court does not have discretion and must grant a repossession order if the ground is proved to exist. In the case of all these grounds (except number (8) below), the tenant must have been given advance written notice that the landlord might require possession on the ground in question; in the case of grounds (1), (2) and (9), however, the court has discretion to dispense with this notice[8]. The onus of proof that the ground exists is on the landlord. The mandatory grounds are:

(1) Requirement of the house by an owner-occupier for himself or a member of his family. The owner must have resided in the property

---

20 Rent (Scotland) Act 1984, Sch 2, pt 1, case 8; see also *Kerr v Gordon* 1977 SLT (Sh Ct) 53; *Smith v Penny* [1947] KB 230, [1946] 2 All ER 672, CA.
 1 *Epps v Rothnie* [1945] KB 562, [1946] 1 All ER 146, CA; *Newton v Biggs* [1953] 2 QB 211, [1953] 1 All ER 99, CA.
 2 *Thomas v Fryer* [1970] 2 All ER 1, [1970] 1 WLR 845, CA.
 3 Rent (Scotland) Act 1984, Sch 2, pt III; see also *Abiafo v Lord* (1984) CLY 1920.
 4 See no. 1 of the mandatory grounds below.
 5 Rent (Scotland) Act 1984, Sch 2, pt I, case 9.
 6 Ibid Sch 2, pt I, case 10.
 7 Ibid s 11 and Sch 2, pt II.
 8 *Bradshaw v Baldwin-Wiseman* (1985) 49 P & CR 382, (1985) 274 EG 285, CA.

immediately before granting the tenancy[9]. This provision is designed to encourage owner-occupiers to let their premises temporarily without having to fear that they will be denied possession when they want to return. Where a property was let by two joint owner-occupiers, but only one of them required it back to reside in, it was nevertheless held that the ground was satisfied and the landlords were granted possession[10]. To establish that he 'requires' the property it is not necessary for the landlord to prove that it is 'reasonably required'; it is enough if he can demonstrate that he has a genuine desire and a genuine immediate intention to use the dwellinghouse as his residence or as a residence for members of his family[11]. Repossession will also be granted if the owner-occupier needs to sell the house with vacant possession in order to buy another one that is near his work, or if he has died and a member of his family or his heir require it to live in, or want to sell it with vacant possession.

Where the property is subject to a heritable security and the owner is in default, the tenancy may also be terminated in order to allow the creditor to exercise his power of sale with vacant possession[12].

(2) Where the dwellinghouse was acquired by the landlord in order to occupy it as his residence on his retirement from regular employment, and he now requires it for that purpose. Again there are certain other circumstances where repossession will be granted, eg where the landlord has died and the property is required by a member of his family etc[13].

(3) Off-season lets of holiday premises for a period not exceeding eight months[14]. These should be distinguished from holiday lets, which are not protected tenancies at all (see above section). If a property that was the subject of a holiday let is let outwith the holiday season, the tenancy may be protected in the sense that a fair rent can be registered for it; however, security of tenure is denied in order that the property can become available again for the next holiday season. Also, since leases falling under this and the following ground are by their nature very short, and new regulated tenancies cannot normally be created after 2 January 1989,

---

9 *Pocock v Steel* [1985] 1 All ER 434, [1985] 1 WLR 229, CA.
10 *Tilling v Whiteman* [1980] AC 1, [1979] 1 All ER 737, HL.
11 *Kennealy v Dunne* [1977] QB 837, [1977] 2 All ER 16, CA.
12 Rent (Scotland) Act 1984, Sch 2, pt II, case 11 (as amended by the Rent (Amendment) Act 1985, s 1).
13 Rent (Scotland) Act 1984, Sch 2, pt II, case 12.
14 Ibid Sch 2, pt II, case 13.

these two grounds are already virtually obsolete in relation to regulated tenancies; however, similar grounds now exist for assured tenancies.

(4) A short lease between student lettings for a period not exceeding twelve months. This would cover lets during vacation time of properties normally let to students[15].

(5) Short tenancies[16]. These are considered in more detail below.

(6) Requirement of the house for a minister or a full-time lay missionary[17].

(7) Certain cases where the house is required for a person employed or to be employed by the landlord in agriculture[18].

(8) Where the house has been designed or adapted for use by a person with special needs, is no longer occupied by such a person, and the landlord requires it for occupation by a person who has such special needs[19].

(9) Where the owner requires the dwellinghouse as his own residence and, at the time he acquired the house, as well as at the commencement of the tenancy, he was a member of the British army[20].

Short tenancies[1]. The Tenants Rights Etc (Scotland) Act 1980 (the relevant provisions of which are now incorporated into the Rent (Scotland) Act 1984) created a new style of let known as a 'short tenancy'. In such a case the landlord has an absolute right to a possession order at the end of the period of let, provided that the statutory requirements were complied with. The period of let must be between one and five years. A short tenancy could not be created in favour of an existing sitting tenant without his consent and the landlord, before the commencement of the tenancy, must have given the tenant notice in prescribed form that the tenancy was to be a short tenancy and not a normal protected tenancy. If a fair rent was not already registered for the house (see below), the landlord must have applied for one to be registered within fourteen days of the tenancy's commencement. If the conditions of the Act were

15 Rent (Scotland) Act 1984, Sch 2, pt II, case 14.
16 Ibid Sch 2, pt II, case 15.
17 Ibid Sch 2, pt II, case 16.
18 Ibid Sch 2, pt II, case 17, 18 and 19.
19 Ibid Sch 2, pt II, case 20.
20 Ibid Sch 2, pt II, case 21.
 1 Ibid ss 9, 14 and 14.

fulfilled, the landlord may recover possession at the end of the let by giving the tenant three months' written notice. Failure to give notice will result in the tenancy being continued on a yearly basis by tacit relocation.

Short tenancies were introduced in order to encourage owners to bring properties on to the letting market without the fear of losing possession of them indefinitely. A similar provision has been included in the case of assured tenancies without, of course, the necessity of registering a fair rent[2]. Because their maximum length is five years and because new ones can no longer be created, short regulated tenancies are likely to disappear and be replaced by assured tenancies much more quickly than will be the case with other regulated tenancies.

Part VII protection. In the case of some lets that are not protected tenancies, a more limited protection may be available under Part VII of the Rent (Scotland) Act 1984. The cases this applies to are those furnished lets which are without full protection (eg student lets or where there is board or attendance)[3], and lets where there is a resident landlord, in the latter case even where the let is unfurnished[4]. In cases to which Part VII applies, the rent assessment committee has the discretion to fix the rent on application of either party[5], and also to grant security of tenure for periods of six months at a time[6]. In the case of contracts entered into after 1 December 1980, the power to grant security of tenure rests not with the rent assessment committee but with the sheriff, and the maximum extension he can grant is three months[7].

Since 2 January 1989, no new Part VII contracts can be created[8]. In view of the very limited periods of security of tenure that may be granted, Part VII contracts should disappear fairly quickly, except in cases where the contractual period of the lease was of some length.

Fair rents

As we saw at the beginning of the chapter, the present system of rent regulation was first introduced in 1965. The relevant Scottish

2 See pt 3 below.
3 Rent (Scotland) Act 1984, s 63(1).
4 Ibid s 96 and s 98.
5 Ibid s 66.
6 Ibid s 71.
7 Ibid s 76.
8 Housing (Scotland) Act 1988, s 44.

provisions are now found in Parts IV and V of the Rent (Scotland) Act 1984. These allow for the fixing of fair rents for protected tenancies by local rent officers and rent assessment committees and for the registration of such rents. Rent officers are independent government officials appointed and paid by the Secretary of State. One or more rent officers normally serve for each registration area, which are the areas served by the district and islands' councils[9]. Rent assessment committees are drawn from a large panel of professional and lay people appointed by the Secretary of State, and a typical committee would consist of three members, one legally qualified, another a professionally qualified surveyor or valuer, and the third a lay member; it is, however, possible for a committee to have only two members and, in exceptional cases, the chairman may decide cases on his own[10]. Under the new system of assured tenancies rent assessment committees will continue to have a function, although they will now be working out rents on a different basis[11]; in addition, of course, both rent officers and rent assessment committees will be continuing to fix fair rents for existing regulated tenancies for some time to come.

Registration of fair rent. Where a tenancy is a protected one, either the landlord or the tenant, or both, may apply to the local rent officer to fix a fair rent to be registered for the house[12]. This may be done either during the contractual period of the tenancy, or after the lease has expired and it is continuing as a statutory tenancy. This means that, even if a tenant has already signed a lease at a particular rent, there is nothing to stop him going to the rent officer to have a fair rent registered if he thinks this will effect a reduction. After a fair rent has been registered, that rent will be the maximum that the landlord can charge, and if the tenant pays more he will be entitled to recover the difference from the landlord[13]. During the contractual part of the lease, however, the tenant can hold the landlord to the rent in the lease if it is less than the registered rent. The registration takes effect from the date of registration by the rent officer, except in the case of appeals, where it takes effect from the date of the decision of the rent assessment committee[14].

---

9 Rent (Scotland) Act 1984, s 43.
10 Ibid s 44.
11 See pt 3 below.
12 Rent (Scotland) Act 1984, s 46.
13 Ibid s 28 and s 37; see also *North v Allan Properties (Edinburgh)* 1987 SLT (Sh Ct) 141.
14 Rent (Scotland) Act 1984, s 50.

Any element of the registered rent which is attributable to the use of furniture, the provision of services, or the use of part of the premises as a shop or office or other business purpose must be noted separately on the register if it exceeds 5 per cent of the rent[15].

Either during the contractual or the statutory period of the tenancy, the landlord and tenant may enter into an agreement to increase the rent. However, such an agreement does not affect the tenant's right to have a fair rent registered, and unless the agreement draws the tenant's attention to his statutory rights it will be unenforceable[16]; thus the tenant is offered some protection from being persuaded to pay a higher rent than he needs to because he is ignorant of his rights.

If either the landlord or the tenant is dissatisfied with the figure arrived at by the rent officer, he can appeal to a rent assessment committee by lodging a written objection with the rent officer within twenty-eight days[17]. The committee's decisions are final on questions of fact, but not on questions of law.

Variation of rent. Once a fair rent has been determined for a property, it will remain fixed for a period of three years, unless there is a material change in the condition of the house (eg by the carrying out of a substantial improvement)[18], or in the terms of the tenancy or the quantity, quality or condition of the furniture[19]. After three years has elapsed since registration, either party can apply for re-registration; if an application is made before that, the registration will not take effect until after the three year period has elapsed[20]. If the dwellinghouse in question ceases to be let under a regulated tenancy, the landlord can apply for a cancellation of the registration[1].

Phasing. When a rent is registered (or re-registered), the landlord may not be entitled to charge the new rent right away, but, depending on the size of the increase, may have to phase the increase over all or part of the three year period. Following registration, the existing rent is increased annually by either £104 or 25 per cent of the rent, whichever is the greater, or such lesser amount as is

---

15 Ibid s 49 (2) and (3).
16 Ibid s 34 and s 36.
17 Ibid s 46 and Sch 5, para 6.
18 *London Housing & Commercial Properties v Cowan* [1977] QB 148; [1976] 2 All ER 385, DC.
19 Rent (Scotland) Act 1984, s 46(3).
20 Ibid s 50(2).
 1 Ibid s 52.

necessary to reach the full registered rent[2]. The same formula is applied at the end of each year to the rent being paid in order to determine the rent payable in the succeeding year. These limits may be changed in the future by a further order made by the Secretary of State[3].

Under the Housing (Scotland) Act 1988 the Secretary of State is given power to amend these provisions for phasing, or repeal them entirely, and so it is likely that phasing will disappear in the near future[4].

Determination of fair rent. The fair rent formula is contained in s 48 of the Rent (Scotland) Act 1984:

1. In determining a fair rent, the rent officer or rent assessment committee must have regard to all the circumstances (other than personal circumstances), and in particular apply their knowledge and experience of current rents of comparable property in the area, as well as have regard to the age, character and locality of the dwellinghouse in question and to its state of repair and, if any furniture is provided for use under the tenancy, to the quantity, quality and condition of the furniture.

2. It is to be assumed that the number of persons seeking to become tenants of similar houses in the locality is not substantially greater than the number of available houses.

3. There is to be disregarded:

   (a) Any disrepair or defect of the property or furniture which is the fault of the tenant or his predecessor.
   (b) Any improvements or replacements in respect of either the property or furniture by the tenant or his predecessor.

When it was first introduced, the fair rent formula was criticised as being too vague. This was a deliberate policy, however, in order to avoid the litigation and hair-splitting that might result from a more detailed formula; instead, a great deal was left to the professional discretion of the rent officers and rent assessment committees, and from this point of view the system seems to have worked reasonably well. However, the formula has been amplified to some extent by the decisions of the courts and we will now examine some of the ways in which its wording has been interpreted.

2 Rent (Scotland) Act 1984, s 33; Increase of Rent (Scotland) Order 1980 (SI 1980 1664).
3 Rent (Scotland) Act 1984, s 33.
4 Housing (Scotland) Act 1988, s 41.

1. (a) *All the circumstances.* Examples of relevant circumstances are: (1) the rents of comparable properties, especially those for which a fair rent has already been fixed[5]; (2) the capital value of the property[6], and (3) the terms of the tenancy. In the last case, the fact that a let is a furnished one will normally mean that a higher rent can be fixed.

(b) *Other than personal circumstances.* The tenant's poverty or hardship are not factors that can be taken into account. Nor can the fact that the tenant is in possession of the property and enjoying security of tenure, as this is also considered to be a personal circumstance[7].

(c) *To apply their knowledge and experience of current rents of comparable properties in the area.* These words did not appear in the original fair rent formula and are still not in its English version; they were added to the Scottish version by the Tenants Rights Etc (Scotland) Act 1980, because the Scottish courts had been taking a different line from their English counterparts regarding the need for rent assessment committees to give reasons for their decisions[8]. The change in wording does not absolve rent assessment committees from the need to give reasons, but allows them to use their own judgment and skill in cases where there is insufficient evidence, eg of comparable properties.

(d) *The age, character and locality of the dwellinghouse and its state of repair.* 'Locality' in this context is thought to mean the immediate locality, as that is what is likely to affect the value of the property; in relation to the scarcity element, 'locality' is thought to mean a much wider area[9].

(e) *The quantity, quality and condition of the furniture.* There are various ways in which this could be taken into account, but the method favoured seems to be one based on a return on the capital value of the furniture[10]. In *R v London Rent Assessment Panel ex p*

---

5 *Learmonth Property Investment Co Ltd v Aitken* 1970 SC 223, 1971 SLT 349.
6 *Learmonth Property Investment Co Ltd v Aitken* 1970 SC 223, 1971 SLT 349; *Skilling v Arcari's Exrx* 1974 SC (HL) 42, 1974 SLT 46, reversing sub nom *Mason v Skilling* [1974] 3 All ER 977, [1974] 1 WLR 1437, HL.
7 *Skilling v Arcari's Exrx* 1974 SC (HL) 42, 1974 SLT 46, reversing sub nom *Mason v Skilling* [1974] 3 All ER 977, [1974] 1 WLR 1437, HL.
8 *Albyn Properties Ltd v Knox* 1977 SC 108, 1977 SLT 41.
9 See 'Calculating Fair Rents, by Paul Q Watchman, Journal of the Law Society of Scotland (Workshop Section) p 217 (July 1981).
10 *Mann v Cornella* (1980) 254 EG 403, CA.

Mota[11], it was held that, as long as the tenant was entitled to the use of the landlord's furniture, it could be taken into account in fixing the rent, even though the tenant, with the landlord's consent, had replaced it with her own furniture.

2. *The scarcity element.* This part of the formula, contained in s 48(2) of the 1984 Act, is arguably the single most important element that distinguishes a fair rent from a market rent. Effectively it means that any inflationary effect on rents from housing shortages in the locality should be disregarded. As noted above, 'locality' means not just the immediate area, but a fairly large one, ie 'the area within which persons likely to occupy this class of accommodation, having regard to their requirements and work, would be able to dwell'[12]. As there are very few, if any, areas where there is not some sort of housing shortage, it is normal for the rent to be reduced by a sizeable percentage to take account of scarcity[13].

3. *Tenant's improvements or disrepair caused by the tenant.* It would clearly be wrong if a tenant who added to the property's value by making improvements at his own expense was penalised by being charged a higher rent. Conversely, a tenant whose actions detracted from the property's value should not be able to gain from his actions. It is only improvements and not repairs carried out by the tenant that should be disregarded[14]. It should be noted that the word 'predecessor' in this context means predecessor in title under the same lease, eg where there has been an assignation, or where the tenant has died and has been succeeded in the tenancy by a member of his family. Where the property is being relet under a new lease, anything done to it by the previous tenant will be irrelevant.

3. ASSURED TENANCIES

Definition

As we saw earlier, new tenancies which would formerly have been regulated tenancies, will be classified as assured tenancies if they

---

11 (1988) 02 EG 66.
12 The Francis Committee and the London Rent Assessment Panel, quoted in 'Calculating Fair Rents' by Paul Q Watchman, Journal of the Law Society of Scotland (Workshop Section) p 217 (July 1981); *Metropolitan Property Holdings Ltd v Finegold* [1975] 1 All ER 389, [1975] 1 WLR 349, DC.
13 *Western Heritable Investment Co Ltd v Husband* [1983] 2 AC 849, 1983 SC (HL) 60.
14 *Stewart's Judicial Factor v Gallagher* 1967 SC 59, 1967 SLT 52.

were created after 2 January 1989, when Part II of the Housing (Scotland) Act 1988 came into force. Many of the criteria for determining whether or not a tenancy is an assured tenancy are the same or similar to those under which an earlier tenancy qualified as a regulated one. However, there are significant differences.

The most obvious is the absence of a rateable value limit: this means that the very top end of the housing market, which was excluded from rent regulation, will be caught within the ambit of assured tenancies. But this is a less significant change than it seems: so slight is the protection of tenants under the new system compared with that conferred under the old, that landlords at the top end of the market are hardly likely to notice the difference. In particular, under the system of assured tenancies, they will still be able to charge market rents.

Another obvious difference is that there is no exclusion of bona fide lets with board or attendance. We saw above that, in the case of regulated tenancies, this excepted category provided one of the most fruitful sources of Rent Act evasion[15]. However, this welcome death blow to the bed and breakfast let is also less radical than appearances might at first suggest. The new system so favours the needs of landlords that they no longer have much motive for evasion.

Finally, the 1988 Act expressly provides that the tenant (or at least one of them if there are joint tenants) must occupy the house as his only or principal home[16]. This contrasts with the case of regulated tenancies where a tenant who had sublet the house in its entirety, or even a limited company, could be protected during the contractual (though not the statutory) period of the tenancy[17].

As with regulated tenancies, the general qualification for an assured tenancy is that a house is let as a separate dwelling[18]. Also as before, it does not matter if some of the accommodation is shared with other tenants as long as there is a part that is occupied exclusively by the tenant[19]. Where land is let along with the house (other than agricultural land of more than two acres), the land will be included within the assured tenancy provided that the main purpose of the letting is the provision of a home for the tenant[20].

---

15 See pt 2 above; see also pt 5 below.
16 Housing (Scotland) Act 1988, s 12(1) (a), (b).
17 See pt 2 above.
18 Housing (Scotland) Act 1988, s 12(1).
19 Ibid s 14; see also s 21 for situations where the right to shared accommodation may be terminated or varied.
20 Ibid s 13; Sch 4, para 5.

Excepted categories. There are thirteen categories which do not qualify as assured tenancies. Apart from certain transitional cases, included to cover the changeover period between the two systems, these are all identical, or substantially similar, to cases that were excluded from regulation under the Rent (Scotland) Act 1984[1]. This means that many of the comments made above will also apply here. It is also likely that many of the cases on regulated tenancies will be highly persuasive.

Schedule 4 of the Housing (Scotland) Act 1988 lists the following types of tenancy that cannot be assured tenancies. The numbers correspond to the paragraph numbers in the Schedule:

1. *A tenancy entered into before, or pursuant to a contract made before, Schedule 4 came into force.* This is a transitional provision that allows existing regulated tenancies to remain subject to the older system. There are also certain very limited circumstances where new regulated tenancies can be created[2]. It should also be remembered that the contractual and statutory periods of a regulated tenancy are not considered to be separate tenancies, but to be different parts of the same regulated tenancy[3]. This means that a regulated tenancy entered into prior to 2 January 1989 can convert into a statutory regulated tenancy in the normal manner, even if the contractual period of the let ends after that date.

2. *Tenancies at a low rent.* These are tenancies where either no rent is payable, or the rent is less than £6 a week (or its equivalent, if the payment period is different)[4]. This limit may be varied in the future in a further order made by the Secretary of State. In determining the appropriate level, sums payable by the tenant in respect of services, repairs, maintenance or insurance are to be disregarded.

3. *A tenancy to which the Tenancy of Shops (Scotland) Act 1949 applies*[5]. Under the old system, a sublet of a residential element of a shop tenancy could be protected[6]. That proviso does **not** apply in the case of assured tenancies.

---

1 See pt 2 above.
2 Housing (Scotland) Act 1988, s 42; see also pt 2 above.
3 Rent (Scotland) Act 1984, s 8.
4 Assured Tenancies (Tenancies at a Low Rent) (Scotland) Order 1988, SI 1988/2069.
5 See ch 8 above.
6 Rent (Scotland) Act 1984, s 10(2).

4. *Licensed premises.* This is virtually identical to the equivalent exception in the case of regulated tenancies[7].

5. *Tenancies of agricultural land.* These are tenancies under which agricultural land exceeding two acres is let along with the house. This is also the same as the equivalent exception for regulated tenancies, although the wording has been simplified[8].

6. *Tenancies of agricultural holdings.* This refers to tenancies under which the house is comprised in an agricultural holding within the meaning of the Agricultural Holdings (Scotland) Act 1949[9], and it is occupied by the person responsible for farming the holding; the latter may be either the tenant himself or his servant or agent. This is a new category, and it is not immediately obvious which cases it would include that were not already caught by category 5. Presumably it would extend the exclusion to agricultural holdings of under two acres, eg some market gardens.

7. *Student lets, where the landlord is the student's educational institution.* This is identical to the equivalent exception for regulated tenancies[10].

8. *Holiday lets.* This is also identical to the earlier provision[11].

9. *Where the landlord is resident.* The rather complex wording of this paragraph is again almost entirely identical to its equivalent in the Rent (Scotland) Act 1984[12]. However, the definition of a resident landlord has been refined a little further. We saw above that an ambiguity created by the Rent Act 1974 was later corrected by making it clear that there was a resident landlord where the landlord and tenant each occupied the same house, but not where they occupied separate flats within a purpose built block of flats. But what of the common situation where a large house was originally built as a single dwelling but has later been converted into two or more separate, self-contained flats? In strict terms of the 1984 Act, since they were not originally custom built as flats, a landlord

---

7 See ibid s 10(1); see also pt 2 above.
8 See Rent (Scotland) Act 1984, s 1(3) and s 2(1)(e); see also pt 2 above.
9 See ch 12, pt 1 above.
10 See Rent (Scotland) Act 1984, s 2(1)(c) and s 2 (5); see also pt 2 above. A list of the educational establishments that qualify under this exception is contained in the Assured Tenancies (Exceptions) (Scotland) Regulations 1988, SI 1988/2068.
11 See Rent (Scotland) Act 1984, s 2(1)(d); see also pt 2 above and cases cited there.
12 See Rent (Scotland) Act 1984, s 6 and pt 2 above.

occupying one of them would be considered a resident landlord, and any tenants of his occupying other flats within the same converted house would have no protection. However, under the 1988 Act the wording is amended to make it clear that such a landlord would **not** be classified as a resident landlord, and so a tenancy of another flat in the same building would not thereby be prevented from being an assured tenancy. This is done by adding a condition that, for a landlord to be considered resident, he must have some means of access through the tenant's house or vice versa[13].

10. *Crown tenancies.* This is identical to the equivalent provision in the 1984 Act[14].

11. *Local authority and other tenancies.* These include tenancies by regional, islands or district councils, development corporations, the Scottish Special Housing Association, Scottish Homes, co-operative housing associations and urban development corporations. These (with the exception of housing associations) will all qualify for the more substantial protection conferred by a secure tenancy under the Housing (Scotland) Act 1987[15].

12. *Shared ownership agreements.* This means any tenancy under a shared ownership agreement within the meaning of the Housing Associations Act 1985[16]. This refers to a situation where a tenant has an 'equity share' in the property, ie as well as paying a periodic rent he has paid a capital sum and remains entitled to a percentage of the house's value; in effect, therefore, he is part tenant, part owner. For people who cannot yet afford to take the full plunge into owner-occupation this arrangement provides a useful halfway stage between tenancy and ownership. Such agreements will not be assured tenancies, though presumably the tenant's equity share (if not the terms of the agreement) will give him a measure of security, as the tenancy could not be terminated without him being paid his share of the property's value.

13. *Transitional cases.* These are (a) protected tenancies under the Rent (Scotland) Act 1984; (b) housing association tenancies, and (c) secure tenancies[17]. The first two of these are transitional since

13 Housing (Scotland) Act 1988, Sch 4, para 9(1)(c).
14 See Rent (Scotland) Act 1984, s 4; see also pt 2 above.
15 See ch 14, pt 2 below.
16 Housing Associations Act 1985, s 106(1).
17 See ch 14, pt 2 below.

(apart from the few limited exceptions already noted) there are to be no new regulated tenancies, and future lets by housing associations will be assured rather than secure tenancies. However, other public sector tenancies will continue to be secure tenancies, and it is not immediately clear why they should be described as transitional, unless this is a reference to the government's policy to encourage the transfer of public sector housing to the private sector.

Security of tenure

Statutory assured tenancies. The provisions here are similar to those for regulated tenancies. The contractual period of the tenancy can only be terminated by the landlord serving a notice to quit at least four weeks prior to the termination date[18]. This notice will be invalid unless it contains certain specified information informing the tenant of his legal rights[19]. The tenant under an assured tenancy who remains in possession of the house after the contractual period of his lease has been thus terminated, will continue to have the assured tenancy of the house[20]. He can only be removed if the landlord obtains a court order by the sheriff, based on one of the grounds set out in Schedule 5 of the Act[1]. Although these grounds primarily apply to the termination of statutory assured tenancies, certain of them also apply during the contractual period of the lease, provided that the tenancy terms allow it[2]. The tenant must be given prior written notice of the repossession proceedings and the notice must state the ground of repossession. The period of notice depends upon the ground that is being used. In respect of grounds 1, 2, 5, 6, 7, 9 and 17 below it is two months, and in the case of all the other grounds it is only two weeks. In certain circumstances, the sheriff has discretion to dispense with the need for a notice[3]. The required form of the notice is laid down by the Assured Tenancies (Forms) (Scotland) Regulations 1988.

The notice of repossession proceedings would appear to be a separate requirement from the notice to quit terminating the tenancy. However, there seems to be no reason why the two could not be combined, provided that the combined notice observed the

---

18 Rent (Scotland) Act 1984, s 112.
19 Assured Tenancies (Notices to Quit Prescribed Information) (Scotland) Regulations 1988, SI 1988/2067.
20 Housing (Scotland) Act 1988, s 16(1); see also pt 2 above and cases cited there.
 1 Housing (Scotland) Act 1988, s 16(2).
 2 Ibid s 18(6).
 3 Ibid s 19.

prescribed requirements regarding content and minimum length for each type of notice.

Once more the repossession grounds are divided between mandatory and discretionary ones though, perhaps significantly, this time the mandatory grounds are placed first. Many of these are identical or substantially similar to the grounds of repossession for regulated tenancies, and they should be considered in conjunction with the comments and case citations made in that context[4]. There are, however, important differences. In particular, it is now made easier to get rid of a tenant for rent arrears, or (a new development) persistent late payment of rent, even without accumulated arrears. In some cases eviction for arrears will be mandatory, with the sheriff having no discretion in the matter. Another important new ground of removal is where the landlord requires possession of the house for the purpose of redevelopment.

Despite the similarity to the provisions for regulated tenancies, however, the protection afforded to tenants under assured tenancies may turn out to be less than it initially seems. As we will see below, landlords also have the option of creating short assured tenancies at market rents, with an absolute right to end the lease at its expiry date. If this method is widely used, the security of tenure enjoyed by tenants could be as little as six months in many cases[5].

If a property subject to an assured tenancy has been lawfully sublet, also under an assured tenancy, then the subtenant's tenancy will not be terminated along with that of the principal tenant; instead the subtenant will take the principal tenant's place under the main tenancy[6].

Mandatory grounds of repossession[7]. In these cases the sheriff, if he is satisfied that the ground exists, **must** give possession back to the landlord[8]. In respect of grounds 1 to 5 the tenant must have been given prior written notice that possession might be required under the ground in question; however, in the case of the first two of these grounds, the sheriff has the discretion to dispense with the need for such notice if he thinks it reasonable. The numbers of these mandatory grounds (and of the discretionary ones below) correspond to the paragraph numbers in Schedule 5 of the 1988 Act:

4 See pt 2 above.
5 See section on short assured tenancies below.
6 Housing (Scotland) Act 1988, s 28.
7 Ibid Sch 5, pt I.
8 Ibid s 18(3).

(1) Where the landlord formerly occupied the house as his only or principal home; alternatively where he did not formerly occupy it, but now requires it for himself or his spouse and did not buy the property subject to the sitting tenancy. This is a shift of emphasis from the parallel ground in the case of regulated tenancies. There the ground was only mandatory where the landlord had actually occupied the property, and was otherwise discretionary[9]. Here it is mandatory in each case.

(2) Where the house is subject to a heritable security granted before the creation of the tenancy and, as a result of the debtor's default, the creditor requires to sell the house with vacant possession. The obvious example of this is where the house is repossessed because of the landlord's mortgage arrears.

(3) Off-season lets of holiday premises for a period not exceeding eight months. This is also virtually identical to its equivalent for regulated tenancies.

(4) A short lease between student lettings for a period not exceeding twelve months. This is also the same as its equivalent for regulated tenancies.

(5) Requirement of the house for a minister or a full-time lay missionary. This is also the same as the equivalent ground for regulated tenancies.

(6) Where the landlord intends to demolish or reconstruct the whole or a substantial part of the house, or to carry out substantial works on the house, or a building of which it forms part. This is a new ground. It will not apply where the landlord or his predecessor bought the property for value after the creation of the tenancy. In other words, a landlord who bought the house subject to the sitting tenancy with the purpose of redeveloping the property will not be able to get vacant possession under this ground. It is also a condition of the ground applying that the work cannot be done without the tenant vacating the property; alternatively, it will apply if it is necessary for the tenant to accept a tenancy of only part of the house, or some other variation of his tenancy terms, and he has refused to agree to this. Where a tenancy is terminated under this ground (or under ground (9) below) the landlord is required to pay the tenant's removal expenses[10].

---

9 See pt 2 above.
10 Housing (Scotland) Act 1988, s 22.

(7) Where the tenant inherited the tenancy from a former tenant. The proceedings for recovery of possession must be begun not later than twelve months after the death of the former tenant, or within twelve months after the date when (in the sheriff's opinion) the landlord became aware of the former tenant's death. Mere acceptance of rent by the landlord after the death of the former tenant will not create a new tenancy, unless he has agreed in writing to change the level of rent, the duration of the let or some other term of the tenancy. This is also a new ground, resulting from the more restricted succession rights to assured tenancies, compared with those under regulated tenancies[11].

(8) Both at the date of the service of the notice relating to the repossession proceedings and at the date of the hearing, the tenant is at least three months in arrears with rent. This is a significant new ground. In the case of regulated tenancies, rent arrears is always a discretionary ground. Now it is mandatory for assured tenancies, provided that there are at least three months arrears. This means that, even where there are mitigating circumstances, the sheriff has no power to delay the proceedings to give the tenant time to pay; in theory, eviction could be mandatory even in circumstances where it was not the tenant's fault at all, eg if there was a delay in payment of housing benefit. The only leeway allowed the tenant is the opportunity to bring his arrears below the three months level during the period between the service of the landlord's notice and the date of the hearing; however, since this is one of the grounds where only two weeks' notice is required before the landlord can begin proceedings, this is not giving the tenant very much room for manoeuvre.

Discretionary grounds. Where one of the grounds in Part II of Schedule 5 is established, the sheriff is not to grant an order for possession unless he considers it reasonable to do so[12]. Also, as with regulated tenancies, the sheriff has the power in the case of a discretionary ground to delay the proceedings, including the power to adjourn the case[13]. A new addition is that the sheriff is required to impose conditions with regard to the payment of any rent arrears, and also with regard to payment of rent or other payments relating to the tenant's occupation of the property after the termination of the tenancy, or any other conditions he thinks fit; however, he has

---

11 See pt 4 below.
12 Housing (Scotland) Act 1988, s 18(4).
13 Ibid s 20.

the discretion not to impose such conditions if he considers that to do so would cause exceptional hardship to the tenant or would otherwise be unreasonable[14]. The numbering of these discretionary grounds, as with the mandatory ones above, follows the numbering of the paragraphs in Schedule 5:

(9) Suitable alternative accommodation is available for the tenant or will be available for him when the order for possession takes effect. What is meant by suitable alternative accommodation is set out in Part III of Schedule 5, and is virtually the same as the equivalent provision for regulated tenancies. Factors to be taken into account include the proximity to the tenant's place of work, the rent level and the extent and character of the accommodation. The alternative accommodation must be under an assured tenancy or one giving an equivalent degree of security of tenure; a short assured tenancy or one subject to termination under grounds (1) to (5) above does not qualify as suitable. A certificate by the relevant local authority, new town or by Scottish Homes that they will rehouse the tenant is sufficient evidence that suitable alternative accommodation is available. Where a tenancy is terminated under this ground (or under ground (5) above) the landlord is required to pay the tenant's removal expenses[15].

(10) Where the tenant has given a notice to quit to the landlord and has remained in possession of the house after the expiry of the notice. Proceedings must be begun by the landlord within six months of the expiry of the notice. Also, the landlord will be precluded from using this ground if the tenant has been granted a new tenancy of the house in the meantime. This ground is similar to Case (5) for regulated tenancies, but with an important difference. There it was also a requirement that the landlord, on the strength of the tenant's notice, must have committed himself in some way, eg by contracting to sell or relet the house. In the case of assured tenancies there is no such requirement.

(11) Where the tenant has persistently delayed paying rent which has become lawfully due. This is another new ground, and it applies whether or not there are actually any rent arrears due on the date when repossession proceedings are begun.

(12) Where some rent is unpaid on the date when repossession proceedings are begun. There also must have been unpaid rent on the date when notice of the proceedings was served on the tenant,

---

14 Ibid s 20(3).
15 Ibid s 22.

unless it is a case where the sheriff has used his discretion to dispense with such a notice[16].

(13) Where any other obligation of the tenancy has been broken or not performed.

(14) Deterioration of the condition of the house or any of the common parts of the building because of the neglect of the tenant, or any one of joint tenants, or anyone living with the tenant. The tenant may only be removed for the act or default of a lodger or subtenant where he has failed to take any reasonable steps to remove the person concerned. This is the same as the equivalent ground for regulated tenancies, with the addition of the provisions about common parts of the building and joint tenants.

(15) Conduct in the house, or in its vicinity, which is a nuisance to adjoining proprietors, or where there is a criminal conviction for using the house for an immoral or illegal purpose. Apart from the reference to conduct in the vicinity of the house, this is the same as the equivalent provision for regulated tenancies.

(16) In the case of a furnished let, deterioration in the condition of the furniture because of ill treatment by the tenant or anyone living with him. As with ground (14) above, the tenant may only be removed for the act or default of a lodger or subtenant where he has failed to take any reasonable steps to remove the person concerned. This is also identical to the equivalent provision for regulated tenancies, although the wording has been tidied up a little.

(17) Where the house was let to the tenant in consequence of his employment by the landlord, or a previous landlord, and the tenant has ceased to be in that employment. In the case of regulated tenancies, it was also necessary for the landlord to require the house for another employee. In relation to assured tenancies, that requirement has been dropped.

Rents under assured tenancies

As we have already observed, it is in relation to the rent level that an assured tenancy differs most fundamentally from its predecessor, the regulated tenancy. A tenant no longer has the right to have a fair rent registered with the rent officer. Instead, a market rent will be payable, although rent assessment committees still have a role to

---

16 Housing (Scotland) Act 1988, s 19(1)(b).

play in settling disputes. Opinions will differ regarding the desirability of abolishing the fair rent system; however, for the lawyer at any rate, there is the bonus that the new provisions are very much simpler.

Where the period of let specified in the lease contract is still unexpired, or where the lease is continuing on tacit relocation, the rent will be as stated in the lease document. Since it will presumably be at a level negotiated between the parties, and since the tenant will have no right to go to the rent officer to have it altered, this means that it is likely to be at a market level. After the expiry of the lease contract, when the tenancy is continuing as a statutory assured tenancy, the landlord may at any time serve a notice on the tenant proposing a new rent[17]. If the length of the tenancy was six months or more, the period of notice is six months; if the length was less than six months, the period will be the duration of the tenancy, though not less than one month[18]. After the rent has been increased, it may not be raised again until after a year has passed[19].

The new rent will take effect unless the tenant refers the matter to a rent assessment committee, or the parties negotiate a different level of rent. Section 25 sets out the rent assessment committees' guidelines for fixing a market rent. Since the tenant may feel that the landlord has proposed a rent above the market level, it may well be worth his while to refer the matter to a committee. The appropriate level of rent is that at which the committee consider that the house might reasonably be expected to be let in the open market by a willing landlord under an assured tenancy. It is to be assumed that the tenancy begins at the period when the new rent is to take effect and that the house has been let on terms (other than those relating to rent) that are the actual terms of the tenancy. If a notice or notices have been given that possession might be recovered under grounds (1) to (5) of Schedule 5, that should also be taken into account[20]. There should be disregarded any effect on the rent attributable to (a) the granting of a tenancy to a sitting tenant; (b) an improvement carried out by the tenant or a predecessor in title, unless the improvement was carried out in pursuance of the terms of the tenancy, and (c) the failure by the tenant to comply with any terms of the tenancy[21].

---

17 Ibid s 24(1). For the prescribed form of such a notice, see Assured Tenancies (Forms) (Scotland) Regulations 1988, SI 1988/2109.
18 Ibid s 24(2).
19 Ibid s 24(4).
20 Ibid s 25(1).
21 Ibid s 25(2).

Other tenancy terms

Alteration of terms. During the contractual period of an assured tenancy, the terms will be those in the lease document. Once the tenancy has become a statutory one, the terms (other than those relating to termination of the tenancy or increasing the rent) will initially remain the same as before[22]. They will only be changed if the landlord, within a year of the termination of the contractual tenancy, serves a notice on the tenant proposing different terms[1]. The tenant may refer the notice to a rent assessment committee, who may confirm the new terms or fix other terms that they consider reasonable[2]. If the notice is not referred to a committee, the new terms will take effect three months after the service of the notice, or after such longer period as the notice specifies[3]. Either the landlord in his notice, or the rent assessment committee if the matter is referred to them, may make an adjustment of the rent to take account of the new terms[4]. There are prescribed forms for both the landlord's and the tenant's notices[5].

Assignation and subletting[6]. It is an implied term of every assured tenancy that, except with the consent of the landlord, the tenant shall not (a) assign the tenancy (in whole or in part) or (b) sublet or part with possession of the whole or any part of the house. This provision only applies if there is no provision in the lease dealing with assignation or subletting.

Access for repairs[7]. It is an implied term of every assured tenancy that the tenant will afford the landlord reasonable access to the house and all reasonable facilities for carrying out any repairs the landlord is entitled to execute.

Written lease and rent book[8]. The landlord under an assured tenancy has a duty to draw up a probative or holograph document

22 Housing (Scotland) Act 1988, s 16(1).
1 Ibid s 17(2). For the prescribed forms of notice for both landlord and tenant under this section, see the Assured Tenancies (Forms) (Scotland) Regulations 1988, SI 1988/2109.
2 Ibid s 17(4).
3 Ibid s 17(3).
4 Ibid s 17(5).
5 Assured Tenancies (Forms) (Scotland) Regulations 1988, SI 1988/2109.
6 Housing (Scotland) Act 1988, s 23.
7 Ibid s 26.
8 Ibid s 30.

containing or referring to the tenancy terms, and to give a copy of it to the tenant. This should all be free of charge to the tenant. If the landlord fails to draw up such a document, or to adjust the terms of an existing document where necessary, the tenant can refer the matter to the sheriff. Where the rent is payable weekly, the landlord has a duty to provide a rent book, and a landlord failing to do so will be liable to a fine. The rent book must contain certain information informing the tenant of his legal rights[9].

Short assured tenancies[10]

This is a special type of tenure under which the landlord has an absolute right to possession of the house when the period stated in the lease contract comes to an end. In such cases, therefore, the tenant is denied the right to extended security of tenure as a statutory assured tenant. In order to qualify for this exemption, the term of the let must be at least six months and the tenant must have been given written notice in advance that the tenancy was to be a short assured tenancy[11]. If the tenant is granted a renewal of the lease, or it continues by tacit relocation, no fresh notice will be required to qualify the tenancy as a short assured tenancy[12]. The landlord, however, is entitled to convert such a renewed lease into an ordinary assured tenancy by serving on the tenant a notice to that effect[13].

The same grounds of repossession apply to short assured tenancies as with other assured tenancies. In addition, the sheriff is bound to give an order for possession if he is satisfied (a) that the short assured tenancy has reached its ish (ie its expiry date) (b) that tacit relocation is not operating (c) that no further contractual tenancy is in existence and (d) that the landlord has given a notice stating that he requires possession of the house[14]. The period of notice is two months, or such longer period as the lease specifies[15].

The Act does not make the function of such a notice entirely clear. It cannot be a notice to quit in the normal sense, as it is expressly stated that it may be served before, at or after the termination of the

---

9 Assured Tenancies (Rent Book) (Scotland) Regulations 1988, SI 1988/2085.
10 Housing (Scotland) Act 1988, ss 32-35.
11 Ibid s 32 (1) and (2).
12 Ibid s 32(3).
13 Ibid s 32(4).
14 Ibid s 33(1).
15 Ibid s 33(2).

tenancy to which it relates[16]. However, the sheriff cannot grant the landlord possession where tacit relocation is operating, and the common law relating to notices to quit and tacit relocation is expressly saved by section 52. It will therefore be necessary for the landlord to send a notice to quit at least twenty-eight days prior to the expiry date of the tenancy to prevent the onset of tacit relocation[17].

There seems to be no reason why the two notices cannot be combined in one, provided that their respective functions are met by the single notice. However, although a twenty-eight day notice will stop tacit relocation operating, the landlord cannot raise repossession proceedings until he has given the required notice of at least two months. This means that if the landlord wants to be able to raise proceedings as soon as the lease has ended, he will require to serve his combined notice at least two months before the expiry date.

There are prescribed forms for the various statutory notices required in connection with short assured tenancies[18].

Since the general provisions relating to assured tenancies appear to apply to short assured tenancies as well, it seems likely that many landlords will adopt them as the preferred form of tenure. If landlords opt for short assured tenancies of the minimum length, the greatest security that any tenant will enjoy is for the initial period of six months. If the landlord grants a renewal, it can be for a shorter period[19]. There therefore seems no reason why a landlord could not, for example, grant a lease of six months, followed by one of a shorter period, which could thereafter proceed by tacit relocation until the landlord decided to terminate it or put up the rent. Such a let, however, would still require two months' notice of termination.

There are, however, some disadvantages that a landlord will suffer by opting for a short assured tenancy. For example, if the tenant thinks that his rent is too high, he can refer it to a rent assessment committee to have a market rent fixed during the contractual period of his lease[20]. In the case of a normal assured tenancy, on the other hand, he is stuck with the rent in the lease until the lease has ended and the tenancy has become a statutory one; then, if the landlord serves a notice of increase, the tenant can refer

16 Housing (Scotland) Act 1988, s 33(3).
17 Rent (Scotland) Act 1984, s 112; see also ch 7, pt 1 above.
18 Assured Tenancies (Forms) (Scotland) Regulations 1988, SI 1988/2109.
19 Housing (Scotland) Act 1988, s 32(3).
20 Ibid s 34.

the matter to a rent assessment committee. The right of a tenant under a short assured tenancy to have a market rent fixed by a rent assessment committee is qualified in two ways (1) there must be a sufficient number of similar houses in the locality let on assured tenancies for the committee to use as comparisons[1] and (2) the right can be discontinued in particular areas, or in other specified circumstances, if the Secretary of State makes an order to that effect[2].

One possible advantage to a landlord of opting for a normal assured tenancy, therefore, is that he may be able to get a tenant to agree to a rent above the level that a rent assessment committee is likely to fix as a market rent. In such a case the tenant will be held to that rent until the lease has expired, and even after that, provided that the landlord has not served a notice of increase. The landlord's penalty is that the tenant will get extended security of tenure. Whether many landlords will consider this a worthwhile risk remains to be seen.

There is, however, a more substantial incentive for landlords to steer clear of the short assured tenancy. Under the Business Expansion Scheme introduced by the Government in the Finance Act 1988, companies investing in the provision of dwellinghouses for let become entitled to tax relief. However, short assured tenancies do not qualify for relief under the scheme[3]. This disqualification may, in the short term at any rate, prevent the widespread adoption of short assured tenancies as the normal form of tenure. But the short assured tenancy could well outlast the tax provision, in which case the protection offered residential tenants may end up being more apparent than real.

4. PROVISIONS COMMON TO REGULATED AND ASSURED TENANCIES

Succession to tenancies

Prior to 2 January 1989, the widow or widower of a tenant under a regulated tenancy, failing which a member of the tenant's family who had resided with the tenant for six months prior to the tenant's death, had a right to succeed to the tenancy. Furthermore, there was a right to a second succession after the death of the first successor.

---

1 Ibid s 34(3).
2 Ibid s 35.
3 Finance Act 1988, s 50(3)(b)(ii).

This meant that in some cases security of tenure could span many years, covering two or even three generations of the same family.

The Housing (Scotland) Act 1988 Act gives much more limited succession rights to the tenant under an assured tenancy, basically confining the right of succession to the tenant's widow or widower who lived with the tenant at the time of his or her death[4]. Furthermore, there is no right of succession to a tenant who has already inherited the tenancy; this means, for example, that where a widow or widower succeeds to a tenancy and then remarries, the new spouse will have no succession right.

The 1988 Act similarly curtails succession rights in the case of existing regulated tenancies, so that only a widow or widower of the **original** tenant can now inherit a regulated tenancy[5]. In certain circumstances a member of the tenant's family may still succeed to the tenancy, but what he or she will get is an **assured** tenancy, **not** a regulated one. These circumstances are: (1) on the death of the original tenant's spouse, where the original tenant died **after** 2 January 1989 and the spouse inherited a regulated tenancy; (2) on the death of the original tenant where he or she died after 2 January 1989 but did not leave a spouse, and (3) where the newly-deceased tenant was not the original tenant, but succeeded to a regulated tenancy under the old law prior to 2 January 1989. This means, for example, that where a tenant inherited a regulated tenancy from a parent prior to 2 January 1989, and he dies after that date, his widow can only inherit an assured tenancy; only the **original** tenant's spouse can now inherit a regulated tenancy. In order to qualify for succession to an assured tenancy, the member of the family must have resided with the tenant for two years prior to the tenant's death; to cover transitional cases, a lesser period will qualify, provided that the member of the family resided with the tenant for six months prior to 2 January 1989.

It should be emphasised that these rather complex provisions only apply where the original tenancy was a **regulated** tenancy. As mentioned above, where it started life as an assured tenancy (ie after 2 January 1989) the position is much simpler: only the spouse can inherit.

For the purpose of these provisions, a person who was living with the tenant as the tenant's wife or husband (even though they were not married) will qualify as widow or widower.

---

4 Housing (Scotland) Act 1988, s 31.
5 Rent (Scotland) Act 1984, s 3 and Sch 1; s 3A, Sch 1A and Sch 1B (added by the Housing (Scotland) Act 1988, s 46 and Sch 6, pt I).

The main effect of these amendments will be to hasten the changeover from regulated to assured tenancies. Existing regulated tenancies will not now last beyond the lifetime of the existing tenant or his spouse.

Protection from eviction and harassment

We saw in part two of chapter 7 that a tenant who is unlawfully evicted may have a claim of damages against the landlord at common law. In the case of dwellinghouses, this common law remedy has been greatly reinforced by the Rent (Scotland) Act 1984 and the Housing (Scotland) Act 1988, making the landlord, or other person responsible for the unlawful eviction, liable under both the criminal and the civil law. Moreover, these provisions apply very widely, to all residential occupiers. This means that they apply to **all** leases of dwellinghouses, not only those under regulated or assured tenancies. They also probably apply to residential occupation of property that is not strictly a dwellinghouse, eg a caravan or houseboat, and to forms of tenure other than a lease, eg where the property is occupied under a licence[6].

Criminal liability. The Rent (Scotland) Act 1984[7] makes unlawful eviction or harassment of a residential occupier a criminal offence. There has been unlawful eviction if the landlord, or anyone else, 'unlawfully deprives the residential occupier of any premises of his occupation of the premises or any part thereof or attempts to do so'[8]. The deprivation does not need to be permanent provided that it has the character of an eviction, but deprivation for one day and night only has been held not to be enough[9]. It is a defence if the person accused 'believed, and had reasonable cause to believe, that the residential occupier had ceased to reside in the premises'[10]. Harassment is where either the landlord or someone else, with the intention of getting the occupier to move out of the property, or relinquish any of his rights in connection with it, 'does acts calculated to interfere with the peace or comfort of the residential occupier or members of his household, or persistently withdraws or

---

6 See pt 5 below.
7 Rent (Scotland) Act 1984, s 22 (as amended by the Housing (Scotland) Act 1988, s 38).
8 Rent (Scotland) Act 1984, s 22(1).
9 *R v Yuthiwattana* (1984) 80 Cr App R 55, 128 Sol Jo 661, CA. But see also *Schon v Camden London Borough Council* (1986) 279 EG 859; 53 P & CR 361.
10 Rent (Scotland) Act 1984, s 22(1).

withholds services reasonably required for the occupation of the premises as a residence'[11].

Civil liability. Under the 1988 Act, a landlord who unlawfully evicts or harasses a tenant or other residential occupier is liable in damages to him[12]. 'Eviction' and 'harassment' are given similar definitions to those in the 1984 Act. The liability is stated to be a delictual one[13], but an interesting feature of this provision is that the measure of damages is not the usual one in delict, ie the loss suffered by the claimant. Instead it is the difference in value between the landlord's interest subject to the sitting tenancy, and the value of his interest with vacant possession[14]. In other words, the landlord stands to forfeit any gain that evicting the tenant is likely to bring him. Without this provision, it might in some cases have been in the landlord's interest to unlawfully evict a tenant if damages based on the tenant's loss were likely to be less than what the landlord would gain by obtaining vacant possession.

Cases where the tenant's right to occupy has ended. The above provisions apply to situations where the tenant or other occupier still has the right to occupy the property, ie where his lease has not yet ended, or where he has the right to extended security of tenure as a regulated or assured tenant. However, the 1984 Act also makes provision for cases where the tenant's tenancy or right to use the property has come to an end, and he does not have extended security of tenure. In such cases, the owner of the property must obtain a court order before he can recover possession[15]. This reinforces the common law principle applicable to all leases[16]. This provision does not apply to lodgers, temporary occupants without title, occupiers under holiday lets or occupants of hostels owned by local authorities or other public sector landlords[17].

Rather curiously, section 23 of the 1984 Act does not specify the consequences incurred by a landlord for evicting without a court order in such circumstances. It might be thought that he would be liable to the civil and criminal sanctions for unlawful eviction

---

11 Rent (Scotland) Act, 1984, s 22(2).
12 Housing (Scotland) Act 1988, s 36(1) and (2).
13 Ibid s 36(4).
14 Ibid s 37(1).
15 Rent (Scotland) Act 1984, s 23 (as amended by the Housing (Scotland) Act 1988, s 39).
16 See ch 7, pt 2 above.
17 Rent (Scotland) Act 1984, s 23A (added by the Housing (Scotland) Act 1988, s 40).

referred to above, but the definition of a residential occupier whose eviction can give rise to such liability seems to be confined to those who have a contractual right to occupy, or a statutory right to security of tenure under a regulated or assured tenancy[18]. Presumably, however, section 23 has the effect of reinforcing the civil right at common law to claim damages for unlawful eviction[19].

Prohibition of premiums[20]

These provisions, in relation to both regulated and assured tenancies, make it an offence for the landlord or anyone else to accept any additional payment as an inducement to grant a tenancy, or to grant a renewal or other continuance of it. Payments to obtain an assignation (which could be made either to the landlord or the existing tenant) are also an offence. In each case the person receiving the premium is liable to a fine and to repay the sum involved. The sale of furniture to an incoming tenant at an excessive price may be considered a premium.

It is also illegal for a landlord to charge rent for a rental period that has not yet started, or to demand an advance payment of rent for a period of more than six months[1]. Breach of this will render the landlord liable to a fine and the rent for the prohibited period will be irrecoverable from the tenant[2].

These provisions were originally introduced for regulated tenancies to prevent a possible method of evading rent control; for example, a landlord confined to charging a fair rent might have sought to compensate for this by charging a capital sum in addition to rent. There seems less need for this protection in the case of assured tenancies: since the landlord is allowed to charge a market rent anyway, presumably any housing shortage that might induce a tenant to pay a premium will now be reflected in the rent. Nevertheless, there may still be cases where these provisions will operate to protect a tenant from exploitation.

The future application of these provisions, of course, will be to assured tenancies, since it is normally no longer possible to create new regulated tenancies. However, they may still continue to apply in the case of assignations of existing regulated tenancies.

18 Rent (Scotland) Act 1984, s 22(5); Housing (Scotland) Act 1988, s 36(8)(a).
19 See ch 7, pt 2 above.
20 Rent (Scotland) Act 1984, pt VIII; Housing (Scotland) Act 1988, s 27.
 1 Rent (Scotland) Act 1984, s 89.
 2 Ibid s 89(2) and (3).

5. EVASION OF THE RENT ACTS

For many years the imposition upon landlords of fair rents and security of tenure provisions has naturally caused them to look for loopholes in the legislation. As a result, they have used many devices to evade the Acts, so that they can charge higher rents and be able to regain possession of their properties when they want to. One advantage of assured tenancies (though tenants may think it a dubious one) is that such tactics should generally no longer be necessary: so many of the restrictions on landlords have been lifted that they now have much less motive to get round the legislation. Nevertheless, there are many tenancies entered into before the commencement of the Housing (Scotland) Act 1988 where some of these methods will have been tried, and the question may well arise in the future as to whether a particular attempt at evasion has been successful, or whether it has not worked and the tenancy in question is a regulated one. Also, although they have less motive, landlords may still try to get round the more flimsy protection offered tenants by assured tenancies. For these reasons we will consider briefly two of the more common methods of evasion.

'Bed and breakfast' lets

In the last dozen years or so, many tenants of bedsits and other furnished lets must have been surprised by an apparent concern for their welfare on the part of their landlords. This unexpected generosity usually took the form of a lease obligation to the effect that the landlord would provide the tenant with breakfast, often in a form that was distinctly bizarre: for example, the landlord might agree to deposit a cooked breakfast on the tenant's doorstep in a tinfoil tray, or arrange for him to eat at a local hotel, sometimes not situated very near to the subjects of let. There are probably still many tenants around who have such leases. They should not be fooled. The landlord's motive is not his tenant's welfare, but exactly the opposite. He is attempting to evade the protection of the Rent (Scotland) Act 1984 by claiming that the tenancy is a bona fide let with board, which is one of the excepted cases where the Act does not apply[3].

One would have thought that such a blatant attempt at evasion could not be considered bona fide. Nevertheless, although the exception was probably intended only to apply to cases such as

3 See pt 2 above.

lodgers or the tenants of boarding houses, the Act does not define what is meant by board; as a result 'bed and breakfast' lets have flourished virtually unchallenged since the provisions of the Rent Act 1974 first extended full protection to furnished tenancies. The case law on the subject is sparse and not always consistent. In *Holiday Flat Co v Kuczera*[4], a tenant had the option of having a continental breakfast delivered to his room by a caretaker. It was held that this was a bona fide let with board and the tenancy was not protected. On the other hand, in the English case of *Rita Dale v Adrahill and Ali Khan*[5], where the tenant was entitled to breakfast in a separate building 250 yards from the subjects of let, it was held that the tenancy **was** protected. The only significant difference between these two cases appears to be that, in the first, the breakfast was served on the premises, and in the other it was not; however, the latter case has been reported only in digest form, so it is difficult to be sure.

However, that distinction was confirmed, and the law somewhat clarified, in *Gavin v Lindsay*[6]. In that case the tenant was given two options: the first was to be served with breakfast at a local cafe and the second was to collect the ingredients for breakfast at a nearby shop and make the meal herself. The tenant chose the latter option. It was held that this was **not** a bona fide let with board and that the tenancy was a protected one. After reviewing the sparse authority, Sheriff Kearney provided his own definition of 'board':

> 'I have no doubt myself that, whether in the seaside or urban context the concept of "board" has two elements, viz., service and substance – both provided at or about the time of use. By substance I mean the food and drink. By service I mean the preparation and setting out of that food and drink. How much of each is to be provided before "board" can be constituted is a matter of degree but both elements must be present at least in some degree before the concept of board can begin to be established[7].'

The sheriff approved the case of *Holiday Flat Co v Kuczera*, acknowledging that board might be only partial and that the provision of breakfast alone, even a continental one, was sufficient. However, no matter how spartan the meal might be, it was an

4 1978 SLT (Sh Ct) 47.
5 (1982) CLY 1787.
6 1987 SLT (Sh Ct) 12.
7 1987 SLT (Sh Ct) 12 at 15; see also *Otter v Norman* (1987) 284 EG 372, (1988) 132 Sol Jo 52, CA.

essential element in the concept of board that the landlord should clear up afterwards.

The question of whether the let was bona fide was also raised in that case. The sheriff held that the mere fact of the landlord attempting to use the breakfast provision as a pretext for removing the let from the category of protected tenancy into that of unprotected one was not by itself enough to amount to bad faith.

The case of *Gavin v Lindsay* (if it is followed) does not entirely dispose of the bed and breakfast let, but at least it disqualifies the more extreme manifestations of it. It would appear that the tenant must be served with at least one meal, prepared by the landlord, and that it must be served on the premises. The service of a meal elsewhere (eg in a hotel), or the mere provision of ingredients for the tenant to make the meal himself is not enough.

At any rate, the exception of bona fide lets with board or attendance does not exist in the case of assured tenancies. We can therefore look forward to the gradual disappearance of the bed and breakfast let, along with the demise of regulated tenancies.

Licences

In England, many landlords have for a long time sought to avoid the application of the Rent Acts by attempting to create, not a lease, but a personal licence, to which the Acts do not apply. This practice has not really caught on in Scotland, probably because the concept of a licence, although it exists, is much less developed in Scots law.

A licence is defined by Paton and Cameron as 'a contract, falling short of a lease, whereby not the heritage itself but the right to use a particular part of it or to put a particular part of it to some use is granted'[8]. There are a number of reported Scottish cases, though none of them relate to Rent Act evasion[9]. An important test seems to be whether the landlord has granted exclusive possession to the tenant, or whether he has retained partial possession himself.

In England, where the concept of a licence is much more developed, a similar criterion has been used; until recently, however, it was only one among a number of other tests – none of them conclusive – to decide whether a contract was a licence. For example, it was relevant to consider whether or not the premises were furnished or whether the occupation was permanent or

---

8 *Paton & Cameron* p 12.
9 See *Paton & Cameron* pp 12-15 and cases cited there, particularly *Broomhill Motor Co Ltd v Assessor for Glasgow* 1927 SC 447, 1927 SLT 189 and *Chaplin v Assessor for Perth* 1947 SC 373, 1947 SLT 163.

temporary. Moreover, the name the contractual document gave itself could also be taken into account, and, naturally, a landlord seeking to get round the Acts would want to describe it as a licence. This situation was considerably tidied up by the House of Lords in *Street v Mountford*[10]. In that case, although the contractual document described itself as a licence, the tenant had an exclusive right to occupy the furnished room in question, apart from a limited right, reserved to the landlord, to enter the room for inspection, repair or similar purposes. It was held that the contract was a lease and that the tenancy was a protected one. What the parties called the agreement was irrelevant. As Lord Templeman put it:

'If the agreement satisfied all the requirements of a tenancy, then the agreement produced a tenancy and the parties cannot alter the effect of the agreement by insisting that they only created a licence. The manufacture of a five-pronged implement for manual digging results in a fork even if the manufacturer, unfamiliar with the English language, insists that he intended to make and has made a spade[11].'

The proper test of a lease, his lordship concluded, was whether the tenant had exclusive possession for a term at a rent. It has subsequently been held that there can be exclusive possession which passes the test in *Street v Mountford* where several joint tenants occupy the same property, even although the contract may describe itself as a licence[12].

The test of exclusive possession is therefore common to both Scotland and England. It might be dangerous, however, to equate the law of the two countries too closely. As we have already seen[13], there are established categories in Scots law (eg mineral leases or leases of salmon fishings) where there can be a lease even **without** exclusive possession of the land. Also, the law of licences has not been developed in Scotland in relation to dwellinghouses.

At any rate, the decision in *Street v Mountford* has gone far to plug this loophole in England. It is to be hoped that this and (for landlords) the much more benign regime of assured tenancies will prevent the belated introduction of residential licences into Scotland.

10 [1985] AC 809, [1985] 2 All ER 289, HL.
11 Ibid at p 819.
12 *AG Securities v Vaughan* (1988) 06 EG 112, CA. But see also *Antoniades v Villiers* [1988] 2 All ER 309, CA.
13 See ch 1, pt 3 above.

14 Residential Leases: The Public Sector

1. INTRODUCTION

We saw in chapter 13 that under the various Rent Acts the tenants of most privately let dwellinghouses have enjoyed protection of one kind or another for more than seventy years. At the beginning of that period, the private let was still the most common type of tenure for householders. Since the 1939-45 war, emphasis has increasingly been on the public sector, mainly in the form of council lets, which nowadays far outnumber private leases of dwellinghouses. And yet, until recently, public sector tenants did not have the legal protection from eviction enjoyed by their private sector counterparts. They might have felt in less need of protection, being in the hands of publicly accountable organisations rather than private landlords, but in strict law their tenure was very much at the discretion of their landlords. When the lease contract came to an end, the council, or other public sector landlord, could terminate the let if they chose[1].

This was changed by the Tenants Rights Etc (Scotland) Act 1980 which gave to public sector tenants a statutory right to security of tenure at the end of their leases, along with a number of other rights, collectively nicknamed 'the Tenants' Charter'. This right to security of tenure is similar, but not identical, to the right enjoyed by private tenants under regulated tenancies; paradoxically, the security of tenure rights under the system of assured tenancies introduced by the Housing (Scotland) Act 1988 are now less favourable than those enjoyed by public sector tenants. The first part of this chapter will therefore be concerned with the rights of secure tenants.

Along with security of tenure, a public sector tenant was also for the first time given the right to buy the house he occupied, at a substantial discount. This was the most controversial aspect of the 1980 legislation – prior to that, local authorities did not even have

---

1 *City of Aberdeen District Council v Christie* 1983 SLT (Sh Ct) 57. But see also *Edinburgh District Council v Parnell* 1980 SLT (Sh Ct) 11.

the right to sell their houses if they wanted to, without the consent of the Secretary of State. The second part of this chapter will therefore be concerned with the current statutory rules relating to the right to buy.

Finally, the Housing (Scotland) Act 1988 has introduced a machinery by which council and other public sector tenants have a right to transfer their tenancy to a new landlord, possibly a private one. This 'choose a landlord' scheme is described in the last part of the chapter.

Since 1980 a number of amendments have been made to the initial legislation. With the exception of the most recent changes introduced by the Housing (Scotland) Act 1988, all of the law has been brought together in the Housing (Scotland) Act 1987. The English provisions are similar, but are contained in different legislation.

2. SECURE TENANCIES

The provisions relating to secure tenancies are mainly contained in Part III of the Housing (Scotland) Act 1987, as amended by the Housing (Scotland) Act 1988. For the tenancy to be a secure tenancy, the landlord must be one of the following types of body: (1) an islands or district council; (2) a regional council; (3) a new town or urban development corporation; (4) the Scottish Special Housing Association; (5) Scottish Homes; (6) a police authority; or (7) a fire authority[2].

The tenants of the following also have secure tenancies, but only if the tenancy was entered into prior to the commencement of Part II of the Housing (Scotland) Act 1988 (ie 2 January 1989) or in certain other limited circumstances[2]: (a) the Housing Corporation; (b) a registered housing association (with the exception of co-operative housing associations); (c) a housing co-operative, and (d) any housing trust which was in existence on 13 November 1953. In the case of islands, district or regional councils, the right will also apply where the landlord is not the council itself, but an associated body, such as a joint board or committee of the council, or the common good of the council, or any trust under the council's control[3].

Apart from the exceptions listed below, all tenants of the above

---

2 Housing (Scotland) Act 1987, s 44(2) and s 61(2)(a) (as amended by the Housing (Scotland) Act 1988, s 43(3)).
3 Housing (Scotland) Act 1987, s 61(2)(a) (i) and (ii).

landlords are secure tenants provided that (a) the house is let as a separate dwelling and (b) the tenant is an individual (ie rather than a limited company or other corporate body), and the house is his only or principal home[4]. Joint tenancies will be secure tenancies as long as all the joint tenants of the house in question are individuals and at least one of them occupies the house as his only or principal residence[5]. In *Thomson v City of Glasgow District Council*[6], it was held that a tenant who occupied a bedroom in a council hostel, where all the other facilities were communal, was not occupying a house let as a separate dwelling. One can understand why the tenant might want to claim security of tenure, but in that particular case he had applied to purchase the property!

Excepted categories

Schedule 2 of the Housing (Scotland) Act 1987 contains eight categories of let that are not secure tenancies. The Lands Tribunal for Scotland has expressed the opinion that the underlying intention of the Act is to exclude only the minimum number of houses consistent with the particular authority's functions[7], which means that they should be interpreted fairly narrowly. The excepted cases are as follows:

(1) Where the tenant is the employee of the landlord, or of any local authority or development corporation, and he occupies the house under his contract of employment for the better performance of his duties. This last part need not be expressly stated in the employment contract, but may or may not be implied depending upon the circumstances[8].

(2) Lets made expressly on a temporary basis to people seeking accommodation in the area because they are taking up employment there. The effect of the word 'expressly' is that the lease must make

---

4 Housing (Scotland) Act 1987, s 44(1).
5 Ibid s 44(3).
6 1986 SLT (Lands Tr) 6.
7 *Barron v Borders Regional Council* 1987 SLT (Lands Tr) 36.
8 *Douglas v Falkirk District Council* 1983 SLT (Lands Tr) 21; *Kinghorn v City of Glasgow District Council* 1984 SLT (Lands Tr) 9. See also *Stevenson v West Lothian District Council* 1985 SLT (Lands Tr) 9, *Docherty v City of Edinburgh District Council* 1985 SLT (Lands Tr) 61, *Campbell v City of Edinburgh District Council* 1987 SLT 51 and *Forbes v City of Glasgow District Council* 1988 GWD 31-1330.

it clear that the let is temporary, and it is not enough for it merely to refer to the appropriate schedule and paragraph of the Act[9].

(3) Temporary lets of houses that are due for development. Development could either be a building operation or a material change of use[10].

(4) Temporary lets of alternative accommodation while works are being carried out on the tenant's usual house, to which he has the right to return as a secure tenant. The tenant, however, does have the right to stay on in the temporary accommodation until his previous house is ready for occupation again[11].

(5) Temporary accommodation granted under the landlord's duty, as a local authority, to homeless persons.

(6) Where the house is let along with agricultural land or business premises, ie along with more than two acres of land, or along with a shop, office or premises licensed to sell alcohol.

(7) Rent and rate free lets by police authorities to police constables, and lets by fire authorities to firemen in consequence of their need to live near a particular fire station. Also excluded are temporary lets to other people pending a let to a police constable or fireman.

(8) Where the house is within the curtilage of a building that is not used as housing accommodation. This means that it must be used for the comfortable enjoyment of the other building so as to form an integral part of it[12]. Where the house and the other building are separated by a public road, the house cannot be within the curtilage of that other building[13].

Security of tenure

The effect of a tenancy being secure is essentially the same as with regulated and assured tenancies in the private sector. In other words, the tenant has the right to stay on in the property even though the contractual term stated in his lease has expired. The landlord has only very limited rights to bring the tenancy to an end. The tenant, on the other hand, can terminate the let at any time by

9 *Campbell v Western Isles Islands Council* 1988 SLT (Lands Tr) 4.
10 Town and Country Planning (Scotland) Act 1972, s 19.
11 Housing (Scotland) Act 1987, s 46(2).
12 *Barron v Borders Regional Council* 1987 SLT (Lands Tr) 36. See also *Burns v Central Regional Council* 1988 SLT (Lands Tr) 46.
13 *Fisher v Fife Regional Council* 1989 SLT (Lands Tr) 26.

giving the landlord four weeks' notice[14]. The tenancy may end on the tenant's death, but only where there is no relative entitled to succeed to the tenancy and who wishes to take it up[15]. Otherwise, the tenancy can only be terminated if the tenant abandons the property[16], or the landlord obtains a court order for possession.

Before it can raise court proceedings, the landlord must give the tenant at least four weeks' written notice, stating the ground of termination[17]. The notice will cease to be effective if not used by the landlord within six months[18]. The court will only grant the landlord a possession order on certain limited grounds which are specified below. These are not quite the same as the grounds of possession for regulated and assured tenancies, although there are similarities[19].

Grounds for termination

The grounds entitling the landlord to recovery of possession are set out in Part I of Schedule 3 of the Housing (Scotland) Act 1987. There are sixteen grounds in all. The first seven of these all relate to situations where the tenant could be said to be at fault in some respect. In these cases there is no requirement that other accommodation will be available to the tenant, but the court must be satisfied that it is reasonable to make the order[20]. This therefore gives the sheriff discretion, if he does not think that a landlord is acting reasonably, to refuse it possession even where a ground of termination exists.

The remaining grounds ((8)-(16)) do not involve any fault on the tenant's part, but there is other good reason for him to be moved out. In all of these cases the court, before it can grant an order, must be satisfied that suitable alternative accommodation is available to the tenant[1]. The criteria for suitability are set out in Part II of Schedule 3. The alternative accommodation need not be provided by the landlord itself, but **must** be either under another secure tenancy, or be a protected tenancy under the Rent (Scotland) Act

14 Housing (Scotland) Act 1987, s 46(1)(f).
15 Ibid s 46(1) (a) and (b).
16 See section on abandonment of tenancy below.
17 Housing (Scotland) Act 1987, s 47 (2) and (3).
18 Ibid s 47(4); *City of Edinburgh District Council v Davis* 1987 SLT (Sh Ct) 33.
19 See ch 13, pts 2 and 3 above.
20 Housing (Scotland) Act 1987, s 48(2)(a); *Second WVRS Housing Society v Blair* (1987) 19 HLR 104, CA.
 1 Housing (Scotland) Act 1987, s 48(2)(c).

1984 or an assured tenancy under the Housing (Scotland) Act 1988[2]. The other criteria are not mandatory, but the sheriff must have regard to them in deciding whether or not the accommodation is reasonably suitable. They include the proximity of the new house to the tenant's or a member of his family's place of work, comparability with the tenant's existing house and any special needs of the tenant or his family[3].

The following are the sixteen grounds that may entitle the landlord to recover possession of the house[4]:

(1) Rent arrears or breach of any other obligation of the tenancy.

(2) Use of the house for immoral or illegal purposes.

(3) Any deterioration in the condition of the property or its common parts caused by the neglect or default of the tenant. This will also be a ground if the deterioration was caused by a lodger or subtenant, unless the tenant has taken reasonable steps to have the person removed.

(4) In the case of furnished lets, deterioration of the furniture due to ill treatment. There is a similar provision to (3) in respect of lodgers or subtenants.

(5) Where the tenant and his spouse have been continuously absent from the house for more than six months without reasonable cause, or have ceased to occupy the house as their principal home. In the English case of *Crawley Borough Council v Sawyer*[5], the tenant left the house for about a year and a quarter to stay with his girl friend, then returned after he and his girl friend split up. During the period of his absence, he continued to pay the rent, visited the house about once a month and occasionally lived in it for periods of up to a week. It was held that the landords were not entitled to repossess.

(6) Where the landlord was induced to grant the tenancy because of a false statement made knowingly or recklessly by the tenant.

(7) A nuisance committed in the neighbourhood by the tenant or someone living with him, in circumstances where it is not reasonable for the landlord to have to provide alternative accommodation[6].

2 *Charing Cross & Kelvingrove Housing Association v Kraska* 1986 SLT (Sh Ct) 42.
3 Housing (Scotland) Act 1987, Sch 2, para 2.
4 Ibid Sch 3, pt I.
5 (1988) 20 HLR 98, CA.
6 *Scottish Special Housing Association v Lumsden* 1984 SLT (Sh Ct) 71.

(8) Same as (7) (ie nuisance), in circumstances where the landlord believes that it **is** appropriate for the tenant to be moved to other accommodation.

(9) Overcrowding amounting to an offence.

(10) Demolition of, or substantial work to, the house or the building of which it forms part. If the landlord intends that the tenant should return to the house afterwards, the court will make an order that he is entitled to do so[7]. The tenant will have security of tenure in the alternative house until such time as his original house is ready for occupation again[8]. In England it has been held that, before it can regain possession, the landlord must show a firm and settled intention to carry out the works and also to show that the works cannot be reasonably carried out without obtaining possession[9].

(11) Where the house has been designed or adapted for a person with special needs. This applies only if there is no longer anyone in the house with such needs and the landlord requires the house for someone who has.

(12) Where the house is part of a group of houses intended for persons in need of special social support. This is subject to a similar proviso to that in (11).

(13) Where the landlord is a housing association that caters for the elderly, the infirm, the disabled or people in special social circumstances. Again, there is a similar proviso to that in (11).

(14) Where the landlord is itself a lessee under a lease that has terminated or is about to terminate.

(15) Where the landlord is an islands council and the house is reasonably required for an employee of the council in the exercise of its function as education authority. This applies only if the existing tenancy was granted to a similar employee whose employment has now ended.

(16) Where the landlord wishes to transfer the tenancy to the tenant's spouse or former spouse or a person living with the tenant as husband and wife. This only applies if the other person has applied for the transfer of tenancy, and one of the parties (either the tenant or the other) no longer wishes them to live together. In respect of this ground only, the court has to be satisfied **both** that it

---

7 Housing (Scotland) Act 1987, s 48(5).
8 See excepted category 4 above.
9 *Wansbeck District Council v Marley* (1987) Times, 30 November, 1987 CLY 2229.

is reasonable to make the repossession order **and** that other suitable accommodation is available.

Abandonment of tenancy

We saw above (termination ground (5)) that the tenant's absence from the house for more than six months can be a ground for a court order terminating the tenancy. However, if the landlord has reason to believe that the tenancy has been abandoned, it may be able to recover possession without waiting for six months or obtaining a court order. If it has reasonable grounds for believing that a house let under a secure tenancy is unoccupied and that the tenant does not intend to occupy it as his home, the landlord may take possession of it[10]. It must first serve four weeks' written notice on the tenant of its intention to repossess unless the tenant replies within that time that he intends to reoccupy the house[11]. If the tenant fails to reply, the landlord may, after making any necessary enquiries, serve another notice terminating the tenancy. After that it is entitled to take immediate possession without further proceedings[12]. Pending such termination, the landlord is entitled to enter the house, by force if necessary, to secure it against vandalism[13]. The Secretary of State may make an order regarding custody or possible disposal of property left in the house by the tenant[14].

The tenant may appeal to the court within six months to have the tenancy restored, or be granted alternative accommodation. The grounds of appeal are that the landlord failed to carry out the prescribed procedure or that the tenant had good reason, such as illness, for not replying to the landlord's notice[15].

Succession to tenancy

On the death of a secure tenant, the tenancy will pass by operation of law to anyone qualified to succeed him[16]. Those qualified are (1) the tenant's spouse (2) anyone living with the tenant as husband and wife (3) a surviving joint tenant, if the house was his principal home

---

10 Housing (Scotland) Act 1987, s 49.
11 Ibid s 50(1).
12 Ibid s 50 (2) and (3).
13 Ibid s 49 (2) and (3).
14 Ibid s 50(4).
15 Ibid s 51.
16 Ibid s 52.

at the time of the tenant's death and (4) if there is no-one in the above categories, a member of the tenant's family. In each of these cases the person succeeding must have lived in the house as his or her only or principal home at the time of the tenant's death; in number (4) the successor must have resided there for at least twelve months prior to the tenant's death and have attained the age of sixteen[17]. 'Family' is defined very widely, and includes parents, grandparents, aunts, uncles, brothers, sisters, relationships by marriage and relationships of half blood. As well as children of the tenant, there is included stepchildren and illegitimate children, and in England the equivalent definition has been held to include foster children[18].

In England, the Court of Appeal has held that two women living in a homosexual relationship should not be considered to be living as husband and wife for the purpose of succession to a secure tenancy[19].

If more than one person is qualified to succeed to the tenancy (eg where there is no surviving spouse but two or more children), the tenancy may be transferred to any one of them, or to two or more of them as joint tenants. Who is to succeed will be decided by agreement of all the qualified people. If they cannot agree, the landlord will decide[20].

A person qualified to succeed is entitled to decline the tenancy[1].

A second succession is not allowed, unless it is to a joint tenant[2]. However, if there is someone who would otherwise have been entitled to succeed, he may stay on in the house for up to six months[3].

Fixing of rent levels

Although the 1987 Act confers security of tenure on public sector tenants analogous to that enjoyed under the Rent (Scotland) Act 1984 by tenants of private landlords, there is no general public sector equivalent of rent regulation and the fixing of fair rents. The

---

17 Housing (Scotland) Act 1987, s 52(2); *Peabody Donation Fund Governors v Grant* (1982) 264 EG 925, CA.
18 Housing (Scotland) Act 1987, s 83; *Reading Borough Council v Ilsley* (1981) CLY 1323.
19 *Harrogate Borough Council v Simpson* [1986] 2 FLR 91, (1985) 25 RVR 10, CA.
20 Housing (Scotland) Act 1987, s 52(3).
 1 Ibid s 52(4).
 2 Ibid s 52(5).
 3 Ibid s 52(6).

landlord may increase the rent, without terminating the tenancy, by giving the tenant four weeks' notice of the increase[4].

Local authority landlords (ie district and islands councils)[5] are free to charge 'such reasonable rents as they may determine'[6]. They are directed to review rents from time to time and, in fixing rent levels, must take no account of the personal circumstances of the tenants[7]. After the rent levels have been fixed, however, the latter may be taken into account in determining the eligibility of individual tenants for rent rebates.

Tenants of housing associations and the Housing Corporation have, until recently, been in a special category. Under Part VI of the Rent (Scotland) Act 1984, it is provided that they may have fair rents registered and rent increases phased over three years in the same way as those under regulated tenancies from private landlords[8]. This has now been changed by the Housing (Scotland) Act 1988. Where a tenancy was entered into before 2 January 1989, the tenant will still be able to have a fair rent registered; however, in the case of new tenancies entered into after that date (with a few limited exceptions) there will no longer be that right[9]. Also, the Secretary of State now has power to abolish the phasing of fair rents in respect of existing tenancies[10].

Other tenancy terms

Every secure tenant is entitled to a written lease, probative or holograph of the parties[11]. It is up to the landlord to draw up the lease, free of charge to the tenant, and to supply the tenant with a copy[12]. The parties may later agree to a variation of the terms, which the landlord must record in a similarly formal document[13].

If either the landlord or the tenant wishes to change any terms of the lease (other than rent), but cannot get the other to agree, the party wanting the change may apply to the sheriff court for a

---

4 Ibid s 54(2).
5 Ibid s 338(1).
6 Ibid s 210(1).
7 Ibid s 210 (2) and (3).
8 See ch 13, pt 2 above.
9 Housing (Scotland) Act 1988, s 43 (1) and (2).
10 Ibid s 41.
11 Housing (Scotland) Act 1987, s 53(1).
12 Ibid s 53(2).
13 Ibid s 54 (1) and (6).

variation of the terms[14]. The sheriff may make such variation as he thinks reasonable, taking particularly into account the safety of any person or the likelihood of damage to the property[15].

Where it is the tenant who makes the application for a variation, there are additional criteria to be met, which are, incidentally, very similar to those required for the variation of land obligations by the Lands Tribunal for Scotland (ie that they are unreasonable, inappropriate or unduly burdensome)[16]. The tenant may be ordered to pay compensation to the landlord for any loss caused by the variation[17]. Also, he may be required to serve notice of his application on the owner or tenant of any land who benefits from the term in its existing form, or who would be adversely affected by the change[18].

Assignation and subletting

The landlord's written consent must be obtained before the tenant can assign, sublet or in any other way give up possession of the house to another person, or before he can take in a lodger[19]. The landlord's consent, however, may not be unreasonably withheld. In order to obtain consent, the tenant must serve a written application on the landlord and, if the landlord fails to reply within a month, its consent will be deemed to have been given[20]. If the landlord refuses consent, the tenant may appeal to the sheriff[1].

It is stated that assignees and subtenants will not be entitled to either full protection or Part VII protection under the Rent (Scotland) Act 1984 or to an assured tenancy under the Housing (Scotland) 1988[2]. This makes sense in relation to subtenants, as their immediate landlord will be a private individual and therefore potentially within the ambit of the 1984 or 1988 Acts. It is rather confusing in relation to assignees: as they will be tenants directly under the original public sector landlord, they could not be regulated or assured tenants anyway, and there seems no reason

14 Housing (Scotland) Act 1987, s 54(3).
15 Ibid s 54(4).
16 Ibid s 54(3); Conveyancing and Feudal Reform (Scotland) Act 1970, s 1.
17 Housing (Scotland) Act 1987, s 54(4).
18 Ibid s 54(5).
19 Ibid s 55(1).
20 Ibid Sch 4, para 3(b).
 1 Ibid Sch 4, para 4.
 2 Ibid s 55(4) (as amended by the Housing (Scotland) Act 1988, Sch 9, para 10).

why they should not be regarded as secure tenants under the 1987 Act.

The landlord must be notified of any proposed increase in a subtenant's rent, and may object to it[3].

Repairs and alterations

As with all types of tenancy, the landlord is under an obligation (which can be contracted out of) to keep the premises wind and watertight as well as provide subjects reasonably fit for the purpose of the let[4]. In addition, however, s 13 and Sch 10 of the Housing (Scotland) Act 1987 impose further repairs obligations on landlords of houses let for a period of under seven years. It should be noted that this applies to **all** house lets of under seven years and not just to public sector tenancies. However, as most public sector lets are for less than this period, this provision will generally apply in their case.

The landlord's obligations are to keep in repair the structure and exterior of the house[5], and also all installations for water, gas and electricity supply, sanitation, space heating and water heating[6]. In *Hastie v City of Edinburgh District Council*[7], it was held that the exterior of the building included windows and the tenant was entitled to recover from the landlord the cost of a window broken by vandals. Any attempt by the landlord to contract out of these obligations will be void, although either it or the tenant may apply to the sheriff to have them varied in circumstances where it seems reasonable that this should happen[8].

A secure tenant is entitled to carry out alterations and improvements to the house, including the erection of garages or other outhouses[9]. The landlord's consent is required, but may not be unreasonably withheld. If the effect of the tenant's work is to add to the value of the house, he cannot be charged extra rent in respect of that increase in value; furthermore, the landlord has the power to

---

3 Housing (Scotland) Act 1987, s 56.
4 See ch 3, pt 2 above.
5 *McLaughlin v Inverclyde District Council* 1986 GWD 2-34; *Traynor v Monklands District Council* 1988 GWD 8-327.
6 Housing (Scotland) Act 1987, Sch 10, para 3(1).
7 1981 SLT (Sh Ct) 92; see also *City of Edinburgh District Council v Laurie* 1982 SLT (Sh Ct) 83.
8 Housing (Scotland) Act 1987, Sch 4, para 5.
9 Ibid s 57 and Sch 5.

make a payment to the tenant at the end of his tenancy in respect of any value his improvements have added[10].

3. RIGHT TO BUY

Who may buy

A tenant has the right to buy the house he lives in provided (a) he holds it under a secure tenancy[11] and (b) he has been a tenant for at least two years, which may partly consist of a period in occupation of another public sector tenancy[12]. There are some exceptions to this right to purchase:

(1) Where the landlord is not the owner of the property[13]. The landlord must be the heritable proprietor, and this is interpreted strictly. In *Graham v Motherwell District Council*[14], the District Council was itself a tenant under a 999 year lease. Even though this was in real terms virtually equivalent to ownership, it was held that the council's tenant had no right to buy.

(2) Where the house is one of a group designed or adapted for elderly or disabled persons and the facilities include a call service and a warden (ie sheltered housing)[15]. Where a house has been so designed or adapted, but does not fall within the above definition (eg because it is not part of a group of sheltered houses) there is a right to buy, though the Secretary of State has the power to authorise the landlord's refusal of the tenant's application[16].

(3) In certain cases where the landlord is a registered housing association. These include where the association has less than 100 dwellings for let, in some cases where it is a charity, or where it provides houses for people (such as the mentally ill or physically handicapped) who require a social service or special facilities[17].

The tenant may purchase the house jointly along with another

---

10 Housing (Scotland) Act 1987, s 58 and s 59.
11 See pt 2 above; if the landlord is the SSHA, the right to buy will be from Scottish Homes (Housing (Scotland) Act 1987, s 61(2)(a)(iv) (as amended by the Housing (Scotland) Act 1988, s 3(2))).
12 Housing (Scotland) Act 1987, s 61 (1), (2) and (11).
13 Ibid s 61(2)(b).
14 1985 SLT (Lands Tr) 44.
15 Housing (Scotland) Act 1987, s 61(4)(a).
16 Ibid s 69.
17 Ibid s 61(4).

member or members of his family[18]. The right to purchase may not be exercised by any tenant or joint tenant without the consent of his or her spouse[19].

What is purchased

Section 62 merely gives a tenant the right to purchase 'the house' which he has on lease. 'House' is defined later in the Act to include any part of a building, including a flat, which is occupied or intended to be occupied as a separate dwelling. It is also stated to include 'any yard, garden, out-houses and pertinents belonging to the house or usually enjoyed therewith'[20]. In *Neave v City of Dundee District Council*[1], the landlord's offer excluded the garden ground at the front and back of the house, the reason given being that it was part of a communal area maintained by the district council. It was held that the tenant was entitled to buy the garden ground, but that the ground should be subject to the control of the district council, who could maintain it if they wished.

The position seems to be that the tenant is entitled to buy everything that is included in his lease and possessed by him. This applies even to parts that the council, perhaps inadvertently, have already disposed of. In *Morrison v Stirling District Council*[2], the purchaser was held entitled to a right in common to a mutual path and steps separating the house from the one next door, even though the tenant next door had already been sold his house with the whole steps and path included. In *Popescu v Banff and Buchan District Council*[3], the applicant was held entitled to buy his house free of a servitude right that had been granted in favour of the house next door. The reason was that the lease to him was free of any servitude rights. This produced the rather odd result that the council were compelled to modify their offer to include something that was no longer theirs to sell. But, said the Lands Tribunal, the problem was theirs. They would either have to obtain a discharge of the servitude or be liable in breach of contract for failing to implement their bargain. In contrast, in the case of *Hannon v Falkirk District*

18 Ibid s 61(6).
19 Ibid s 61(5).
20 Ibid s 338(1).
 1 1986 SLT (Lands Tr) 18.
 2 1987 SLT (Lands Tr) 22.
 3 1987 SLT (Lands Tr) 20.

Council[4], the tenant was held not to be entitled to a lockup garage because it and his house were let to him under separate leases.

The purchase price

The price is calculated as follows:

(a) The market price is determined either (i) by a qualified valuer nominated by the landlord and accepted by the tenant or (ii) by the district valuer, the choice of which being up to the landlord. It is to be calculated as if the dwellinghouse were available for sale on the open market with vacant possession[5].

(b) No account is to be taken of any element in the market value of the house which would qualify as an improvements reimbursement at the end of a secure tenancy[6]. Otherwise the tenant would be paying for this element in the value twice.

(c) A discount is deducted from the market value. The discount for houses is 32 per cent of the market value plus an additional 1 per cent of the market value for every year beyond two of the tenant's continuous occupation, up to a maximum discount of 60 per cent. In the case of flats, there is a higher discount; for them, the minimum discount is 44 per cent and rises at a rate of 2 per cent per year, up to a maximum of 70 per cent[7]. The Secretary of State has the right by statutory instrument to vary the minimum and maximum discounts and the annual percentage increase[8]. Where the tenant wishing to buy has succeeded to the tenancy (eg from his father) the period when he occupied the house as the tenant's child will be taken into account in calculating the discount, both in relation to his present and previous houses[9]. However, those years before the child reached the age of sixteen will be excluded[10].

(d) The tenant's earlier occupation of another public sector house or houses can be taken into account in ascertaining the relevant number of years for calculating the discount. The earlier tenancies which may be used for this purpose include those where there is a

4 1987 SLT (Lands Tr) 18.
5 Housing (Scotland) Act 1987, s 62 (as amended by the Housing (Scotland) Act 1988, Sch 8, para 2).
6 Housing (Scotland) Act 1987, s 62(2); see also pt 2 above.
7 Housing (Scotland) Act 1987, s 62(3).
8 Ibid s 62(5).
9 *Motherwell District Council v Gliori* 1986 SLT 444.
10 Housing (Scotland) Act 1987, s 61(10)(a).

right to buy – ie those which qualify as secure tenancies in Scotland – but extend to a number of other public sector tenancies as well. These include tenancies from English local authorities and government lets to prison officers or members of the armed forces[11]. Thus, for example, a tenant may buy a Scottish council house with a discount partly calculated from his previous occupation of a council house in England. Likewise, a member of the armed forces may not have a right to buy the house let to him by the Crown, but his period of occupation there may be taken into account if he later exercises his right to buy another public sector house.

(e) If the house is a fairly new one, or the landlord has in the recent past spent substantial sums in improving it, a situation could arise where selling it at a large discount might result in the landlord incurring a loss. In other words, the amount spent on building or improving the house could exceed the sale price after deduction of the discount. This is more likely to happen if the costs were incurred recently; if they were incurred some years before, the effect of inflation is likely to have brought the price above any outstanding costs, even after deducting the discount. In order to minimise the chance of a loss occurring, it is provided that the price may not be less than any outstanding costs incurred within the landlord's five previous financial years, worked out on a basis to be determined by the Secretary of State in a statutory instrument. If, however, the market value before deduction of discount is itself less than the outstanding costs, then that market value is what will be paid[12].

These provisions were introduced by the Housing (Scotland) Act 1988 in place of those in the earlier legislation which performed a similar function, the relevant figure then being known as the 'outstanding debt' on the house. Where a landlord in its offer erroneously deducted the full discount, overlooking the fact that the outstanding debt was higher, it was held that the contract of sale was void and that the landlord could not be held by the tenant to the lower figure[13].

If any of the costs are not known, the landlord should make an estimate of them[14].

The Secretary of State also has power to make an order substituting a different period for the five years stated, and to make

---

11 Ibid s 61(11).
12 Ibid s 62; and ss 6A and 6B (added by the Housing (Scotland) Act 1988, s 65); see also *Murdoch v Gordon District Council* 1985 SLT (Lands Tr) 42.
13 *McGroarty v Stirling District Council* 1987 SLT 85.
14 Housing (Scotland) Act 1987, s 62(10).

different provisions in relation to different cases or circumstances, or different areas[15].

Purchase procedure

The tenant must submit to the landlord an application to purchase, including a statement of his relevant period of occupancy and the name of any joint purchaser[16]. The landlord must make the tenant an offer within two months[17] after which, within one month, the tenant may request the landlord to alter any terms he considers unreasonable or have a new term added[18]. The Secretary of State has power to direct either landlords in general or particular landlords that certain types of term are unreasonable[19].

The landlord may not include a pre-emption provision, ie one giving the landlord first option to buy if the house is ever resold by the tenant[20]. The reason for this is to prevent landlords who were reluctant to sell (probably for political reasons) using a pre-emption provision in order to regain ownership of the property at a later date. There is an exception to this rule in the case of houses adapted or designed for elderly or disabled persons[1]. Also, the Secretary of State has power to sanction pre-emption provisions in certain rural areas, if it appears necessary to stop houses purchased by sitting tenants being resold as holiday houses[2].

If the landlord refuses the offer or fails to amend its offer when requested, the tenant may within one month appeal to the Lands Tribunal[3]. Where he is seeking to vary a condition of a landlord's offer, this does not entitle him to challenge the market value[4]. The landlord is entitled to refuse if it believes that the tenant's application contains incorrect information[5], and also if the house is reasonably required for someone employed by an islands council as

15 Housing (Scotland) Act 1987, ss 6A and 6B (added by the Housing (Scotland) Act 1988, 5 65(2)).
16 Housing (Scotland) Act 1987, s 63(1).
17 Ibid s 63(2).
18 Ibid s 65(1).
19 Ibid s 78.
20 Ibid s 64(4).
 1 Ibid s 64(4).
 2 Ibid s 64 (6) and (7) (as amended by the Housing (Scotland) Act 1988, Sch 9, para 11); see also *Pollock v Dumbarton District Council* 1983 SLT (Lands Tr) 17.
 3 Housing (Scotland) Act 1987, s 68(4) and s 65(2); see also *Keay v Renfrew District Council* 1982 SLT (Lands Tr) 33.
 4 *Macleod v Ross and Cromarty District Council* 1983 SLT (Lands Tr) 5.
 5 Housing (Scotland) Act 1987, s 68(2).

part of its educational function[6]. The Secretary of State may also give the landlord permission to refuse where the house is designed or adapted for the needs of an elderly person[7]. As we saw above, where the house is part of a group of sheltered housing, there is no right to buy at all.

The tenant is entitled to a loan in order to purchase the house. Where the landlord is a new town or urban development corporation, the Scottish Special Housing Association, the Housing Corporation or a district or islands council, the landlord is obliged to grant the loan if applied for; where the landlord is a registered housing association, the loan is to be granted by the Housing Corporation or Scottish Homes (depending upon which one of them the association is registered with); in all other other cases the loan is to be granted by the relevant local authority, ie the islands or district council. In the event of a refusal, the tenant may appeal to the sheriff court[8].

If the tenant enters any proceedings against the landlord in connection with his right to sell, he may be able to obtain financial or other assistance from the Secretary of State in order to fight his case[9].

In England, a situation arose where a tenant submitted an application to buy and then, after the application but before the sale had been concluded, the landlord raised an action to terminate the tenancy. It was held that the landlord was entitled to do so, provided that there was a statutory ground of termination[10].

Clawback on resale

It would be an obvious abuse of the Act if a tenant were to purchase at a substantial discount and immediately, or very soon thereafter, resell the house at the full market value. Accordingly, if a tenant sells within three years, the discount, or a proportion of it, is recoverable by the landlord at the following rate:

Within the 1st year:	100 per cent
Within the 2nd year:	66 per cent
Within the 3rd year:	33 per cent[11]

---

6 Ibid s 70.
7 Ibid s 69.
8 Ibid s 216 (as amended by the Housing (Scotland) Act 1988, Sch 2, para 13).
9 Housing (Scotland) Act 1987, s 79.
10 *Enfield London Borough Council v McKeon* [1986] 2 All ER 730, [1986] 1 WLR 1007, CA.
11 Housing (Scotland) Act 1987, s 72.

There is no liability to repay the discount where: (a) the house is being sold by the executor of a deceased owner; (b) where the house is being compulsorily purchased, or (c) the house is being transferred free of charge to a member of the owner's family who has lived with him or her for the previous twelve months[12].

If the house is sold for a second time within the three year period, there will be no liability to repay discount on that second occasion[13].

4. RIGHT TO TRANSFER TO NEW LANDLORD

General

Part III of the Housing (Scotland) Act 1988 provides the legal machinery by which a public sector tenant may have his tenancy transferred to a new landlord. The latter may be Scottish Homes (the new housing authority set up by the 1988 Act) or may be a housing association or a private landlord. It is also suggested that tenants might form co-operatives with their neighbours to purchase their homes[14]. The choice of landlord has to be approved by Scottish Homes (unless they themselves have been chosen as landlords) and it is also contemplated that Scottish Homes will have a role to play in introducing tenants to prospective new landlords[14].

The stated aim of the government is that tenants who are not content with their housing conditions or the standard of management offered by their public sector landlord should have the right to choose to transfer their tenancy to a landlord who might be able to do a better job[15]. This suggests that the initiative in seeking the transfer will normally be taken by the tenant (or perhaps by a group of tenants). However, the procedure laid down by the Act is for the prospective new landlord to apply to the existing public sector landlord to purchase the property, in very much the same way as a tenant may apply to them under the right to buy provisions. Presumably this formal application by the new landlord might happen because an informal approach has been made to it by the tenant. It seems equally possible, however, that a commercial landlord might approach a tenant (or, more probably a group of

12 Housing (Scotland) Act 1987, s 73.
13 Ibid s 72(4).
14 Housing: The Government's Proposals for Scotland (Nov 1987) (Cmnd 242), para 6.10.
15 Housing: The Government's Proposals for Scotland (Nov 1987) (Cmnd 242), para 6.9.

tenants) proposing a transfer. In any case, a transfer cannot proceed without the tenant's consent.

This process (like a tenant's right to buy) can be carried out against an unwilling public sector landlord. In other words, provided that the proposed new landlord has been given the necessary approval, and the tenant's consent has been obtained, the existing landlord does not normally have the right to refuse an application. This should be distinguished from a situation where a local authority or other public sector landlord may want **voluntarily** to sell a house or group of houses with sitting tenants to a new owner; for that, the tenants' consent is not a legal requirement, although they may be consulted.

The procedure laid down is for applications to be made on an individual basis, so that it would be possible for even a single flat in a block to be transferred to a new landlord. However, it seems likely that private landlords would be more interested in buying houses in a group, and the Act makes provision for Scottish Homes to give their general consent for a new landlord to buy all the houses within a particular category, eg all those in a particular area[16].

As we saw in the early part of this chapter, public sector tenants generally enjoy security of tenure under a secure tenancy, in terms of the Housing (Scotland) Act 1987. It should be noted that tenants transferring out of the public sector to a private landlord, or to a housing association, will cease to have secure tenancies[17]. This will be the case, not only where the transfer occurs as a result of the 'choose a landlord' provisions described in this section, but also in any other situation where a tenancy is transferred out of the public sector. Although Section 45 does not actually say so, such tenancies would normally qualify as assured tenancies instead[18]. A tenant transferring to Scottish Homes would normally continue to enjoy a **secure** tenancy[19].

There are several factors that a tenant thinking about transferring to the private sector should keep in mind: (1) The security of tenure provisions are less favourable under assured tenancies than they are with secure tenancies[20]; (2) the Act makes no provision for a tenant to be transferred back to the public sector should he want to, so a transfer to a private landlord may be an irrevocable step, and (3) the landlord chosen by the tenant can dispose of his interest to yet

16 Housing (Scotland) Act 1988, s 57(2).
17 Ibid s 45.
18 See ch 13, pt 3 above.
19 See pt 2 above.
20 See ch 13, pt 3, and this chapter pt 2 above.

another landlord, and although the consent of Scottish Homes will be required for this, the tenant's consent is not necessary for any such subsequent transfer. The tenant, therefore, has no guarantee that he will remain with the landlord whom he has chosen.

Acquisition procedure

The public sector landlords to whom an application can be made are: (a) an islands or district council; (b) a development corporation, including an urban development corporation; (c) the Scottish Special Housing Association; (d) the Housing Corporation, and (e) Scottish Homes[1]. As with the right to buy, there are exceptions in respect of special categories of properties, eg those adapted for persons with special needs, or those situated in designated rural areas[2]. The applicant may be either Scottish Homes or a person or body approved by them[3].

The application must contain a statement that the applicant seeks to exercise the right conferred on him under the Act and be accompanied by the written consent of the tenant[4]. Unless the landlord disputes the applicant's right, the landlord must reply with an offer to sell containing the market value of the house and other conditions of the sale[5]. The applicant must send a notice of acceptance within two months, which will have no effect unless he has already entered into a lease with the tenant, conditional upon the sale proceeding[6].

Price

The price is to be the market value of the house as determined either by a qualified valuer nominated by the landlord and accepted by the applicant, or by the district valuer, the choice of which being up to the landlord[7]. The market value is to be the price which the house would realise if sold on the open market by a willing seller, but subject to a number of assumptions, including that the only prospective purchasers are Scottish Homes or the approved applicant, and also that the applicant will, within a reasonable time

1 Housing (Scotland) Act 1988, s 56(3).
2 Ibid s 56(5).
3 Ibid s 57.
4 Ibid s 58(1).
5 Ibid s 58(5).
6 Ibid s 60.
7 Ibid s 58(6).

carry out any repairs required to fulfil the landlord's repairing obligations. Provision is also made for the price to be nil, or even a negative amount. This means that a public sector landlord could in some circumstances be compelled to pay a prospective private landlord to acquire a particular house or houses[8].

It is clear from these provisions that the government contemplates situations where run-down properties, of little or no market value, will pass into the hands of private landlords and be upgraded. However, this need not be so, in which case the first of the two valuation assumptions mentioned above seems rather strange. It would seem to mean, for example, that a well-maintained house in a good area, for which there might be considerable market demand, would still have its price calculated on the assumption that no-one was interested in it apart from the applicant or Scottish Homes. This could have the effect of producing a price that was well below the real market value, giving private landlord applicants a considerable bargain. It would, of course, be open to Scottish Homes to refuse consent to a transfer in such cases.

Reference to Lands Tribunal

As with the right to buy, the Lands Tribunal for Scotland has been given jurisdiction to settle disputes that may arise at different stages of the process:

(1) Where a landlord served with an application fails to issue timeously either an offer to sell or a notice of refusal[9].

(2) Where the landlord has refused to strike out or vary any condition which the applicant thinks unreasonable[10].

(3) Where the landlord has served a notice of refusal on the applicant[11].

(4) Where the landlord has served an offer to sell which does not comply with a requirement of Part III of the 1988 Act[12].

The Lands Tribunal, if it considers the applicant's complaint to be justified, has the power to serve an offer to sell, or take any other appropriate action in the landlord's place[13].

---

8 Ibid s 58(8).
9 Ibid s 62(1)(a).
10 Ibid s 59(3) and s 62(1)(b).
11 Ibid s 61(3) and s 62(1)(c).
12 Ibid s 62(1)(d).
13 Ibid s 62(2).

Index